Florida Dreams:
All About the Amazing Rise of the Sunshine Mega-State

PATRICK GRADY

Published by

Global Economics

in the

United States of America.

Copyright © 2019 Patrick Grady

All rights reserved.

Cover photo is of the Vivante at Punta Gorda clubhouse and pool.

ISBN-13: 9781793105011

DEDICATION

To my favorite granddaughter Brooke, who stuck a post-it® on my desk soliciting a book dedication. To be worthy of such an honor, she had to pass the traditional Florida rite of passage. Sorry Kyle!

CONTENTS

	Acknowledgments	i
	Preface	iii
1	Land of Dreams	1
2	Dreams Fuel Strong Population Growth	5
3	The Economic Rise of the Sunshine Mega-State	10
4	The Economic Climate is Almost as Good as the Weather	23
5	Waves of Retirees Wash Up, and Not Only on the Beaches	33
6	The Southeast Florida Ola	42
7	African-American Dreams	50
8	The Indians Never Gave Up on their Florida Dreams	53
9	Snowbirds: More than Tourists, But Not Quite Residents	59
10	The Rich Share in the Dreams	62
11	Opening the Dream to the Young	66
12	The Tourism Juggernaut	73
13	Miami: The Emerging Capital of Latin America and the Caribbean	82
14	Wall Street Joins in the Dream	90
15	The Real Estate Bust Only Temporarily Spooked the Dream	94
16	Florida Developers Dream Big	98
17	The Dreams of Entrepreneurs Drive Development	101
18	Transportation Moves the Dream	108
19	Energy Required to Power Dreams	112

20	The Military Has Brought Many Dreamers to Florida and Created Countless Jobs	120
21	The Dream of Good Health	126
22	Crime Is Not Part of the Dream	132
23	Neither is Poverty and Homelessness	136
24	Fading Dreams for Agriculture and the Fisheries	139
25	How Many People Can Share in the Florida Dream?	150
26	Dreams Threatened by Environmental Challenges	153
27	Red or Blue Dreams?	165
28	The Florida Dream Lives On	171
	Postscript: "Dreams" as a Motivating Force in Economics	174
	Bibliography	176
	About the Author	205

ACKNOWLEDGEMENTS

I'd like to thank my wife Jean who helped me edit *Florida Dreams* and took most of the pictures included to make it more visually appealing. I'd also like to thank my son-in-law Dan Felton for some of the photos. I'm especially grateful to Professor Larry Brand of the University of Miami, the leading scientific expert on red tide, who graciously took the time to provide comments and suggestions on the red tide section of Chapter 26, which is based largely on his published work. Adam Gelber, the Director of the Office of Everglades Restoration Initiatives, in the Department of the Interior, helped by explaining that no permission was required to reproduce the Everglades flow chart in Chapter 26. Peter Robbins, Director of Nuclear Communications Marketing & Communication for FPL, kindly allowed me to use their picture of the Turkey Point Nuclear Plant, after an unsuccessful attempt to get close enough to take my own picture. Finally, I'm indebted to the many Floridians who have taken the time over the years to enlighten me on the esoteric aspects of the local culture and the conditions that make our state so distinctive and fascinating.

PATRICK GRADY

PREFACE

Florida Dreams have a strange way of growing on you over the years. My first exposure to Florida was over a half century ago, when, as a young college student, I hitchhiked down from Illinois to Florida for the winter break with a college friend. After camping for the night outside Knoxville, only to wake up the next morning covered in snow, we finally made it to Fort Lauderdale, where to our great disappointment, it was too cold for the beach. Pushing on to Key West, where the road ends and the quirky congregate, we met up with a young Cuban exile who invited us to stay with him on his "yacht." It was only a half-sunk fishing boat, with bullet holes in the gunwale, that had been used for rescue runs to Cuba. But it was at least scuttled in a beautiful spot, near the Navy base, and provided us a roof over our heads for our sojourn on the isle. Thus, in the town of Papa Hemingway, did my fascination with Florida begin.

It was another quarter century before I returned to Florida on the first of many annual visits. The occasion was my in-laws' acquisition of a modest cinder block bungalow in Port Charlotte on the Gulf Coast. They had been down visiting my father-in law's cousin at his winter home in the Municipal Trailer Park, across the Peace River in Punta Gorda, and had decided to buy their own small piece of paradise. This solid little house served as our Florida base for 22 years, until it was rendered uninhabitable by Hurricane Charley in 2004. To be honest, it was the black mold growing over everything that finally did it in. A leaking roof, not so well covered by one of the ubiquitous blue FEMA tarps, combined with the summer heat, had turned the house into a giant petri dish for mold spores to grow.

As my career as an economic consultant began to wind down, and as my wife, Jean, needed to provide more frequent support for her aging mother, Ruth, we purchased a condominium at Vivante in Punta Gorda in 2008 (as pictured on the cover, but without the alligator, which so far has stayed in the lake). Like many snowbirds, we wintered in Punta Gorda for a few years before finally taking the plunge and becoming year-rounders in 2012. By that time, I was already solidly under the thrall of my Florida Dreams, even though I still had much to learn about my new home state.

I present this book to you as my homage to Florida. It draws on my Florida knowledge and experience, and my own interests and enthusiasms as an economist, to interpret the developments that have transformed Florida from an exotic Southern backwater to the world's leading subtropical vacation destination, as well as the center of the nation's biennial national political circus. And, of course, I wouldn't be very much of an economist, if I failed to offer my assessment of the challenges, like red tide, hurricanes, and sea level rise, that cast a shadow over the Sunshine Mega-State's continued rise.

A word of warning. Some of the early chapters of this book (Chapters 3 and 4) contain the material that could be more difficult reading for the non-economist (so my wife tells me), although it doesn't seem so technical to me, but only has a lot of charts. But if you do have difficulties, I encourage you to jump right from Chapter 1, the introduction, and Chapter 2 on population growth, to Chapter 5 on the wave of retirees coming to the state, particularly if you are of that demographic and are considering the option yourself. You might also want to hop around the book a bit, exploring those chapters that look most interesting. Finally, be sure not to miss Chapter 26 on environmental challenges. It deals with the most important issues currently facing the Sunshine Mega-State and threatening its rise. It's something you need to know if you're going to be an informed citizen of the Sunshine State. Our prosperity and health are both at stake. Also if you want more information on any of the topics discussed, you should consider taking a look at the Kindle version of this book, it's chock full of intriguing hyperlinks, shedding even more light on all things Florida, and, as an added bonus, the photos and charts are all in living color.

1
LAND OF DREAMS

"All our dreams can come true, if we have the courage to pursue them."
Walt Disney

Since the discovery of the New World, and well before Walt and Mickey took the state by storm, people have been coming to Florida in pursuit of their dreams. Ponce de Leon, who was responsible for christening the peninsula, explored the land, looking for gold and, more idiosyncratically for a Spanish conquistador, the Fountain of Youth. Tragically, he didn't find either, but instead got, what some would say he deserved, a fatal arrow in the neck from the existing inhabitants who were not pleased by the arrival of his armed band of invaders. Fortunately, many subsequent dreamers, who have prudently established less confrontational relations with the locals, have fared better.

Henry Flagler came to Florida in 1880 and liked it so much he moved down, and, in effect, took over, using the fortune he had made as John D. Rockefeller's partner in Standard Oil. The railroad Flagler built down the east coast, which, naturally enough, came to be called the Florida East Coast Railway, brought an annual seasonal migration of many of America's Gilded Age grandees to St. Augustine where they filled his newly constructed 540-room Ponce de Leon Hotel. The railroad was then pushed on to Palm Beach, and eventually to Miami, and Key West. The Palm Beach "Season" at the Royal Poinciana Hotel and the Palm Beach Inn (renamed the Breakers) came to rival the summer social swirl up in Newport.

Another Henry, at around the same time, Henry B. Plant also built railroads, but on the west coast of Florida, opening it up as well. People flocked from up north to stay in his Tampa Bay Hotel and several smaller hotels that he owned. The Army General Staff liked Plant's Tampa Bay Hotel so much that they launched and ran the Spanish American War from it. Famous guests, who came down for the season to the end of his railway in Fort Myers, and built homes, included Thomas Edison, Henry Ford and Harvey Firestone. A tour of their homes reveals that they sure caught some monstrous tarpon, which might have been what kept them coming back every year.

Not only rich people were attracted to Florida. Starting in the 1920s, when automobiles became the rage, the "Tin Can Tourists" motored down the Dixie Highway from the Mid-West and other northern states, their trailers and campers in tow, earning their names by their practice of eating out of cans, which were too often left behind to litter their camp sites.

People, suffering through the long snowy winters and cold and rainy falls and springs, were drawn to Florida like a magnet by its semitropical, yet dry winter climate, lush vegetation, expansive beaches, and exotic animals. Especially the plethora of alligators. Well, maybe not so much alligators.

The stifling Florida summer heat and swarms of mosquitos, on the other hand, did a pretty good job of dampening the dreamers' attraction to Florida and discouraging migration.

The appeal of Florida thus remained largely seasonal until after World War II when fortuitously air conditioning was developed, and DDT and other pesticides began to be utilized on a large scale. For the first time, this made Florida seem habitable to other Americans who had become accustomed to living in a relatively bug-free temperate climate and not near mosquito-infested swamps.

The population of Florida ballooned after the war from 2.8 million in 1950, to 21 million in 2017. Florida went from the smallest and most insignificant of the former Confederate States of America to the 3rd largest state, after only California and Texas, edging out New York.

With more population comes more electoral votes and increasing attention on the national political stage every four years when the President is elected. Florida has picked up at least one electoral vote in every census since 1930. The only states that got two more votes from the 2010 census were Florida and Texas.

The 2000 election was only settled in favor of George W. Bush after the US Supreme Court heard extensive legal arguments about vote counting, and the esoterica of hanging chads, before rendering a decision to stick with the original vote count. The margin in Bush's favor was a scant 537 out of 6 million votes.

Florida also played an important role in the 2016 election. The margin in Donald Trump's favor of 116 thousand votes or 1.2 per cent gave him 29 electoral votes which helped to push him over the top. The dreams of two recent Democratic presidential candidates were thus dashed in the Florida polling booths. And in the 2018 mid-term, President Trump helped elect Ron DeSantis and Rick Scott as Governor and Senator, defying a national blue mini-wave.

As a swing (or purple) state, the demographics of Florida is a favorite topic of pundits. Is the state becoming bluer because of Hispanic immigration and Puerto Rican migration, both of which tend to vote Democrat? Or is it becoming redder because of the inflow of retirees who are more likely to vote Republican and turn out at the polls in greater numbers? And what about the ex-felons who regained the right to vote with the passage of Amendment No. 4?

Florida is the only one among the lower 48 US states that has a semitropical climate. State Highway 60, which stretches from Tampa to Vero Beach, corresponds roughly to the frost line. Unlike in northern states where the frost line measures how deep the ground freezes in winter, the frost line down here indicates the southernmost reaches of hard freezes. The ground doesn't freeze at all. It also marks the boundary below which the citrus industry has mostly migrated in its efforts to avoid making prematurely frozen orange juice.

FLORIDA DREAMS

Florida also has a very fragile environment. Its coastal lands are low-lying and exposed to sea-level rises caused by global warming and the melting of the polar ice caps. It is also buffeted by hurricanes, which could be increasing in frequency and intensity. A shortage of fresh water is also a potential problem because the natural flow of water down the peninsula has been disrupted by drainage canals and dams for development and agriculture, which have introduced pollutants in the water. The reduction in water flow has led to some salinization of the water table in Southeast Florida and the increased nutrients have fed the red tide on both coasts, and the toxic green algal blooms, which flow out of Lake Okeechobee with increasing regularity and longevity. These pollute the water and air, and kill fish and marine mammals, transforming beaches into no-go zones, hurting the tourist industry and other coastal developments. The environmental implications of poorly managed growth pose the single greatest threat to the continued rise of the Sunshine State. Yet they need not transform dreams into nightmares and stifle the hopes of Floridians if, as will be explained later, the proper steps are taken.

There are five categories of dreamers that have contributed most to the rise of Florida featured in this book: retirees; immigrants, largely from Latin America, including most notably Cuba; tourists; snowbirds; and entrepreneurs and business people.

The other mega-states, California, Texas and New York also benefit from these categories of people, but there are important differences. California and Texas also attract a lot of Hispanic immigrants, but largely from Mexico and Central America. New York has a more diversified flow of immigrants from all over the world. California and New York are both losing more people than they gain from interstate migration, whereas Florida and Texas are both gaining.

The Florida economy, powering the rise of the Sunshine State, differs significantly from the economies of the other mega-states. All the economies of the mega-states are diversified to a large extent and no state has a monopoly on any industries. But as California is known for Silicon Valley and Hollywood, Texas for oil and gas, and New York for Wall Street and the media, Florida is most closely linked in the public mind with Disney World and retirement communities where the nation's elderly can live out their golden years basking in the sun.

Even though there is a core of truth to these simplifications, there is much more of the story to be told. Florida is Cape Canaveral and the Space Coast, and cutting-edge high-tech industries. Miami is a thriving bilingual Spanish-English megalopolis that dominates the Caribbean and Latin America with its dazzling Hispanic culture, and global business links. It is also the Hispanic media and cultural center of the United States. And while the traditional Florida industries of citrus, cattle, agriculture, mining and lumbering have dwindled in importance, they still contribute wealth and provide jobs.

Florida was built on dreams. Some like those of Walt Disney had the power to transform the whole state. Others like those of the hundreds of thousands of Cubans fleeing the tyranny of Castro collectively built a vibrant, and dynamic Miami, the 7th largest metropolitan area in the country inhabited by 6.2 million people, out of a small Southern city. And the dreams of millions of retirees, largely from the Mid-West and East Coast, have created unique retirement communities like The Villages and Celebration, which are, at the same time, both old-fashioned and modern. Yes, Florida is a strange mix of Tomorrowland and Yesterworld, young and old, English and Spanish speakers, Red and Blue. And that is what makes it so interesting, and what inspired me to write *Florida Dreams*.

2
DREAMS FUEL STRONG POPULATION GROWTH

Florida Takes 3rd Place

Florida overtook New York to be the third largest state in 2014. This was a huge improvement in position for a state that had ranked 33rd in 1900 and 20th in 1950. The usually phlegmatic US Census Bureau heralded this milestone for Florida with an uncharacteristically catchy release (Chart 1). It trumpets the steep upward trajectory of Florida, compared to the stagnation of New York and Illinois, both trends that, by the way, have continued. And, while California seems to be moving up in the chart too, it's an optical illusion, folks. It's only because the Golden State is so large, and the scale is linear. California is growing much more slowly than Florida in percentage terms. Only Texas is growing more rapidly than Florida, and only by a titch.

The big difference among the states is interstate migration (people moving from one state to another). Over the 1990 to 2016 period, 3.9 million more people moved into Florida from other states than out, whereas 4.4 million more people moved out of California, 3.8 million more people moved out of New York, and 420 thousand out of Illinois. It's not only the weather that's behind these outflows. Escaping higher taxes is also a motivation. And the cost of living including housing is another factor in California and New York. Texas is the only mega-state with substantial net in-migration and even there, at only 2.6 million, it falls far short of Florida, even though it is a much larger state.

From an even longer-term perspective, the forty-fold population growth from the turn of the last century to the present is nothing less than extraordinary. So is the more than seven-fold population growth since the end of the World War II (measured from 1950). Up to 2010, population growth ranged between 18 per cent and 79 per cent per decade (Table 1). The Florida population rose much more rapidly than the overall population of the United States. Florida has gone from being one of the smallest states east of the Mississippi to the 3rd largest in the country. Since 1900, only Nevada and Arizona have experienced more rapid population growth. The population of Florida rose from 0.7 per cent of the U.S. population in 1900, to 1.82 per cent in 1950, to 6.44 per cent in 2017. Florida's population growth is expected to continue to be relatively high, registering 14.2 per cent in the current decade.

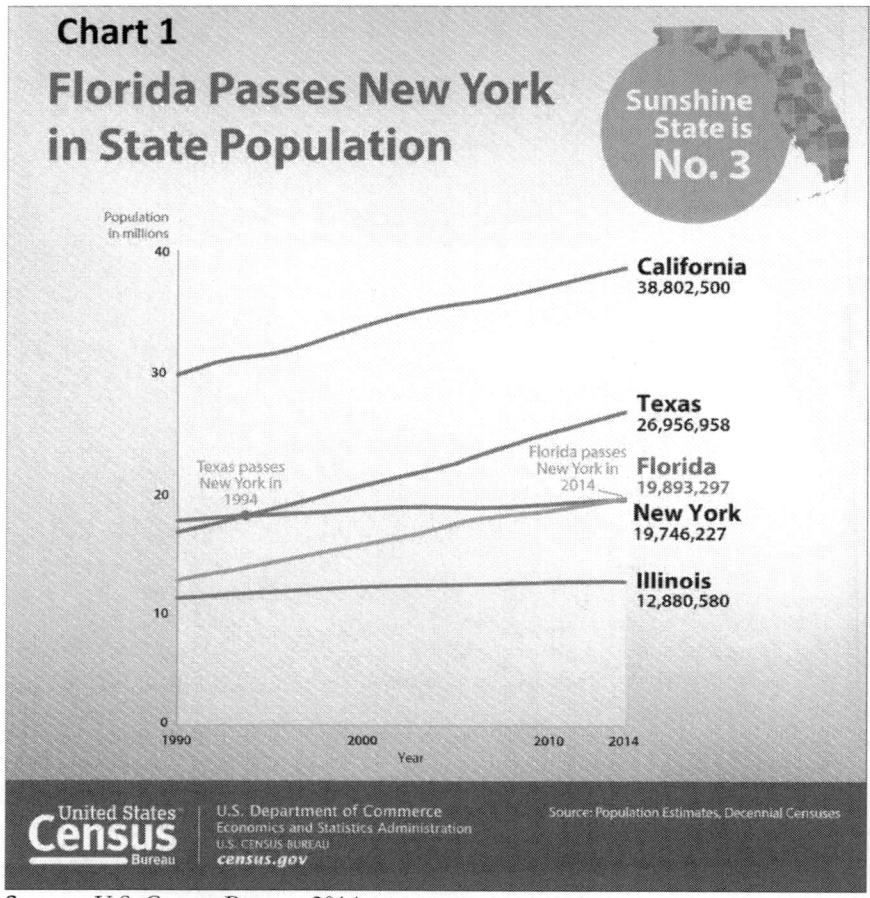

Chart 1: Florida Passes New York in State Population

Sunshine State is No. 3

- California: 38,802,500
- Texas: 26,956,958
- Florida: 19,893,297
- New York: 19,746,227
- Illinois: 12,880,580

Texas passes New York in 1994. Florida passes New York in 2014.

Source: Population Estimates, Decennial Censuses. United States Census Bureau, U.S. Department of Commerce, Economics and Statistics Administration, U.S. Census Bureau, census.gov

Source: U.S. Census Bureau, 2014.

Population grows to the extent that births and in-migration, both of which increase population, exceed deaths and out-migration, which decrease it. The natural increase in population is defined as births minus deaths. This contributed to the growth in Florida's population, particularly following World War II when births spiked producing the baby boom through the 1960s, and subsequent "baby boom echo" in the 1990s. But the main reason for Florida's rapid population growth has been net in-migration, which accounted for over 85 per cent of the state's population growth from 1970 to 2014. The largest share of in-migrants come from other states, but immigration from foreign countries, most notably in Latin America and the Caribbean, but also in Asia, is also a source of in-migrants. It accounted for almost 30 per cent of in-migration from 1955 to 2000 (Smith, 2005). And they just keep coming. In 2016, an average of 2,285 moved to Florida every day from other states or other countries (U.S. Census Bureau, American Community Survey, 2017).

Table 1: Florida Population Growth, 1990-2020			
Year	Population	Decade Change	Percent Change
1900	528,542		
1910	752,619	224,077	42.4
1920	968,470	215,851	28.7
1930	1,468,211	499,741	51.6
1940	1,897,414	429,203	29.2
1950	2,771,305	873,891	46.1
1960	4,951,560	2,180,255	78.7
1970	6,791,418	1,839,858	37.2
1980	9,746,961	2,955,543	43.5
1990	12,937,926	3,190,965	32.7
2000	15,982,378	3,044,452	23.5
2010	18,846,461	2,864,083	17.9
2017e	20,984,200		
2020p	21,526,500	2,680,039	14.2

Note: e is an estimate and p is a projection.

Source: Bureau of Business and Economic Research, University of Florida, Smith (2005), and Rayer and Wang (2018).

New York was by far the largest source of in-migrants in the final decades of the 20th Century. Other large source states were New Jersey and Pennsylvania in the Northeast and Ohio, Illinois and Michigan in the Midwest. The only leading source state in the South was Georgia, and in the West, California. (Aisch, Gebeloff and Quealy, 2014).

Florida is one of the states with the smallest native-born population. In 2012, scarcely more than one-in-three residents was born in Florida. Only Nevada had a smaller share. In the same year, 43 per cent of the Florida population was born in other states and 21 per cent abroad. Only New York and California had a larger share of the population born abroad.

Florida is a state where everybody comes from somewhere else. But don't worry, in the Panhandle and the hinterlands away from the large cities and coastal tourist towns, there are still enough proud, old-fashioned Florida crackers to keep Old Florida alive. And don't forget the two federally recognized Indian Tribes in Florida, the Seminoles and Miccosukees, who are headquartered in South Florida, and proudly maintain their traditions (including the internationally renowned Florida tourist attraction of alligator wrestling), as well as run lucrative casinos.

The growth in population over the 20th century and even after World War II has been concentrated in the center and south of the state with the northern regions falling behind. Since 1980, however, the growth in the Southeast (Miami metropolitan area) has lagged, and the growth in the much smaller Southwest region (Sarasota metropolitan area and the Fort Myers-Cape Coral metropolitan area) has been the strongest.

The Miami metropolitan area, which includes Fort Lauderdale and West Palm Beach, grew from 694 thousand in 1950 to 6.2 million in 2017, making it the 7th largest in the country. The Tampa-St. Petersburg metropolitan area had 3.1 million people in 2017 and the Orlando metropolitan area 2.5 million. Florida has become not only one of the largest states, but one with some of the largest cities.

Florida's population is concentrated around its major cities (Chart 2). The darkest area in the southeast of the state is Miami-Dade County. The Tampa-Saint Petersburg metropolitan area is spread across counties in the center west of the state. The Orlando metropolitan area is largely in Orange County to the north and east of Tampa along the I-4 corridor. The Jacksonville metropolitan area is in Duval County, which is the darker area in the far northeast of the state.

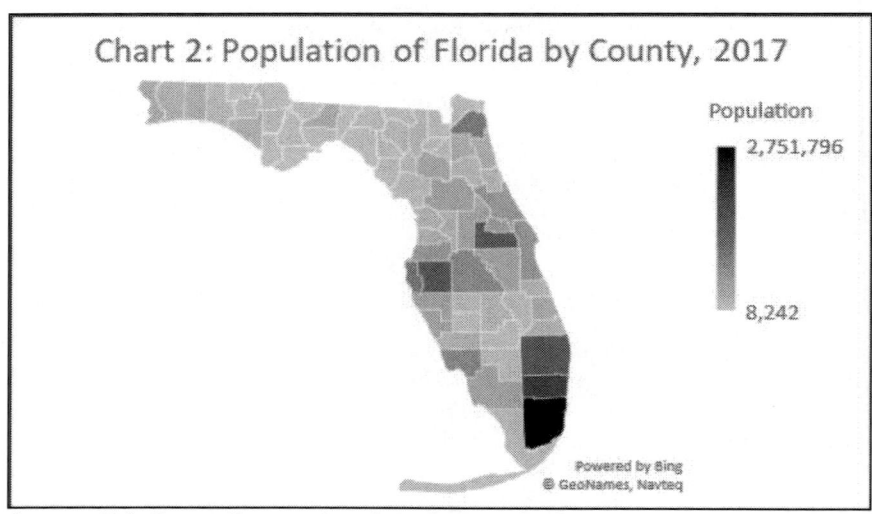

Chart 2: Population of Florida by County, 2017

Population
2,751,796

8,242

Source: U.S. Census Bureau, American Community Survey, 2017.

The Myth that Only Old People Move to Florida

In 2017, there were 3,807,480 people 65 and over living in Florida. This comprises 20.1 per cent of the population, making Florida the state with the highest proportion of senior citizens in the country, ahead even of West Virginia, the next highest state, which has 19.7 per cent elderly. Florida has a significantly higher share of elderly than the 15.6-per-cent national average.

The two larger mega-states California and Texas have much smaller elderly population shares, at 13.9 per cent and 12.3 per cent respectively, primarily because of the large influx of young foreign migrants. Even New York, with a 15.9 per cent senior share, is a lot lower than Florida. (U.S. Census Bureau, 2017).

There is a common misperception that most of the people moving to Florida are elderly and that is what makes the Florida population so old. This is, in fact, not true. Most of the people who migrate to Florida are not over age 65 even though Florida does get a larger share of seniors than other states. However, while the average age of migrants to Florida is lower than the age of the population in general (only 37.1 years old in 2016), the average age of people leaving the state is even younger. So, it is net in-migration, not gross, that has contributed to the aging of the Florida population and helped to make Florida's population one of the oldest in the nation. The median age of 42.1 years in 2016 was only exceeded by four states (Maine, 44.6 years; New Hampshire, 43; Vermont, 42.7; and West Virginia, 42.2). Moreover, it is 4.2 years higher than the 37.9 years median for the country. (U.S. Census Bureau, 2017).

The most important factor depressing the aging of the population is the birth rate. This is because of the simple fact that babies join the population at an age of zero which can offset the one-year increase in age of a lot of other people. Unfortunately, the birth rate has been decreasing because babies don't feature so prominently in people's dreams anymore. Instead they are making a lifestyle choice to get married later (or not at all) and to postpone or even forego having children.

The "natural increase" of the population because of births exceeding deaths is already being turned on its head in many places in the United States, including especially Florida where Stefan Rayer, a University of Florida demographer, has coined the term "natural decrease" to describe a situation where deaths exceed births. He reports that "While natural increase is still positive for the state overall, in 2014, for the first time, more Florida counties (37) experienced natural decrease than natural increase (30)." (Rayer, 2016). This is a growing, and worrying, trend in Florida and elsewhere in the country.

While Florida is further down the road towards an older population, the aging of the population is a problem facing the United States. And it is expected to get worse over time because of low birth rates and the aging of older larger population cohorts such as the "baby boomers." This has major implications for the supply of labor, the production of goods and services, and the funding of social programs like Medicare and Social Security, which permit many retired people to live out their Florida Dreams.

3
THE ECONOMIC RISE OF THE SUNSHINE MEGA-STATE

Florida GDP Growth Surges Ahead

The Florida Chamber of Commerce boasted that the Florida GDP (Gross Domestic Product or the sum of all the goods and services produced in the state) reached the landmark level of a $1 trillion at annual rates in the fourth quarter of 2017 (but not yet then for the whole year). They went on to claim that, if Florida was a country, this would give it the 17th largest economy in the world ahead of such states as Saudi Arabia, the Netherlands, Switzerland and Argentina. (Ousley, 2018). This is true if GDP is measured in U.S. dollars at market exchange rates. And it is even not too much of a stretch if GDP is measured in terms of purchasing power parity exchange rates, as is usually done in international comparisons of GDP levels. Regardless, it's a pretty impressive achievement for a state that had less than a million people a hundred years ago. But while Florida has the 3rd largest population of all the states, it falls back to 4th behind New York in terms of the size of its economy, which, of course, is still pretty good (Chart 3).

Florida attained this lofty trillion-dollar level of GDP by steadily growing over many years. Over the thirty years between 1987 and 2017, the Florida economy more than doubled in real terms (adjusted for inflation), increasing by 127 per cent or 2.8 per cent per year (Chart 4).

Most of the growth in the Florida economy occurred in private service-providing industries, which over the 20-year period ending in 2017 grew 70.9 per cent, far outpacing the private goods-producing industries, which only grew 22.8 per cent over the same period (Table 2). By 2017, the private service sector accounted for 77.7 per cent of all economic activity and the private goods producing sector only 11.2 per cent. The service sector growth stemmed from the strong performance of: the information sector; professional and business services; wholesale and retail trade; finance, insurance, real estate rental and leasing; and educational services, health care, and social assistance. The goods sector growth was led by manufacturing, which exhibited solid growth. Construction, the other industry accounting for a large share of goods sector output, grew very weakly over the period. And natural resources, including agriculture, forestry, fishing, and mining also grew slowly, especially mining, quarrying and oil wells, which declined.

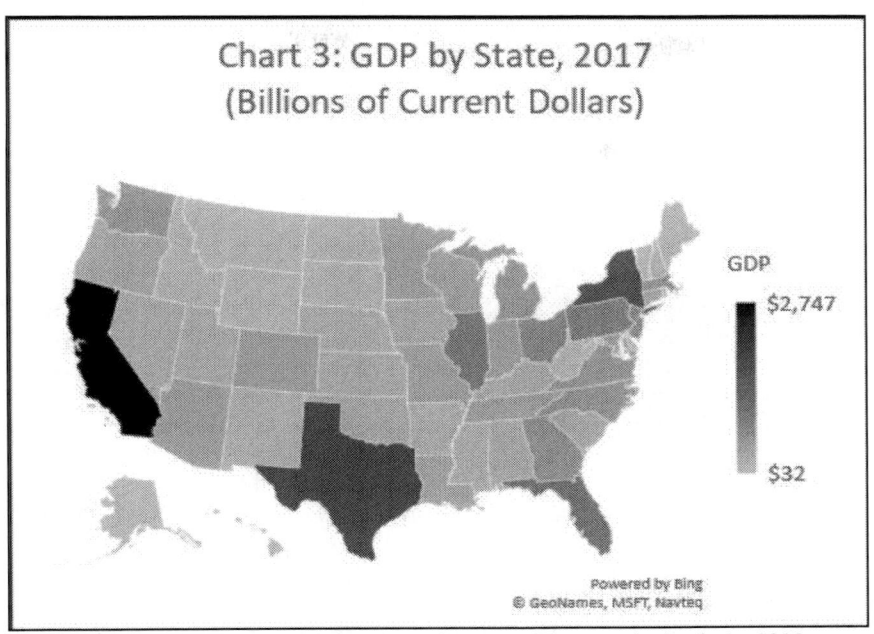

Chart 3: GDP by State, 2017 (Billions of Current Dollars)

GDP
$2,747
$32

Source: U.S. Department of Commerce, Bureau of Economic Analysis, 2018.

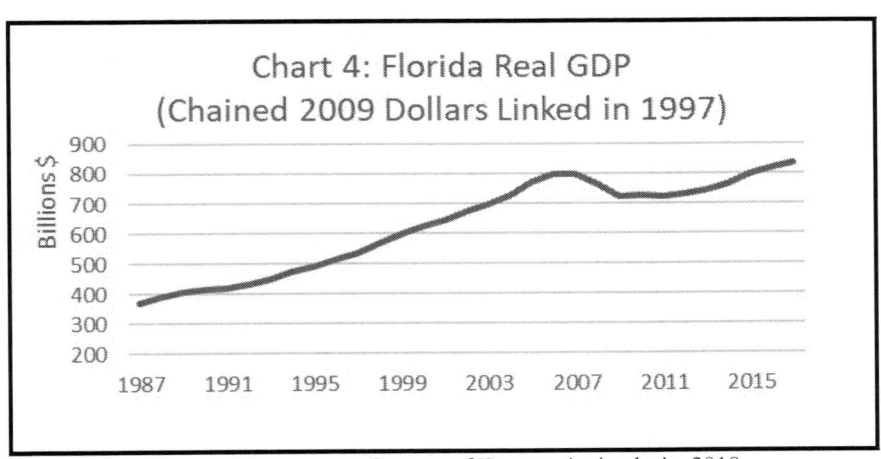

Chart 4: Florida Real GDP (Chained 2009 Dollars Linked in 1997)

Source: U.S. Dept. of Commerce, Bureau of Economic Analysis, 2018.

The largest industries in the private sector of the Florida economy, according to this broad industry breakdown, are, in descending order of their share of GDP:

finance, insurance, real estate, rental, and leasing; professional and business services; educational services, health care, and social assistance; retail trade; wholesale trade; arts, entertainment, recreation, accommodation, and food services; and manufacturing; construction; and information.

Exports Are Important for the Growth of Manufacturing and Latin America Is the Biggest Customer

Florida exported $55 billion in goods originating in the state in 2017 (origin is used to exclude goods produced in other states that are exported through Florida ports). This made Florida only the country's 8th biggest exporting state, ranking behind all the other mega-states, including Texas ($264 billion) ranked 1st, California ($172 billion) ranked 2nd, and New York ($75 billion) ranked 4th (Chart 5) (Enterprise Florida, 2018). Texas's main exports are petroleum and petroleum products, California is more diversified, but has a concentration in high technology exports. Washington State ($77 billion) is such an important exporter, showing darker on the map, because of its exports of aircraft, mainly from Boeing (U.S. Census Bureau, 2018).

While Florida is not as large of an exporter of goods as would be expected based on its position as the state with the 4th highest GDP, such a ranking, which only takes into accounts goods exports, underestimates Florida's true importance as a source of export earnings for the United States because it doesn't count services, most notably tourism, which for Florida is a big export industry.

The biggest customers for U.S. exports shipped from Florida are Brazil, Canada and Mexico in that order (Chart 6). (Note that, because of the availability of data, this is not the same basis as Florida origin, as it includes exports shipped from Florida originating in other states.) Germany and China are also important customers. But the striking thing about U.S. exports from Florida is their heavy concentration in Latin America and the Caribbean (including Mexico), which took 54 per cent of the state total in 2017 (Enterprise Florida, 2018). Florida, and particularly Miami, have very close economic and social ties to the region. Indeed, as will be argued in Chapter 13, Miami has become the emerging unofficial capital of Latin America. In contrast, Europe only took 19 per cent of U.S. exports shipped from Florida in 2017, and Asia and the Middle East only 17 per cent.

The top 25 U.S. Harmonized System (HS) commodities shipped from Florida, which encompasses Florida origin exports but also transshipments, includes: high-tech products like aircrafts and parts; telephone equipment and cell phones; non-monetary, unwrought gold; digital and network products like computers and other electronic devices; perfumes and toilet water; medical instruments; and boats and yachts (Table 3).

Table 2: Florida Real GDP by Industry (Millions of chained 2009 $)

Industry	2017	Per Cent Change from 1997	Per Cent of Total in 2017
All industry total	836,056	55.6	100.0
Private industries	743,274	62.9	88.9
Agriculture, forestry, fishing, and hunting	5,295	18.9	0.6
Mining, quarrying, and oil and gas extraction	1,487	-7.6	0.2
Utilities	14,113	1.5	1.7
Construction	40,840	2.8	4.9
Manufacturing	45,964	59.2	5.5
Wholesale trade	57,419	73.3	6.9
Retail trade	67,261	72.7	8.0
Transportation and warehousing	24,853	44.6	3.0
Information	40,115	149.9	4.8
Finance, insurance, real estate, rental, and leasing	183,873	73.8	22.0
Professional and business services	111,473	84.2	13.3
Educational services, health care, and social assistance	79,270	71.9	9.5
Arts, entertainment, recreation, accommodation, and food services	49,929	51.9	6.0
Government and government enterprises	93,272	12.5	11.2
Addenda:			
Natural resources and mining	6,806	14.8	0.8
Trade	124,663	72.7	14.9
Transportation and utilities	39,199	26.8	4.7
Private goods-producing industries	93,550	22.8	11.2
Private services-providing industries	649,478	70.9	77.7

Source: Bureau of Economic Analysis, 2018.

Chart 5: U.S. Exports by State of Origin, 2017

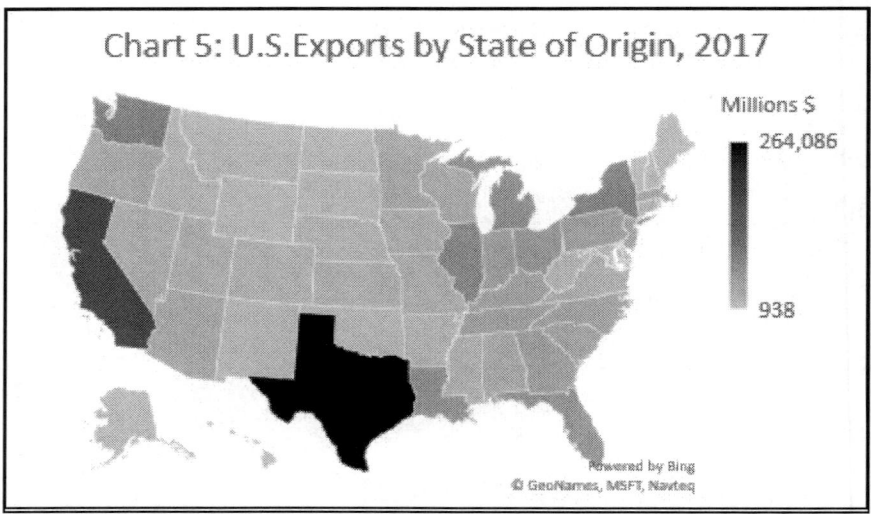

Millions $
264,086
938

Source: U.S. Department of Commerce, U.S. Census Bureau, Foreign Trade Division, as cited in Enterprise Florida, 2018.

Chart 6: Top 25 Destinations for U.S. Exports Shipped from Florida, 2017

Billions $
4,086
738

Source: U.S. Census Bureau, 2018.

Some of these commodities are only being transshipped from other states to, especially, Latin America, which places a lot of its orders through Florida or gets them shipped out of Florida ports. But a strong Florida-based manufacturing industry has developed and has also been contributing to export growth. The proximity of Florida to many U.S. airbases and Cape Canaveral has developed a globally competitive aerospace and high technology industry in Florida, which shows up at the top of the export list (see Chapter 20 on the military for more of a discussion of the links between the military and Florida's industry). This has helped Florida to grow its manufacturing sector during a time when other states with more traditional manufacturing sectors have been experiencing slower growth, or even declines, in production. Motor boats and yachts are natural exports for a state surrounded by water. Fertilizers (commodities containing phosphate and phosphorus on the list) long produced by Florida's mining industry, most notably Mosaic, continue to be an important export. Orange juice and sugar aren't on the list as they are mainly exported to other states and not so much internationally.

Per-Capita Income Growth Is Not So Good

Florida's growth in real GDP is much less impressive if you look more closely (Chart 7). This is because most of the increase in Florida's real GDP came from the strong increase in population, and not so much from increased real GDP per person. Nevertheless, the Florida economy was chugging along very solidly until it was hit by the real estate meltdown in 2007-2008. The dip in per-capita GDP that began then and continued through 2010 was led by a collapse of construction activity. The subsequent recovery, while more rapid than in most other states, has not been enough to make up for the ground lost due to the recession. Over the whole period, Florida per-capita-GDP fell from 91.4 per cent of the United States' average to 77.6 per cent.

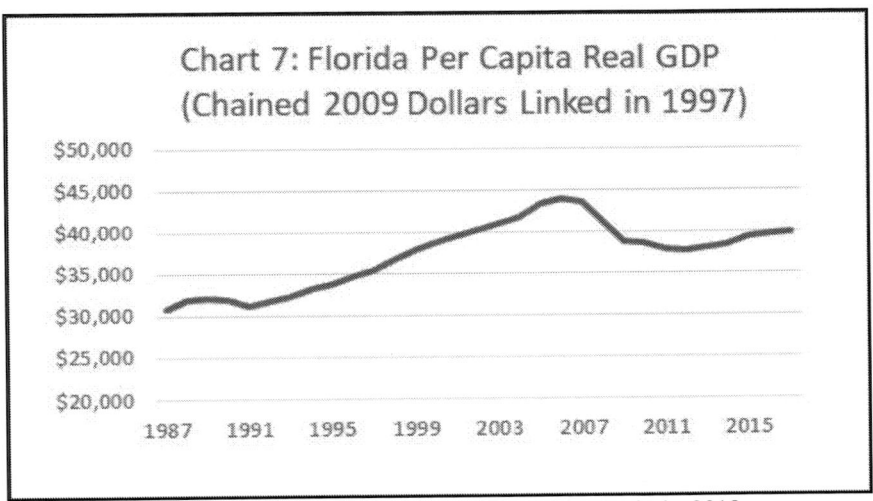

Chart 7: Florida Per Capita Real GDP (Chained 2009 Dollars Linked in 1997)

Source: U.S. Dept. of Commerce, Bureau of Economic Analysis, 2018.

Florida's per capita real GDP is also low in 2017 relative to other states (Chart 8). At $39,842 in 2017, Florida only ranks 40th out of the 50 states, even though it is higher than the other Southeast states except for neighboring Georgia ($45,925). The other mega-states have much higher per-capita real GDP (California, $60,359; Texas, $53,737 and New York, $65,220), not to mention the District of Columbia where Federal Government spending and employment has boosted per capita real GDP to a stratospheric $159,607. High-tech Massachusetts ($66,500), and energy-rich North Dakota ($64,911), Alaska ($63,610), and Wyoming ($61,091) (and most of the other

Table 3: Top 25 Exports Shipped from Florida (Origin of Movement) (Millions $)

HS Code	Description	2017
880000	Civilian aircraft, engines, and parts	6,326
851712	Phones for cellular networks or for other wireless networks	3,027
710812	Gold, nonmonetary, unwrought, NESOI	2,219
854231	Processors and controllers, electronic integrated circuits	952
851762	Telephone equipment	935
847130	Portable digital automatic data	885
330300	Perfumes and toilet waters	619
847330	Parts & accessories for ADP machines	605
901890	Instruments & appliances for medical surgical dental veterinary, NESOI	594
310540	Ammonium Dihydrogenorthophosphate	558
310559	Fertilizers containing nitrogen and phosphorus, NESOI	554
310530	Diammonium Hydrogenorthophosphate (DAP)	532
390810	Polyamide-6,-11,-12,-6,6,-6,9,-6,10 or -6,12	531
841199	Gas turbine parts, NESOI	482
870323	Passenger vehicles spark-ignition integrated components	433
711319	Jewelry and parts thereof, of other precious metals	430
950450	Video game consoles & machines, exclusive of subhead 9504.30	422
870899	Parts and accessories of motor vehicles, NESOI	400
847170	Automatic data processing storage units, NESOI	373
470321	Chemical woodpulp, soda etc. non-dissolvable semi bleached & bleached coniferous	311
844399	Parts & accessories of printers, copiers and fax machines, NESOI	304
890392	Motorboats, other than outboard motorboats	301
970110	Paintings, drawing and pastels by hand	283
210690	Food preparations, NESOI	260
890399	Yachts etc. for pleasure/sport, NESOI	259

Notes: HS Code here is a 6-digit code used to classify exports under the Harmonized System used in international trade.
NESOI is an acronym, which means "Not Elsewhere Specified Or Included."

Source: U.S. Census Bureau, 2018.

states for that matter) all have higher per capita real GDP. That's what being ranked 40th means. Only 10 states have lower per-capita real GDP.

The Florida Dreams Wage Paradox

Florida's relatively low per-capita income is a conundrum. How does Florida attract so many migrants if its level of income is so low? And how come Florida seems to be doing so well when real GDP per capita, one of the most widely used indicators of prosperity, suggests otherwise?

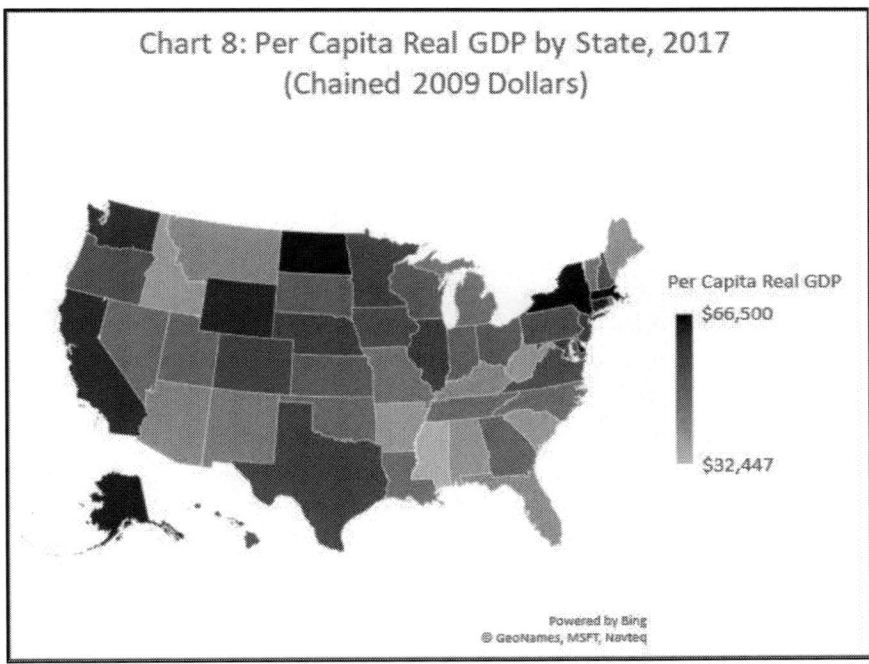

Chart 8: Per Capita Real GDP by State, 2017 (Chained 2009 Dollars)

Per Capita Real GDP
$66,500
$32,447

Source: U.S. Department of Commerce, Bureau of Economic Analysis, 2018.

The first and most obvious answer is that large numbers of people come to Florida because of the warm, sunny climate to retire, not to look for jobs. This is confirmed by a survey done by the Bureau of Business and Economic Research at the University of Florida that found that 40.6 per cent of in-migrants to Florida aged 65 years and older cited the climate as the main reason for moving to Florida. (Smith, 2005). Elderly migrants bring their pensions and accumulated wealth with them to finance their retirements, and don't need good-paying jobs. While the median net worth of Florida households estimated by a Census Bureau study (Chenevert, Gottschalck, Klee, and Zhang, 2017) is not great, indicating many people don't have a lot of assets, the mean level of net worth in 2013 was quite high ($1.8 million) putting Florida in 13th place. This suggests that quite a few people in Florida have a lot of money saved up and that many of them are probably choosing to spend it on their retirement dreams in Florida.

Moreover, the cost of housing in Florida is much lower than in the northern states where most of retirees come from. The same Bureau of Census study estimates that the median cost of housing in Florida was only $153,300, making it the 20th cheapest among all the states.

Another important group of migrants are those who come to Florida from overseas especially from the Latin America and Caribbean countries that have tropical or semitropical climates like Florida. Many of them come to Florida under Family-based immigration programs to join their families already here. Migrant social networks that help to integrate immigrants are also important factors encouraging immigration. And Florida has very large communities, which speak the languages of the countries that so many immigrants come from. This makes the immigrants feel right at home. Miami has become a city where Spanish speakers are in a majority. And many other Florida cities and towns also have large Spanish-speaking majorities. Florida Dreams are widespread throughout Latin America and the Caribbean because Florida is a place where people know they can make a much better living than in their home countries. And, sure, maybe they would make more if they immigrated to, say, Alaska, but it's cold up there, and who could they talk to?

According to a study by the Center for Immigration Studies (Vaughan, 2017), more than half of the immigrants coming to the United States in recent years came to join family members who are already here in what's called "chain migration." This includes the sponsorship of spouses and parents, which is unrestricted by law, as well as siblings and adult children, which is restricted and can result in long wait periods. The "migration multiplier," or the number of sponsored relatives for each immigrant, has averaged 3.45 in recent years and 6.38 for Mexicans who have the highest rate of "chain migration." This type of immigration is not responsive to the level of wages but has a momentum of its own.

Income hasn't grown as much in Florida because much of the demand for labor has been for lower skilled workers required to provide services to retirees and tourists and much of this demand has been met by immigrants willing to work for relatively low wages. This has kept wages down and at the same time enabled the labor market to absorb large numbers of new workers. The phenomena of low, relatively-flat wages persisting with high in-migration can be called the Florida Dreams Wage Paradox.

The median hourly wage in Florida in 2017 was $16.07. This means that half the workers in the state earned more than this and half less. Florida ranked 43rd among the states according to this indicator (Chart 9). It was much lower than in the other three mega-states (California, $19.70; Texas, $17.39; and New York, $21.00). It was even lower than in neighboring Georgia ($16.85).

The resulting dynamism of the Florida labor market is evidenced by the strong employment growth in Florida over the last three decades (Chart 10). Over the whole 1987 to 2017 period, employment in Florida grew by over 74 per cent or an average of 1.9 per cent per year. Even the setback in 2008 and 2009 resulting from the Great Recession was quickly made up by the pick-up in growth to 2.2 per cent per year over the course of the ongoing recovery. The only other mega-state that's in the same league as Florida with respect to employment growth since the crisis and over the longer run is Texas. And only a handful of smaller states such as Arizona, Colorado, Idaho, Nevada and Utah have managed to beat Florida's growth rate over the three decades.

The Florida labor market was able to provide employment for its fast-growing labor force without upward pressure on the unemployment rate over the last three decades. The only exception to this was during the period of cyclical weakness from 2008-2011 when the unemployment rate rose to over 11 per cent. As the economy recovered, employment growth picked up and the unemployment rate declined to a new low level (3.4 per cent in October 2018).

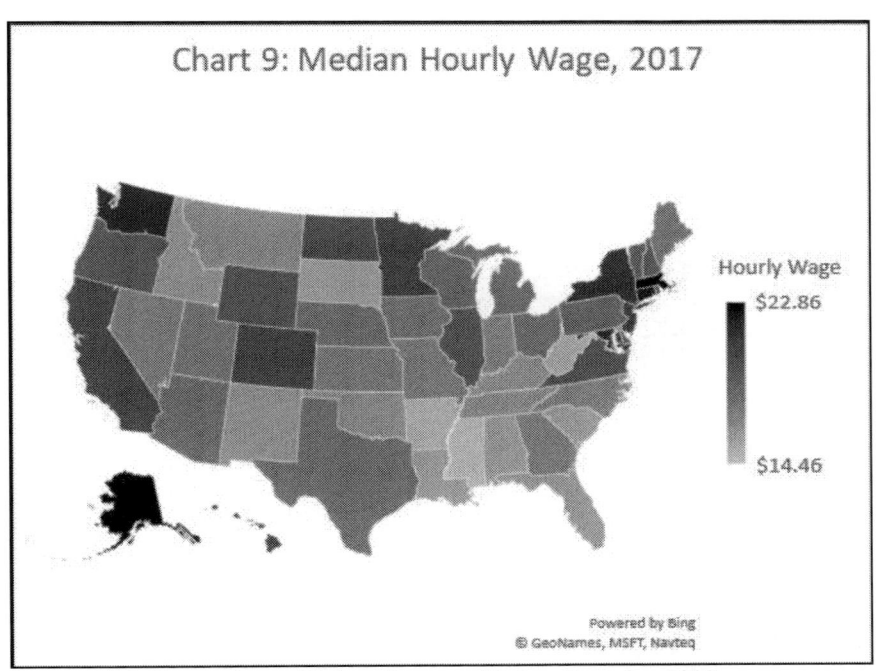

Chart 9: Median Hourly Wage, 2017

Hourly Wage
$22.86

$14.46

Powered by Bing
© GeoNames, MSFT, Navteq

Source: U.S. Department of Labor, Bureau of Labor Statistics, 2018.

While Florida only ranked 21st in terms of the lowness of its unemployment rate in 2017, it still was one of several states with exceptionally low unemployment rates and was below the United States' average of 4.4 per cent for the year (Chart 11). Overall the Florida labor market has been performing very well of late.

Which Industries Provide the Jobs?

The jobs in Florida are almost 90 per cent in the service producing industries and only 10 per cent in the good producing industries (Table 4). This is even more weighted towards services than the distribution of GDP. That's because productivity per worker is lower in services than in goods so that more employees are required per unit of output than in goods production.

Chart 10: Florida Employment (Millions)

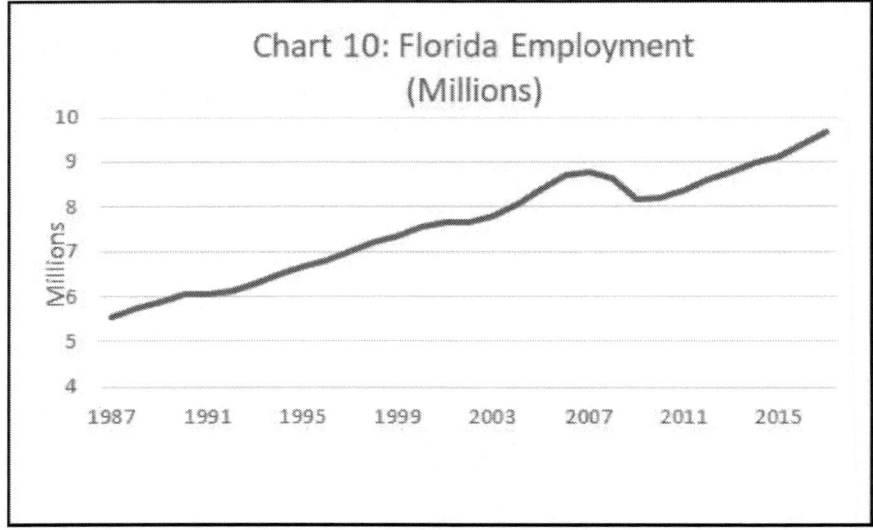

Source: U.S. Department of Labor, Bureau of Labor Statistics, 2018.

Chart 11: Unemployment Rate by State, 2017 (Annual Average)

Source: Department of Labor, Bureau of Labor Statistics, 2018.

Employment in the service industry grew strongly over the last two decades, whereas employment contracted in the goods producing industries. This is not because Florida produced less goods. On the contrary, goods production expanded. It's because output in the service industries grew so much more rapidly than goods, and productivity per worker increased slightly more slowly.

Employment in mining and manufacturing has been declining for decades. Construction employment has made a comeback from the 2007-2009 Great Recession but has grown much more slowly than GDP over the period.

The largest increases in jobs have been in business and professional services, education and health services, and leisure and hospitality (Table 4). Education and health services employment has been increasing in response to the surge in spending in these areas and the weakness of measured productivity gains. Leisure and hospitality includes accommodation, food services and drinking places, all of which have benefitted from the expansion of tourism.

What about Tourism?

Much data has been presented on the Florida economy, and yet no numbers for tourism, the goose that lays the golden egg. The data above show the real GDP, exports, and employment by broad industry categories. It fails to reveal, however, the overwhelming importance of the tourism sector for the Florida economy. That's because tourism is not a single nicely contained industry that fits in any of the traditional industry boxes. Rather it is a demand-side activity that includes all the spending of tourists on such diverse things as accommodation, food, entertainment, transportation, and shopping. Consequently, it's spread around all the industries affected in the economic accounts, and can only be added up through painstaking analysis, which requires many heroic assumptions. Nevertheless, only a fool would deny the obvious that tourism is Florida's number one generator of value and jobs. That's why to do it justice takes a whole chapter. If you can't wait to find out, you can always jump ahead to Chapter 12.

Table 4: Florida Employment by Industry, 2017

Title	2017	Per Cent Change From 1998	Per Cent of Total in 2017
Total Non-Agricultural Employment	8,566,800	29.6	100.0
Total Private	7,460,200	31.9	87.1
Goods Producing	873,800	-6.8	10.2
Service Producing	7,693,000	35.6	89.8
Private Service Providing	6,586,400	39.6	76.9
Mining and Logging	5,700	-20.8	0.1
Construction	504,500	13.1	5.9
Manufacturing	363,600	-24.5	4.2
Trade, Transportation, and Utilities	1,742,700	19.6	20.3
Wholesale Trade	343,800	11.5	4.0
Retail Trade	1,111,800	23.2	13.0
Transportation, Warehousing, and Utilities	287,100	16.8	3.4
Information	138,100	-14.2	1.6
Financial Activities	561,900	24.8	6.6
Professional and Business Services	1,321,900	75.8	15.4
Education and Health Services	1,272,700	58.9	14.9
Leisure and Hospitality	1,201,400	45.9	14.0
Other Services	347,800	26.6	4.1
Total Government	1,106,600	15.9	12.9
Federal Government	139,100	15.5	1.6
State Government	256,100	24.9	3.0
Local Government	711,500	13.1	8.3

Source: Florida Research and Economic Information Database Application (FREIDA), Current Employment Statistics, 2018.

4
THE ECONOMIC CLIMATE IS ALMOST AS GOOD AS THE WEATHER

Florida's Low-Tax, Business-Friendly Economic Climate

It's not only the nice, warm, sunny weather that draws people to Florida but the low-tax and business-friendly economic climate. Florida is not a place where people are embarrassed by old-fashioned American values like liberty, individualism, responsibility and self-reliance. Hard work is still rewarded without being subject to state income and estate taxes, piled on top of confiscatory federal taxes. People can pass their hard-earned wealth on to their heirs without the state government taking a bite. Free-market capitalist dreams are welcomed in the Sunshine Mega-State. Hand-outs by the state government are few and far between in comparison with what goes on in the Northeast and on the West Coast.

Economic growth in Florida has been as strong as it has largely because the government stays out of the way. In contrast, California and New York are big-government states with higher taxes and more generous social welfare systems. Their slow recent growth is no coincidence. Let's look more specifically at the difference between Florida and the other states.

No Big Government for Floridians

Per-capita spending by state and local governments in Florida was only $8,130 in 2015 (the latest year for which actual data are available) (Chart 12). This is the 3rd lowest level of spending in the country. It is way below the level of the two big-government mega-states of California and New York. In 2015, California spent $13,124 and ranked 5th highest among the states. New York spent $16,231 or twice as much per-capita as Florida and ranked 3rd highest among the states. The need to finance their higher levels of spending is the reason why California and New York must impose so much higher taxes than Florida. Even Texas, another smaller-government mega-state, spends $8,828 per capita or more than Florida. And Florida even spends less per capita than the other parsimonious Southern states, except for Georgia. The highest spending state is Alaska, which spends $22,700 per capita financed by their bountiful natural resource revenue.

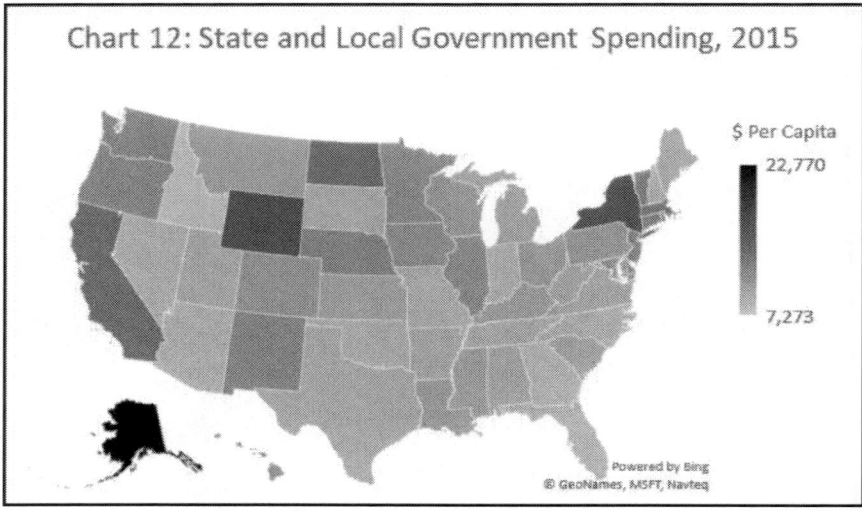

Chart 12: State and Local Government Spending, 2015

$ Per Capita
22,770

7,273

Source: usgovernmentspending.com, December 2018.

Not only is Florida a low-government-spending state in general, but it's also among the least generous in welfare spending that supports those either unable or unwilling to work (Chart 13). At $325 per capita in 2015, Florida ranked the 5th lowest in the nation. Only South Carolina, Alabama, Missouri, and Georgia spent less, and not by much. On the other hand, California and New York followed Alaska in topping the list of big welfare spenders with outlays of $1,075 and $991 per capita, or more than three times Florida. Texas, which ranked 6th lowest, only spent an insignificant $6 per-capita more than Florida.

A low-level of welfare spending is particularly important for a rapidly growing state attracting immigrants. Nobel-Prize-winning free-market economist Milton Friedman's off-the-cuff comment that "You cannot simultaneously have free immigration and a welfare state" may have touched on one of the keys to Florida's success. The meager welfare provided ensures that people only come to Florida if they are looking to work or otherwise can pay their own way. Handouts are not a part of the Florida Dream.

Floridians Get the Low Taxes They Demand

Since Florida is a state with low state and local government spending, it should be no surprise that Florida is also a low-tax state. A comprehensive measure of how much revenue state and local governments raise from their taxpayers is own-source revenue per capita, which is compiled annually from U.S. Census Bureau data by Florida Tax Watch, and "counts all direct revenue, including taxes and non-tax revenue such as charges for services, special assessments, impact fees, and net lottery revenue." (Florida Tax Watch, 2018, p.5). In Fiscal Year 2015, which runs from July 1, 2014 to

FLORIDA DREAMS

June 30, 2015, Florida collected $5,679 per capita (Chart 14). This was less than the $7,061 state average and put Florida at 42nd, near the bottom of the states in terms of the own source revenue collected. In contrast, California collected $8,379 and was ranked 8th, and New York raised $11,513 and was ranked 3rd. The tax burden on many in high-tax states will be increased further by the SALT cap in the 2017 Tax Cut and Jobs Act, which limits the deduction of state and local taxes from Federal Income Tax to a maximum of $10,000.

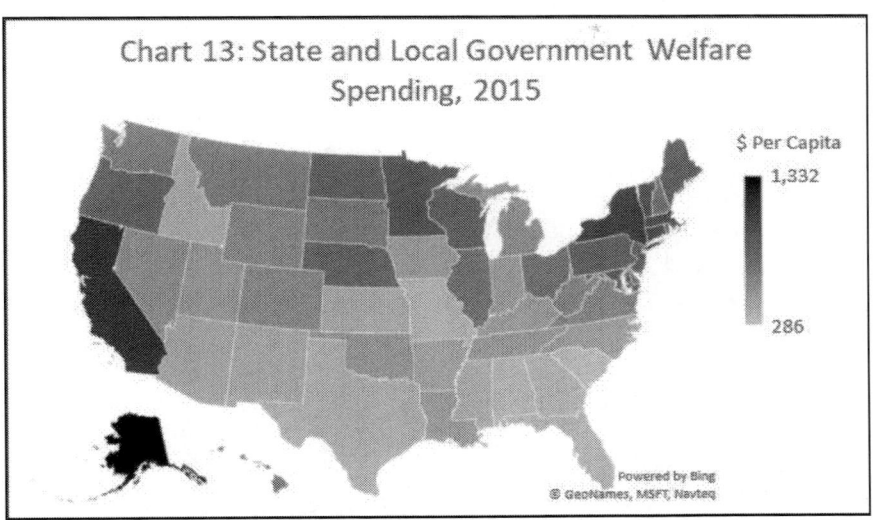

Chart 13: State and Local Government Welfare Spending, 2015

$ Per Capita
1,332
286

Source: usgovernmentspending.com, December 2018.

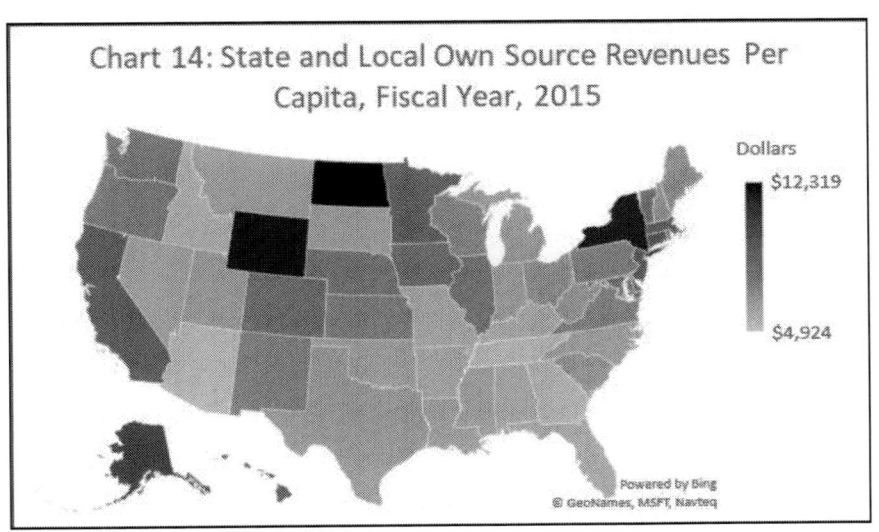

Chart 14: State and Local Own Source Revenues Per Capita, Fiscal Year, 2015

Dollars
$12,319
$4,924

Source: Florida Tax Watch, 2018.

Floridians can sleep peacefully in their beds not worrying that they will be paying any income, estate or inheritance taxes in the foreseeable future since such taxes are prohibited by Article VII, Section V of the State Constitution (as amended in 1968). And if Floridians have any doubts, they can take solid comfort in the fact that all five ways of revising the constitution set out in Article XI (Legislative Proposal, Revision Convention, Initiative, Constitutional Convention, Taxation and Budget Reform Commission) still require the approval of sixty per cent of voters in the next general election. My personal bet is that hell would freeze over first before that many Floridians would agree to pay an income tax.

Florida obviously comes out looking pretty good in any comparison of state income tax rates (Chart 15). Like Texas it has a zero top marginal income tax rate (since both have no state income tax). Zero is much lower than the top rate of 13.3 per cent in California, 8.82 per cent in New York, and 4.95 per cent in Illinois. To be fair, the highest top rate in California and New York is only for those making over a million dollars, but, in California, it is still 9.3 per cent over $53,980, and, in New York, 6.33 per cent over $21,400, which is still a lot higher than zero.

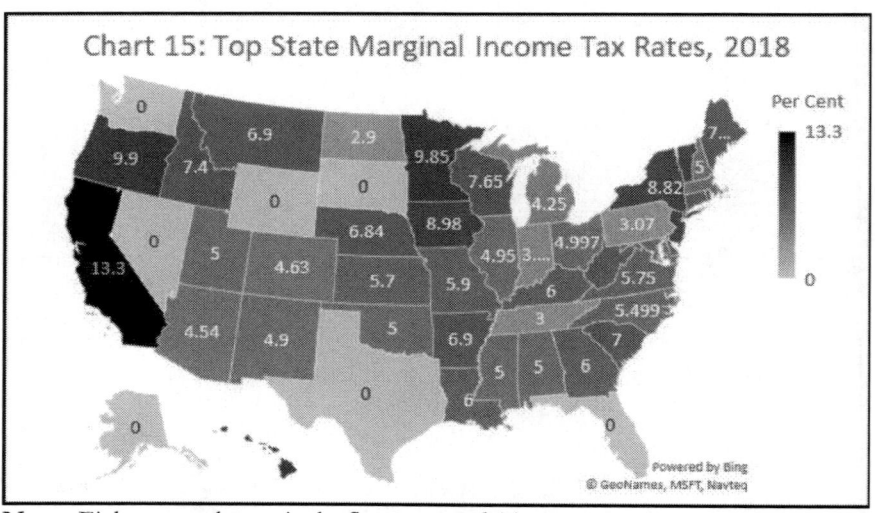

Chart 15: Top State Marginal Income Tax Rates, 2018

Note: Eight states have single flat rates and Tennessee only taxes interest and dividends.
Source: Scarboro, National Tax Foundation, 2018.

Florida's corporate income taxes are also relatively low according to data collected by the Tax Foundation (Chart 16). The corporate income tax rate in 2017 (and which remains the same) was 5.5 per cent. This is at the low end of the range of state corporate income taxes and certainly below the 8.84 per cent in California and the 6.5 per cent in New York. Texas does not impose a corporate income tax, but instead levies a gross receipts tax, which is considered to be a more economically-damaging tax by many economists. Moderate corporate income tax rates along with no personal income taxes give Florida's corporations and unincorporated businesses a competitive edge.

FLORIDA DREAMS

Florida's collection of local property taxes at $1,244 in Fiscal Year 2015 was in the middle of the pack, but below the average of $1,474 (Florida Tax Watch, 2018, p.42). They were also well below those in New York, which was near the top of the list at $2,697, but not so far below California which at $1,402 was also below the average as a result of the restrictions imposed in 1978 by Proposition 8 and subsequent propositions.

Chart 16: Top Corporate Income Tax Rate, 2017

Source: Scarboro, National Tax Foundation, 2017.

There are two important features of the Florida property tax system that make the burden on residents less than it might appear at first glance. The first is the Homestead Exemption that allows a Florida resident to shield $25,000 of a property's assessed value from property tax and an additional $25,000 exemption for the taxable value greater than $50,000 up to $75,000, for all tax levies except school district levies. The second feature that reduces the property tax burden is the Save Our Homes Act that caps the increase in assessment of a homesteaded residence at the lesser of the increase in the consumer price index or 3 per cent. These two measures ensure that a disproportionate (and admittedly unfair) share of property tax is paid by snowbirds and other seasonal residents who don't have the vote.

Not all taxes are rock bottom in Florida. Florida levies a state sales tax at 6 per cent and allows local governments to tag on an extra up-to 2 per cent (Chart 17). The combined tax rate (calculated by the Tax Foundation) averages 6.8 per cent, which puts Florida in the middle of the pack with a rank of 28th. But Floridians need not despair as this still puts their state below the 8.55 per cent rate in California and the 8.49 per cent rate in New York, which again are near the top. More surprisingly, usually low-tax Texas is, at 8.17 per cent, not far behind California and New York. And the situation in Florida is even better than it looks. Florida is a state with lots of tourists and a higher sales tax rate is a good way to shift some of the tax burden onto them. The Florida Legislative Office of Economics and Demographic Research estimated that in Fiscal Year 2015-16, 13.0 per cent of sales tax revenues (or almost $2.86 billion) could be attributed to spending by tourists.

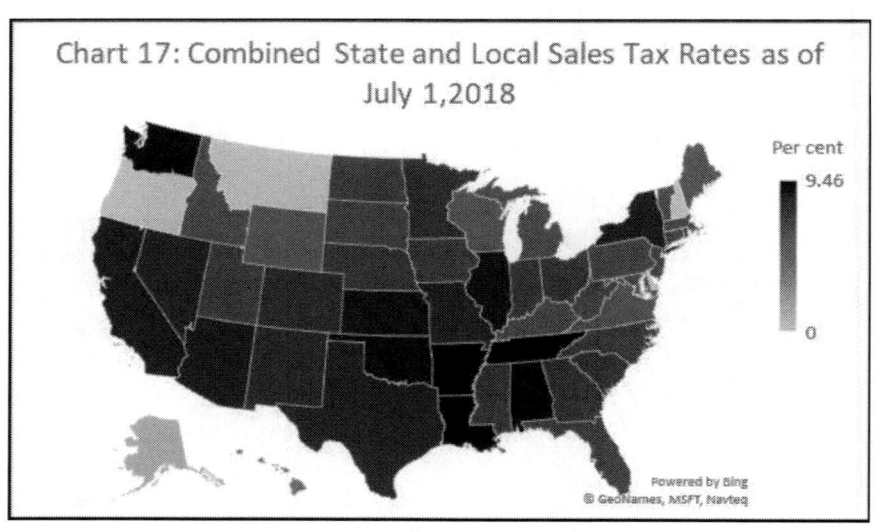

Chart 17: Combined State and Local Sales Tax Rates as of July 1, 2018

Source: Walczak and Drenkard, Tax Foundation, 2018.

Florida Has a Very Healthy Fiscal Position

A good overall assessment of the fiscal health of state governments across the United States has been prepared now for four years by the Mercatus Center at George Mason University (Norcross and Gonzalez, 2017). This assessment calculates an indicator used to rank the states based on the fiscal solvency of the states in five separate categories: cash solvency or the ability to pay short-term bills; budget solvency or the ability to finance budget spending out of revenues; long-run solvency or the ability of the state to cover its long-term spending commitments; service solvency or the ability to satisfy demands for needed increased spending; and trust fund solvency or the magnitude of a state's unfunded pension and healthcare liabilities. The indicators in these categories are combined into a single more comprehensive indicator that can be used to rank the fiscal health of states.

According to the Mercatus study, Florida was ranked as the healthiest state government in 2017, or 1st (Chart 18). This was because the state had plenty of cash on hand (almost too much in Mercatus's view), a small budget surplus, low liabilities and debt, and only relatively modest unfunded pension liabilities (Norcross and Gonzalez, 2017, p.39). In contrast, California and New York came in at the low end of the Mercatus ranking at 43rd and 39th respectively. Texas, on the other hand, ranked in the middle of the pack at 23rd.

FLORIDA DREAMS

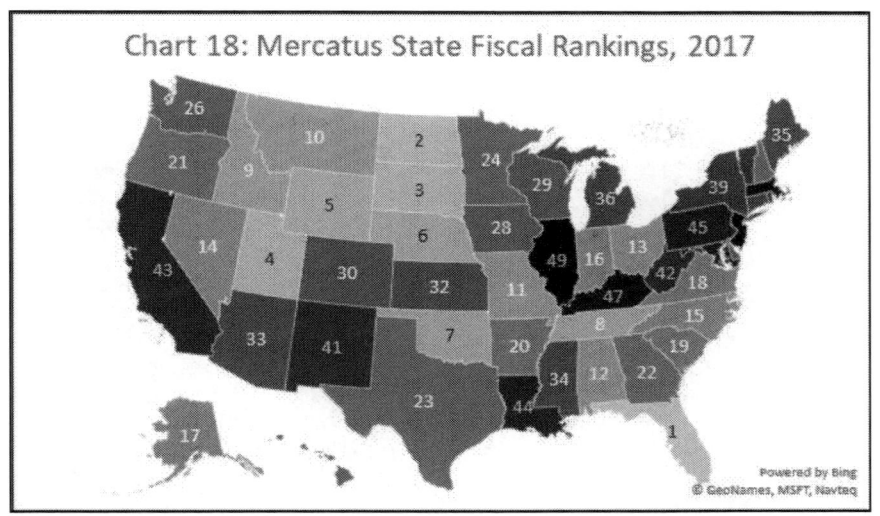

Chart 18: Mercatus State Fiscal Rankings, 2017

Source: Mercatus Center, George Mason University.

A key ingredient in Florida's fiscal health is the extent to which its public pensions and other post-employment benefits (such as healthcare) are not as underfunded as in other states, such as California, New York, Illinois and New Jersey. This is because public employees are not paid as well in Florida and the Florida state government has been much less generous in promising future pensions and benefits in order to attract and retain employees.

Another good indicator of the fiscal health of a state is its credit rating. These are prepared regularly and published by credit rating agencies such as Standard and Poor's, Moody's, and Fitch. Standard and Poor's state credit ratings, which are considered here (Chart 19), classify states by their ability to pay their debts, and the strength of the state's economy. Like back in school, it then assigns a letter grade to each of the states. Fifteen states, including Florida, get: the highest rating of AAA, which means an "extremely strong" capacity to repay; 13 states get AA+, 13 AA, 6 AA-, all of which mean lessening degrees of "very strong;" 1 gets A+, 1 gets A-, which represent lessening degrees of "strong;" and 1 gets BBB-, which means "adequate." These rating levels for state governments are all considered "investment grade." BB+, which comes below BBB-, indicates that the government "faces major future uncertainties," and that its bonds are considered "speculative" or "junk," as they are flippantly called by those in the trade.

Florida's fiscal health at AAA is the same as Texas, but significantly better than the big-government mega-states New York at AA+ and California at AA-. The state with the BBB- is Illinois. It's another big-government state with huge unfunded pension liabilities that was downgraded iJune 2017 and that could have its debt classified as "junk" if it doesn't get its act together.

Chart 19: Standard & Poor's State Credit Ratings, 2017

Source: Standard & Poor's; Pew Charitable Trust, 2017; Ballotpedia. Updated from press reports for downgrades in AK, IL and NJ.

The small-government, low-tax, fiscally-responsible, no-deficit, anti-debt ethos that has shaped Florida government policy over the years under both Republican and Democratic governments (but maybe not so much under any future more progressive Democratic governments) is the reason that Florida has had the most market-oriented, business-friendly economic climate of all the major states. This has been one of the keys to the state's phenomenal economic growth. Floridians don't believe so much in the spend-now-pay-later philosophy that has gotten other states like California, New York, Illinois and New Jersey in fiscal trouble and weighed down their credit ratings.

In 2018, Florida was named the 2nd best place to do business in the United States by Chief Executive Magazine behind only oil-rich Texas. And the worst? You guessed it. California came in dead last, just behind New York and Illinois. You're getting the picture.

A Very Flexible Labor Market Facilitates Job Growth

Another factor in the state's phenomenal growth is its flexible labor market. Florida is a right-to-work state. This is a state that has outlawed closed union shops and prohibits employers from forcing workers to join, or financially support a union, as a condition of employment. There are 27 such states, largely in the south and west central areas of the country but also including some in the Midwest (Chart 20). The states without right-to-work laws include the large states like California on the West Coast, New York and Pennsylvania in the Northeast, and Ohio and Illinois in the Midwest, all of which, except for California, are rustbelt states where unions used to be very dominant, even if not quite so much anymore.

FLORIDA DREAMS

Chart 20: Right-to-Work States, 2018

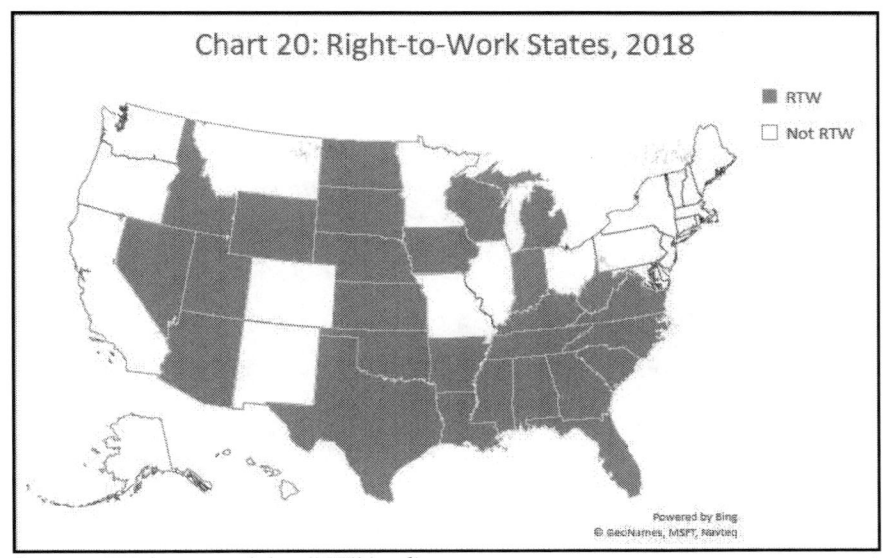

Source: "Right-to-work law," Wikipedia.

As a right-to-work state, Florida has a low level of unionization. In 2017, only 5.6 per cent of employed workers were members of a union (Chart 21). This was only a quarter of the 23.8 per cent unionization rate in the old industrial mega-state of New York and less than half the 15.5 per cent in California with its heavily unionized public sector. The Sunbelt states like Florida, except for Nevada and California, all have relatively low levels of unionization.

While Florida's minimum wage of $8.25 per hour in 2018 only puts it in the middle of the pack, it is not too far above the states clustered at the bottom of the minimum wage table. Moreover, it is still probably low enough that it should not interfere with the demand for low-skilled labor. This is important because much of the increased immigrant supply of labor coming into the state is low skilled and has only been able to find employment at low wages, as was explained in Chapter 3. On the other hand, California and New York, which also have many low-skilled immigrants who must find low wage jobs, have higher minimum wages at $11 and $10.40 per hour respectively, but also have higher costs of living. Moreover, both states buckling under pressure from the "Fight for $15 Movement" have legislated increases in their minimum wages which will take them to the $15 target. The risk is that such a high level of minimum wage will induce many employers to cut back on the number of people hired, particularly at the entry level, if the productivity of those workers happens to be less than the legally required wage. This will make it more difficult for many new immigrants and young people just entering the labor market to find jobs.

Walt Disney World recently signed a contract with the unions representing 38,000 service employees to hike its minimum wage for service employees from $11 to $15 by 2021 (Langone, 2018). While this may resemble an increase in the government mandated minimum wage, its economic impact is quite different because it is based on labor market conditions and reflects Disney's need to attract employees and have good relations with its unions.

In 2016, Miami Beach approved an incremental increase in the minimum wage to $10.31 an hour in 2018 and to $13.31 an hour by 2021. This increase, however, is being challenged in the courts by the state government and business groups who claim that local governments cannot set higher minimum wages than the state level because it runs counter to a "preemption law" (Saunders, 2018).

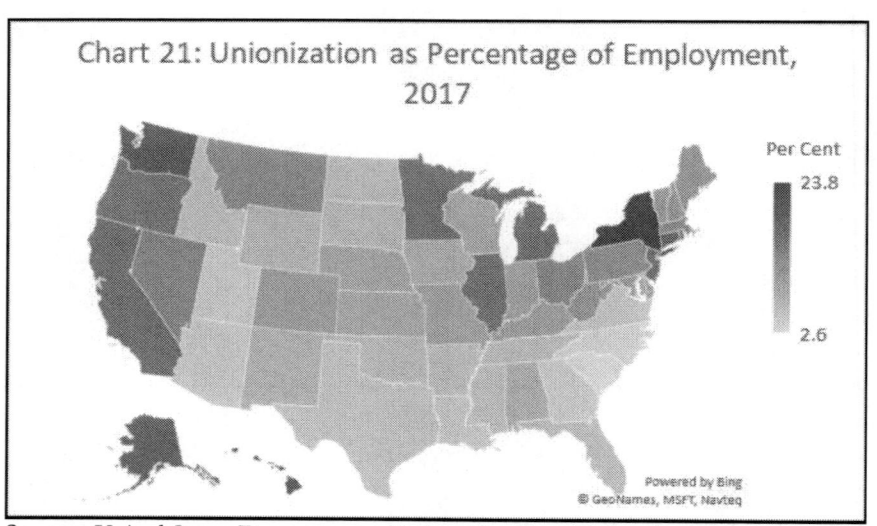

Chart 21: Unionization as Percentage of Employment, 2017

Source: United States Department of Labor, Bureau of Labor Statistics.

5
WAVES OF RETIREES WASH UP, AND NOT ONLY ON THE BEACHES

Florida is the Mecca for America's senior citizens. Like a giant magnet, it pulls in far more retirees than any other state. They come to escape the cold northern winters in warm and sunny Florida. And many, particularly the more affluent, also seek to get out from under the burden of the income and estate taxes levied in their home states.

According the American Community Survey carried out annually by the U.S. Census Bureau, 850,843 people 55 years of age and over moved to Florida over the 2011 to 2016 period. This is an average of 388 people every day over the six-year period. Not all these people were retiring. In fact, 18.3 per cent of Floridians 65 and over remained in the labor force in 2017 (Bureau of Labor Statistics, 2018). But most seniors coming to Florida were retiring, or at the very least, planning to cut back on their work or only do volunteering. People 55 and over made up 27 per cent of the 3,149,920 people who took up residence in Florida over this period. And in 2016, these senior migrants, who came over this period 2011 to 2016, already constituted 12.5 per cent of the 6,820,180 people 55 and over living in Florida in 2016, resulting in more than half the growth in this senior demographic group over the period.

The biggest wave of all now coming to Florida is the baby boomers (those born after World War II from 1946 to 1964). The leading-edge boomers started arriving a decade or more ago. And the tail-enders will continue to struggle in for another decade or so. In Florida, they will join an already large cohort of aging boomers and others on the cusp. The population of Florida will continue to grow older. The Florida Department of Elder Affairs projects that the population in the state 60 and over will grow to 7.3 million by 2030, a 42 per cent or 2.2 million increase from the 2016 level (Florida Department of Elder Affairs, 2016).

While we come in all races and ethnicities, boomers like myself are mostly, and disproportionately, white (88 per cent of the population over 60 in 2015 were white according to the Florida Department of Elder Affairs). This reflects the demographic composition of the country back around the time we were born. We've gone through our lives moving up the population pyramid and carelessly shaking up American society to the roots as we went. It started with overcrowding in maternity wards. Then the school building boom of the 1950s. Who could forget the way many embraced sex drugs and rock and roll in the 1960s. And the anti-war protests that rocked our nation and brought down a President. Birth control was the catalyst of the sexual revolution. It facilitated sex out of marriage and small families, both of which were welcomed by the me-generation. The tech boom led by the likes of Bill Gates, Steve Jobs, Jeff Bezos fundamentally transformed our economy and society first making computers widely available and then magically putting them in all our hands as phones, thereby tethering us 24/7 to social networks, games and cute cat videos.

Politically, many of us have run the full spectrum from liberal anti-war protesters of the 1960s to the Trump deplorables of today. Others have stuck with their youthful liberalism and become the liberal journalists, professors, and teachers who have taken over our cultural and educational institutions, overturning the country's traditional conservative and religious values, and pushing our society in an increasingly liberal direction. However, the experience of having our country attacked on 9/11 in New York and Washington and witnessing the Twin Towers crash down on our television screens was a gut-wrenching shock that restored at least temporarily a semblance of the patriotism our parents had felt during WWII. But, with time, this too has passed.

And, now, baby boomers are turning their focus on the main task remaining before we check out, and I'm not talking about picking out tombstones, but rather radically reshaping the meaning of retirement. People are living longer and are in better physical condition. They are attracted by the year-around active lifestyles possible in Florida. It's not unusual for boomers to participate in 5 and 10K runs while their friends up north are hunkered down in their ice and snow covered homes. Reliving our youth, or making up for what we missed, we play on tennis and pickleball teams and in golf and bocce leagues in large numbers.

In my home town of Punta Gorda, some boomers even join in the annual July 4th Freedom Swim, which is 1 ½ miles across Charlotte Harbor. Well, to be honest, swim is something of an exaggeration. It's more of a happening with an armada of floaties, kickboards and plenty of beer in floating coolers. Skinny-dipping was dropped from the celebration as the participants aged. Instead, bathing suits, many red-white and blue or star spangled, became the preferred costume.

In the good old days, retirement was not a multi-decade period filled with travel, adventure, entertainment, and the good life, in a totally different part of the country. Rather, it was a few quiet years that people could spend close to their grown-up children and grandkids, continuing to do favorite but routine activities in local groups, clubs, churches, health permitting. Rarely would someone pull up stakes and move to a completely different state, and take up a raft of new, unfamiliar pastimes. This, as you will see, is something that boomers moving to Florida have taken to a whole new level. While they are insatiably looking for something new and exciting, they also feel more secure and comfortable in familiar, almost Rockwellesque, surroundings. This means building new communities based on just the right mixture of conservative and liberal values. But, since we are getting older, the emphasis will naturally shift over time more to the conservative. The tastes of many of these retirees understandably lean towards Yesterworld, which is where we grew up.

Themed Communities for Retirees

Florida, which has learned a thing or two from Walt, has taken the bull by the horns and hastened to accommodate the deepest and most nostalgic desires of baby boomers with a proliferation of 55 plus communities (more than 300 by one count). These are age restricted communities, which, to qualify under the Federal Housing for Older Persons Act, must have 80 per cent of homes with at least one person 55 or older, and which can prohibit children under 18 from living in the community. Some of these communities have even taken advantage of Chapter 190 of the Florida statutes, which confers broad local governmental powers on the developer, at least for a time, to impose additional restrictions.

Many retirees like age-restricted (or age-segregated to use a blunter term) communities because they find them much more peaceful without all the bothersome resident children running around, screaming, whining, fighting, playing, and splashing in the pool as kids everywhere so love to do. Of course, most seniors like to see their own grandchildren for a while at least, but they also take comfort that the little devils don't visit for so long and that peace and quiet will soon be restored. That's why God made it impossible for old people to have children.

There are also the obvious financial advantages to living in a community with no children. Taxes and new housing impact fees are lower because no money needs to be raised to pay for schools or playgrounds. Finally, some people just prefer being around people like themselves, of their own age, with similar values and interests. Even so, most people retiring to Florida don't chose to live in age restricted communities, maybe because they like being around people of all ages, in an age integrated community, or maybe because that's just what they're used to, and what seems like a less artificial and more normal way of life. The Florida Dream may be of a life without children for some seniors, but not for most.

Many retirement communities, age restricted or not, have been built right out of the swamp, or at least on nearby scrublands, to recreate the small-town communities of yesteryear where many retirees grew up, or visited their grandparents, and still pine for. The gates, which were absent in the past, are a conspicuous concession to the more dangerous and exclusionary times we live in, but in most areas of Florida are not necessary.

Many of Florida's 55 plus communities are rated the best in the country. Cision PR Newswire (2015) published a list of the 55 best 55 plus communities in the United States in 2015 and 21 or 38 per cent of them were in Florida. The Florida communities considered among the country's best were:

- The Villages – The Villages, FL
- On Top of the World – Ocala, FL
- Solivita – Kissimmee, FL
- Stone Creek – Ocala, FL
- Sun City Center – Sun City Center, FL
- Kings Point – Sun City Center, FL
- Del Webb Ponte Vedra – Ponte Vedra, FL
- Del Webb Naples – Ave Maria, FL
- Timber Pines – Spring Hill, FL
- Pelican Preserve – Fort Myers, FL

- Sweetwater – Jacksonville, FL
- The Plantation At Leesburg – Leesburg, FL
- Valencia Lakes – Wimauma, FL
- Southshore Falls – Apollo Beach, FL
- Heritage Isle – Viera, FL
- Oak Run – Ocala, FL
- Del Webb Orlando – Davenport, FL
- Tampa Bay G&C Club – San Antonio, FL
- Spruce Creek CC – Summerfield, FL
- Ocala Palms – Ocala, FL
- King Isles – Port St. Lucie, FL

Where Retirees Settle

Retirees tend to huddle together in their communities concentrated in certain areas of the state (Chart 22). The darkest county on the map sticking out up in the center of the state is none other than Sumter where a hefty 56.9 per cent of the population was over 65 in 2017. This is where The Villages, the mother of all Florida retirement communities, is centered (although the community also extends into neighboring Lake and Marion counties). It's 60 miles northwest of Orlando. The two darker counties on the southwest coast are my own county, Charlotte, which has 39.4 per cent of the population over 65, counting me and my wife, and Sarasota, which has 36.1 per cent. Unlike Sumter, there is no dominant 55 plus community in these areas, just a lot of retirees living in proximity. The dark county east of them is Highlands, which has 34.8 per cent of the population over 65. It also has no dominant 55 plus community but has a concentration of smaller ones around Sebring.

The Mother of All Retirement Communities

From a modest start as the Orange Blossom Gardens mobile home park, The Villages was aggressively promoted and marketed by its founder Harold Schwartz and especially his son H. Gary Morris, an ex-Chicago advertising executive (whose last name was that of his mother's second husband). Now in 2017, it has reached a population of 125,165. More importantly, it has become the best known 55 plus community in the United States, if not the world. Republican (but not Democratic) presidential and vice-presidential candidates, including Mitt Romney, Sarah Palin, Paul Ryan, and Mike Pence, have all come calling at election time to speak and get the obligatory photo op with that much-cultivated demographic – the old retired white voter who votes Republican two to one and can be counted on to turn out 80 per cent of the time

The Villages, which bills itself as Florida's Friendliest Hometown, is one of the fastest growing communities in the United States. From 2010 to 2017, the main portion in Sumter county grew by about a third or over 4 per cent per year. The formula behind its success has been to offer a wide variety of homes with price tags from as low as $100,000 to over a million (with a median home value of about $250,000). The homes range from manufactured homes, to condominiums and town houses or villas, to some magnificent estate homes.

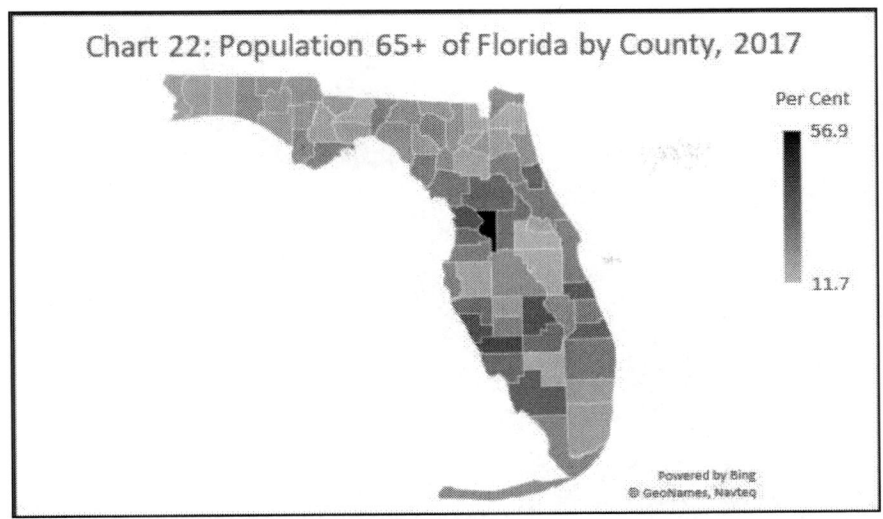

> **Chart 22: Population 65+ of Florida by County, 2017**
>
> Per Cent
> 56.9
> 11.7

Source: U.S. Census Bureau, QuickFacts, 2018.

Retirees who live in The Villages are not millionaires. They're just ordinary middle-class people. The 42,040 taxpayers filing in the two Villages zip codes (32162 and 32159) reported an average adjusted gross income on the 1040s they submitted to the IRS in 2016 of $80,429. This is enough to afford a comfortable dream retirement in the Florida sun, but certainly doesn't qualify as high income.

The Villages is laid out, in Disneyesque fashion, with three themed town centers: Spanish Springs Town Square has a southwestern, Spanish colonial look; Lake Sumter Landing Market Square resembles a lakeside Key West; and the newest Brownwood Paddock Square is supposed to be an Old Florida cow town. The town centers come complete with made-up histories conspicuously displayed on plaques, which I think emphasizes the artificiality of the place, but which evidently appeals to aging baby boomers seeking links to the past, however tenuous they may be. The restaurants in the town centers lean toward the chains, and the stores are the same type as those found in the garden variety-upscale Florida mall. The Villages also has its own house organs: radio station, WVLG; and newspaper, The Villages Daily Sun.

The over 60 neighborhoods collectively making up The Villages are, not surprisingly, called villages. They are governed as community development districts under Chapter 190 of the Florida statutes. This law confers municipal-like powers to raise revenues and provide infrastructure, without having to become incorporated as a city or town. And the town centers are set up as separate central community development districts. The developer owns the town centers 100 per cent and thus exercises total control over them, as well as has control over the individual community development districts for several years until they are transferred to the residents. This centralization of decision-making authority in the developer's hand, in contrast to the citizens' participation in regular incorporated municipal governments, has given rise to concerns about a democratic deficit. But most Villagers seem to be happy to let the

Statue Containing the Ashes of The Villages' Founding Father.

developer run everything and get on with living their Florida Dreams.

The biggest attraction of The Villages is the many activities it offers retirees who have become accustomed to busy lives, and do not want to idle away their remaining years like their grandparents did in rocking chairs on their front porches. Leaving their cars at home, they buzz around the 100 miles of paths, busily flitting from one activity to another, in their celebrated customized golf carts. There are: 11 country clubs and 30 executive golf courses for the golfers, delivering on the promise of "free golf for life;" 200 tennis courts and 100 pickleball courts for the racquet sports enthusiasts; and 90 recreation centers that offer the whole range of activities from water sports, dance, exercise, yoga, Pilates, cards, board games, arts and crafts, and you name it. Three major centers offer live entertainment in addition to the nightly free entertainment in the town squares, which includes the always popular line dancing. Tribute bands are all the rage in The Villages, indeed all over Florida, if the real thing isn't available, which it seldom is. All in all, The Villages is a pretty lively place for aging boomers. Maybe too lively for some.

Sexual activity is a common pastime wherever there are post pubescent people of any age. Its manifestation in The Villages has caught the eye of the tabloid paparazzi. The *New York Post* published an article in 2009 claiming that "wild retirees" sex was causing a major STD outbreak in The Villages. This shocking allegation, which was taken from a book about The Villages called *Leisureville* (Blechman, 2008), caused quite a sensation, pandering as it did so successfully to the liberal reading public's prurience and dislike of largely conservative old people. Blechman was tipped off about this story by an informant he hung with who was called Mr. Midnight (not the man's real name but the moniker he gave his favorite appendage). Seriously, I'm not making this up. Not surprisingly, the topic of promiscuous geriatric sex and STDs just won't go away and keeps coming up wherever people gather to talk about The Villages and retirement communities in general, even in Punta Gorda, which, by the way, is not totally inhabited by puritans.

So, is The Villages a modern-day Sodom and Gomorrah for retirees? The data on STDs from the Florida Department of Health strongly suggest not. In 2015, the latest year available, Sumter County, where The Villages is located, had the lowest rate of STDs (Gonorrhea, Chlamydia & Infectious Syphilis) in all of Florida. The Villages' alarming STD epidemic is more fake news, folks.

This, of course, is not to deny that there have been a couple of reported incidents (which provided fodder for *Leisureville*) of sex in the golf carts or other awkward and inappropriate public places. Seniors living in The Villages and elsewhere, like everyone else, are facing the issue of their own sexuality and their need for meaningful sexual relationships, some more responsibly than others, like everywhere else. (Jane Bloom, 2014).

There are other more real issues that The Villages face, like, for example, Florida sinkholes. In an article on their science, *Smithsonian Magazine* reported The Villages was a "hotbed" with dozens and dozens erupting over the past couple of years (Bodenner,2018). And then there's the little matter of the IRS investigation of The Villages use of tax-free community development bonds, which has been festering for almost a decade. But don't worry, it will probably be worked out now that the IRS is out of Democratic hands.

And, if Golf gets boring, why not try polo?

Ryan Erisman wrote *Inside the Bubble: The Unauthorized Guide to Florida's Most Popular Community*, which, by the way, people seriously interested in The Villages should get. It contains the information they need to know before making the move, and not just the developer's sales pitch.

As an aside, a Villages' commercial on TV caught my cousin Paul's eye. He told me he might like to retire there. Sadly, he died before he was able to go down and check it out. While The Villages isn't everyone's cup of tea, the people who live there seem to have lots of fun and love it.

Jimmy Buffet, the laid-back troubadour of the Keys, has spawned a devoted following called ParrotHeads who swarm to his concerts and can't seem to get enough of him. Buffet has capitalized on his popularity by establishing a large chain of Margaritaville-brand restaurants, bars, resorts, and casinos all over America and the Caribbean. And now, in partnership with Minto, he is going head-to-head with The Villages and other retirement communities under the brand "Latitude Margaritaville" in Daytona and near Panama City (Storey, 2018). Retirement communities have become a very lucrative and competitive big business that is attracting a lot of developers and investors, like bees to honey.

How Much Does It Cost?

While it's not cheap to retire to Florida, it's not expensive either. There are a wide variety of lifestyles depending on the retiree's budget and preferences. An idea of the costs has recently been provided by Hillary Hoffower in *Business Insider*. There she presents illustrative budgets required for a couple to retire in three Florida cities, that get progressively costlier. Jacksonville, at the bottom of the scale, cost $50,536 per year, then comes Orlando at $54,884, and finally the most upscale, Boca Raton, at $72,425. If the couple considered in the illustrative example were to receive $27,000 in Social Security benefits between the two of them, the remainder, that they would have to pay out of their investments or pensions, would be $23,536 in Jacksonville, $27,884 in Orlando, and $45,425 in Boca Raton. (Hoffower, 2018). Living a Florida Dream of a sunny, warm retirement is clearly within the reach of many middle-class Americans provided they have built up a nest egg or equity in a strong housing market somewhere up north.

Retirees Bring Money and Bolster the Economy

The elderly are less likely to be poor than other Florida residents. Only 545,904 or 10.6 per cent of them live below the poverty line. The fact that seniors qualify for Social Security benefits is the main reason why they experience a lower incidence of poverty than the rest of the population. But they also usually have private pensions, IRAs, 401-Ks or other investments to support themselves.

Retirees bring an enormous amount of money into Florida from Social Security. In 2017, residents of Florida received $5.9 billion in old age, survivors, and disability insurance program (OASDI) benefits. This made Florida the state with second largest amount of benefits, behind only California, which only received $7.5 billion despite its much larger population. Texas received the 3rd most benefits at $5.15 billion, and New York was 4th with $4.8 billion. Florida is clearly the winner in the Social Security sweepstakes. This is a key ingredient in supporting the lifestyle of retirees and provides needed fiscal stimulus to the Florida economy.

The contribution that retirees make to the Florida economy was confirmed in a study done for the Florida Department of Elder Affairs by the Bureau of Economic and Business Research at the University of Florida. It shows that those 65 and over contribute virtually the same per-capita revenues as other Floridians, but that, while seniors require more health spending per capita, they utilize less expensive education services, are incarcerated less often, and don't add so much to the congestion on roads. The study estimates that, on balance, the per-capita net fiscal benefit to the state in Fiscal Year 2010 was $2,850 for those 65 and over compared to a per-capita net fiscal cost of $818 for those age 18 to 64 (Denslow and Schaub, 2013).

Retirees have their Florida Dreams and the wherewithal to turn them into reality. They are expected to continue to be an important source of fiscal resources for the state government. And meeting their needs will be one of the leading growth sectors for the Sunshine State.

6
THE SOUTHEAST FLORIDA OLA

Florida was first visited and colonized by Spain shortly after Christopher Columbus set foot in America. St. Augustine, the putative first European town in North America, was established in 1565 by Pedro Menéndez de Avilés. Florida has had a strong Hispanic presence and influence from the time it entered the European orbit (which is not to say its establishment, as that would be to deny the presence of Indians who had lived here for millennia). Hispanics were the first Europeans with Florida Dreams. Unfortunately, in those harsher times, most of them never achieved their dreams, like Ponce de Leon whose reward was only a tomb in San Juan.

The numbers of what we would now call Hispanics have ebbed and flowed as the territory seesawed between the Spanish and the British, and later from the Spanish to the United States. However, since Fidel Castro took over in Cuba in 1959 and imposed a Communist dictatorship on the people, a giant ola (wave in Spanish) of Cubans has come to Florida seeking refuge.

Cuban Refugees

The first groups who came were wealthy and professional, families who still had the wherewithal to pull up stakes and pay for their plane tickets to Miami. There, many had to start life over with nothing but what was in their suitcases. The Cuban government confiscated the property that had to be left behind. Over the 1960 to 1962 period, a group of around 14,000 unaccompanied Cuban children were flown to the United States and admitted under a Catholic charitable program called Operation Pedro Pan. Many of these children, who expected their parents soon to join them, were separated for years, if not permanently. Subsequent groups of refugees, who had delayed or may have not had much to begin with, took Freedom Flights, if they were fortunate, or had to resort to more risky means of transport like small boats, rafts, and even sailboards (Knight Ridder/Tribune, 1994). From 1959 to 1974 an estimated 650,000 Cubans sought refuge in the United States. Over the same period, the U.S. Government spent almost a billion dollars on the Cuban Refugee Program.

FLORIDA DREAMS

The Freedom Tower in Miami was called El Refugio by the Cuban refugees, who were welcomed there by the Cuban Assistance Center, and given a wide range of services, including housing, health, education and financial support.

The Marielitos Were More Problematic

Another group of 125,000 Cuban refugees came almost twenty years later between April and September 1980 in the Mariel Boatlift. Castro had released them from Cuba's prisons and asylums and they were taken to the port of Mariel for transport to the United States. Moved by their plight, Cubans, and other supportive Floridians, mobilized a fleet of boats of varying degrees of seaworthiness to pick them up and take them back to Florida. Once here, U.S. governments at all levels were overwhelmed by the task of processing them and, not knowing exactly what to do with so many people, kept them in the Orange Bowl, before moving them to a temporary tent city under I-95. Eventually, governments got their act together and the Marielitos were finally processed and released to look for work and to settle in to their new home. This was facilitated by the large number of fellow Cubans, including family members, who went out of their way to help their less fortunate compatriots out.

The arrival of 125,000 Marielitos in the Southeast Florida labor market has been embraced by economists as a "natural" controlled experiment of the impact of an exogenous increase in the supply of unskilled immigrant labor on the wage and unemployment rates of competing unskilled native workers. David Card (1990) of Berkeley first examined the impact of the Marielitos on wages and unemployment in Miami in comparison to four other cities and concluded that there had been no impact on the wages and unemployment of natives with a high school education or less. Card's methodology and findings were challenged by George Borjas (2017) of Harvard, himself a Cuban refugee, using data that focused more specifically on the wages of non-Hispanic high school dropouts, which showed a 10 to 30 per cent decline. More recently, Michael Clemens (2017) of the Center for Global Development has come to Card's defense and attributed Borjas's results to modifications to the wage survey methodology by the Census Bureau made in 1981. Clemens argued that this added a larger share of black men with less than a high school education to the sample, depressing the wages of the unskilled, which he claimed accounted for Borjas's findings.

Almost 40 years later, economists are still not in agreement about the impact of the Mariel Boatlift on the Miami labor market, which is, you may be surprised to hear, not all that rare of an occurrence. However, they do seem to agree that the wages of low skilled Cuban workers already in Miami were reduced by competition from the Marielitos and that the migration of workers from elsewhere in the United States slowed after the Boatlift. So much for the esoteric issue of the impact of the Marielitos on the Miami labor market.

Most Cubans Outside of Cuba Are in Florida

Cuban refugees and immigrants have continued to trickle in over the years, and the Cuban-American population has also continued to grow naturally by births exceeding deaths. The result is that Florida, in general, and Miami, where most live, is now home to the largest population of Cuban ethnicity outside of Cuba, numbering over 1.53 million in 2017, according to the 2017 American Community Survey (Chart 23). Florida is unique among states in the preponderance of Cubans in its Hispanic community, as distinct from Mexicans and Puerto Ricans, who make up most Hispanics in other states.

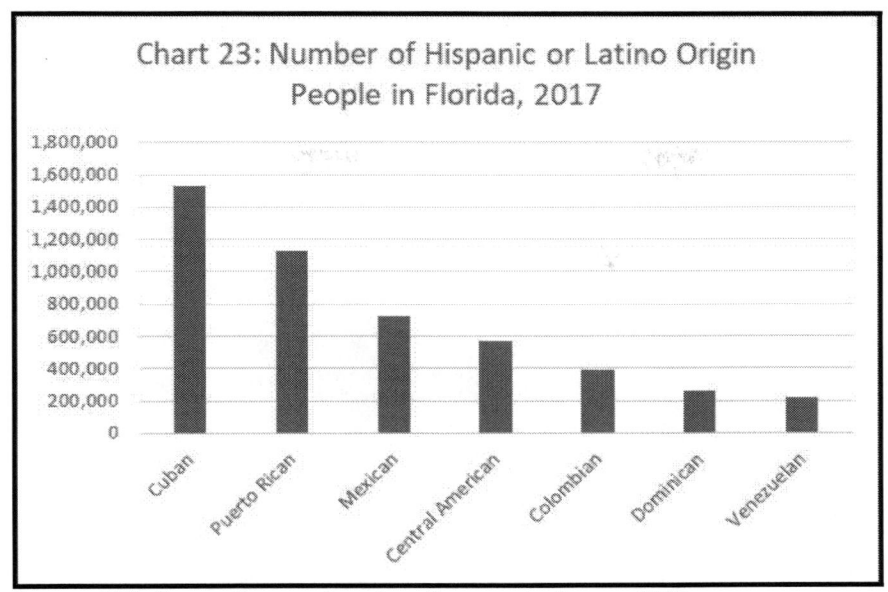

Chart 23: Number of Hispanic or Latino Origin People in Florida, 2017

(Bar chart showing, from largest to smallest: Cuban, Puerto Rican, Mexican, Central American, Colombian, Dominican, Venezuelan)

Source: U.S. Census Bureau, American Community Survey, 2017.

Puerto Ricans, Mexicans and Others

The second largest group of Hispanics in Florida are Puerto Ricans who numbered 1.13 million in 2017 (Chart 23). As Puerto Rico has been a U.S. territory since it was acquired in the Spanish American War of 1898, Puerto Ricans are U.S. citizens by birth and have the same rights to relocate to Florida as other U.S. citizens from the 50 states. Many of them have chosen to settle in the I-4 corridor around Orlando.

The poor state of Puerto Rico's financially strapped economy has been a push factor in the out-migration of Puerto Ricans. And many more came to Florida after Hurricane Maria devastated their island in 2017. A company called Teralytics estimated, based on smartphone data provided by a carrier, that around 150 thousand came to Florida following the disaster in September 2017, but that by February 2018 most had returned home (Echeniique, Martin and Luis Melgar, 2018). A rough estimate based on taking Florida's 43-per-cent share of the initial outflow and applying it to the number of those remaining in the U.S. suggests that only about 20,000 remain in Florida.

People of Mexican ethnicity numbered 727 thousand and are the third largest group of Hispanics in Florida (Chart 23). They too have immigrated to Florida over many years as well as raised Mexican-American families. Many Mexicans came to work in the center of the state in the agricultural sector and spread out into lawn maintenance and construction and other service sector jobs. From there, many have continued to climb the job ladder. Mexican restaurants have proliferated and become very popular in Florida.

The Central American countries of Nicaragua, Honduras, Guatemala, El Salvador and Costa Rica together provide 573 thousand of Florida's Hispanics. Columbia and Venezuela are also important countries of origin, providing 391 thousand and 222 thousand respectively. Finally, 260 thousand originated in the Dominican Republic in the Caribbean. (Chart 23)

In 2017, there were 5,370,860 Hispanics or Latinos in Florida, representing 25.6 per cent of the total population. Most of these (83 per cent) also identify as white. While the Non-Hispanic white population was only 11,288,419 or 54 per cent of the total, the white population, including white Hispanics, was 15,768,315 or 75 per cent of the total. The answer to the question of whether the white population of Florida is moving quickly to minority status thus turns out to be less straightforward than many might think. As white Hispanics learn English and adopt American cultural ways, they become indistinguishable from other white Americans and assimilate like generations of immigrants before them into that mainstream majority demographic.

A Growing and Diverse Hispanic Population Are Making It Economically

The Hispanic population of Florida has grown by almost a quarter over the 2011 to 2016 period. Important sources of this growth have been the migration of 454,141 Hispanics from other states and territories and the immigration of 481,004 from abroad. This added 935,145 new Hispanics in addition to the natural increase from births exceeding deaths. That's an average of 427 every day over the most recent six-year period.

The origin of Florida's Hispanics is quite different from California and Texas. In these two mega-states, most of the Hispanics have origins in Mexico and Central America in contrast with Florida which draws most of its Hispanics from Cuba, Puerto Rico and Latin America. Hispanics with origins in these countries tend to have higher levels of educations. Consequently, they can earn more money and be more easily integrated and assimilated.

In the U.S., Hispanics have been "climbing up the economic ladder" according to a CNN report. It cited a study carried out by Harvard, Stanford and Census Bureau researchers that found that Hispanics were doing better than their parents and getting ahead faster than blacks (Luhby, 2018).

In Florida, Hispanics have also been doing all right. They have gotten more education over the last decade (2007-17), with the percentage not completing high school dropping from 26.9 to 19.9 per cent and the percentage with some higher education rising from 44 to 51.1 per cent (Census Bureau, 2018).

The incomes and earnings of Florida Hispanics have largely kept pace despite the large increase in their numbers. While their median household income and mean earnings, as reported in the Census Bureau's American Community Survey, remained only about four-fifths of Non-Hispanic whites in 2017, this still represents a big increase in income for recent immigrants coming from Mexico and Latin America, where per-capita GDP and hence income levels are only a sixth, or even less, of those in the United States. And the improvement in prospects was even greater for immigrants coming from economic basket cases like Cuba, Venezuela, or Nicaragua where the economic situation can best be described as dire. Most Hispanic immigrants must feel that their standard of living is better in Florida, or they probably wouldn't come and stay. And, then there are those who have been spectacularly successful. The Florida Dream lives for Hispanics.

Where Do Hispanics Live?

Many Hispanics in Florida tend to live in ethnic enclaves with others from their origin country (not unlike retirees who seek each other out). This results in clusters of Hispanics in specific counties (Chart 24). The largest concentration is in the southeast corner of the state in Miami-Dade County where 68.6 per cent of the population was Hispanic in 2017. And, of course, the largest part of this group is Cubans, who are so predominant that Miami has gone way beyond being a city with Hispanic enclaves to being a Cuban-American dominated city.

The darker area in the middle of the state south of Orlando is Osceola County (53.7 per cent Hispanic), where many Puerto Ricans have settled. The two darker areas in the Southwest part of the state are Hardee (43.7 per cent Hispanic) and Hendry (53.2 per cent Hispanic) counties, which have concentrations of largely Mexican agricultural workers. Some of the other more shaded counties have Hispanic population shares over a quarter.

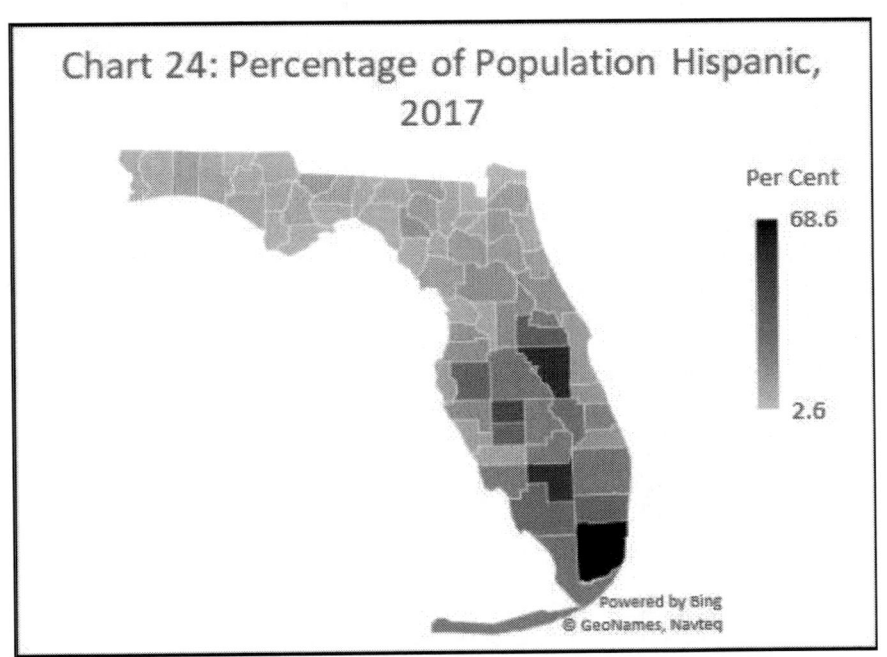

Chart 24: Percentage of Population Hispanic, 2017

Per Cent 68.6 – 2.6

Source: U.S. Census Bureau, QuickFacts, 2018.

Spanish Anyone?

In 2017, 81.5 per cent of Hispanics living in Florida spoke in their home a language other than English, which is obviously Spanish. In addition, 36.7 per cent admitted to speaking English "less than 'very well'." While both percentages were down over the preceding decade, they remain high. (Census Bureau, American Community Survey,

2007 and 2017)

The American Community Survey doesn't shed any light on the extent to which Spanish is spoken outside the home, in say Miami, but casual observation, when visiting the city, suggests it is quite prevalent especially in small businesses. Even in larger businesses and government offices, service is almost always available in Spanish. Is Miami-Dade becoming bilingual? The answer is not *de jure*, but certainly *de facto*.

Over the years, the growing number of Hispanics and the increasing use and visibility of the Spanish language has caused some tensions. Concern caused by the arrival of the Marielitos led to the passage of a Miami-Dade County ordinance prohibiting "the official use of any language but English." This was only overturned thirteen years later. In the meantime, the Florida Constitution was amended by Initiative Petition to make English the official language of Florida. Article II Section 9 declares that "English is the official language of the State of Florida .... The legislature shall have the power to enforce this section by appropriate legislation."

The intensity of feeling behind this is indicated by the fact that an Initiative Petition must be signed by 8 per cent of the voters in each of half the 27 congressional districts of the state and in the state itself, and that this one had no trouble getting over the hurdle of the 342,939 signatures required. Furthermore, it passed in the 1988 general election in a landslide garnering 84 per cent of the vote. (Greenspan, 1994).

Once passed, however, the English as official language amendment has turned out to be a paper tiger and has not been actively enforced. If it had been, though, it could have run afoul of Federal laws such as the Fourteenth Amendment and the Civil Rights and Voting Act Rights. But its real importance is as a symbol of the desire of the English-speaking population not to become an officially bilingual state like, say, Canada, to take the example with which I am most familiar. If Spanish is ever going to be proposed as a second official language, it's going to be quite the cockfight. The constitutional marker has been laid down.

In 2013, the Mayor of Doral, a Miami suburb, which was predominantly Hispanic, unsuccessfully tried to make Spanish the town's second official language. His proposal was rejected by every council member and by large numbers of his Spanish-speaking constituents (Fox News, 2013).

Spanish usage is growing in Florida because of immigration from Latin America. But, at the same time, it is dwindling among the descendants of the Hispanic immigrants. It's not uncommon for a grandparent to speak to a child in Spanish, only to have the child respond in English. The public-school system is, as it always has been, a powerful force for spreading the English language. The Miami-Dade School system is having problems teaching Hispanic children their native tongue (Viega, 2015). According to a Pew Research Institute study, nationwide, the share of children age 5 to 17 speaking English "only" or "very well" has grown from 73 per cent in 2000 to 88 per cent in 2014 (Krogstad, 2016). While Spanish usage is likely to be on the rise as immigrants from Latin America continue to arrive in droves, it will not necessarily displace English as the primary language, even in Florida.

However, Florida is sailing in uncharted waters. The number speaking Spanish exceeds any previous non-English languages in the United States and could easily lead to Spanish becoming the *de facto* official language, at least in Miami-Dade County. This would encourage English-speaking people to leave because of their inability to function in Spanish. This is what happened in Montreal, Canada after French was

FLORIDA DREAMS

made the sole language by the Quebec provincial government. Indeed, to a significant extent, Anglo flight has already begun in Miami. But so far, everything has gone smoothly with relatively little backlash.

7
AFRICAN-AMERICAN DREAMS

Many African-Americans in Florida, particularly in the northern part of the state, are descended from slaves who toiled on the plantations of the Florida Panhandle. Their aspirations were for freedom and equality. They faced violence from the Ku Klux Klan in 1949 in Groveland where black homes were shot at and set afire over an alleged assault of a local white girl. In 1951, they endured a KKK bombing that killed civil rights leader Henry T. Moore and injured his wife. In standing up for their rights, they encountered the same resistance as other Southern blacks. They participated in demonstrations in Tallahassee to desegregate buses in 1956. Martin Luther King Jr. came to St. Augustine to lead a sit-in at a segregated lunch counter in Woolworths and demonstrations to desegregate the beach and a swimming pool.

Florida was fortunate to have had some exceptional governors like Leroy Collins and Reubin Askew during the time of desegregation and the struggle for civil rights. Other southern states weren't so lucky. Governors Lester Maddox (Georgia), George Wallace (Alabama), John Bell Williams (Mississippi) all stirred the pot of racial hatred and tried to block change. Even Florida's U.S. Senators were resistant. Senators Spessard Holland and George Smathers filibustered the Civil Rights Act when it came up for a vote in the Senate in 1964.

Racial tensions have erupted in Florida in more recent years. Following the arrival of the Marielitos, there was a riot in the predominantly black Liberty City neighborhood of Miami. In 1996, years before the establishment of Black Lives Matter, riots broke out in St. Petersburg following a police shooting of a black youth.

The Black Population is Growing Through Immigration

Not all blacks came from old-line African-American families deeply rooted in Florida and the United States. Others, especially many of those in Southeast Florida and the Keys, came from the Bahamas and the Caribbean (and even Latin America although they usually identify more as Hispanics). While Caribbean blacks also faced discrimination and longed for equality, they had come to Florida for another dream – making a better living for themselves in a new land that offered more opportunities than their small impoverished island homes.

At the beginning of the 20th Century, blacks made up 44 per cent of the Florida population. But over the years, the black share of the population decreased because the in-migration was predominantly white and Hispanic. In 2017, blacks or African-Americans alone counted for 16.2 per cent of the population (17.6 per cent in combination with other races). Now the black population is growing more quickly than the white Non-Hispanic, but nowhere near as rapidly as the Hispanic. That is because the black population is benefitting from a greater percentage growth from immigration than the white. In 2017, almost 23 per cent of blacks were foreign born. An important component of the foreign born black population is Haitians who number over 300,000 (Man, 2017).

Where Blacks and African-Americans Live

Blacks and African-Americans are also concentrated in certain Florida counties (Chart 25). There's a high proportion of blacks in counties in the north of the state along the Florida-Georgia line where some of the old plantations used to be situated. The highest percentage of blacks is in Gadsden county with 55.9 per cent, but also in Leon, Jefferson, Madison, and Hamilton to the east, where the black share of the population ranges from 30 to almost 40 per cent. Proceeding east, Duval County on the east coast, where Jacksonville is located, has an over 30 per cent black population. In the Southeast, Miami-Dade has a 19 per cent black share and Broward 27 per cent. This includes many Haitians and other Caribbean blacks. Florida has the largest population of Haitian Americans in the U.S. and the second highest Jamaican-American population. In 2015, there were over 386 thousand people who spoke Haitian Creole, making it the third most common language in Florida after English and Spanish.

Incomes Keeping Up, but not Catching Up

The black population of Florida has seen their income go up at about the same rate as whites and Hispanics over the last decade (2007 to 2017), but still has median household income of only 69 per cent of whites and mean earnings of 65 per cent of whites. Thus, while they're not closing the income and earnings gaps significantly, at least the large share of blacks coming from the Caribbean where the standard of living is much lower are realizing their Florida Dreams of making much more money.

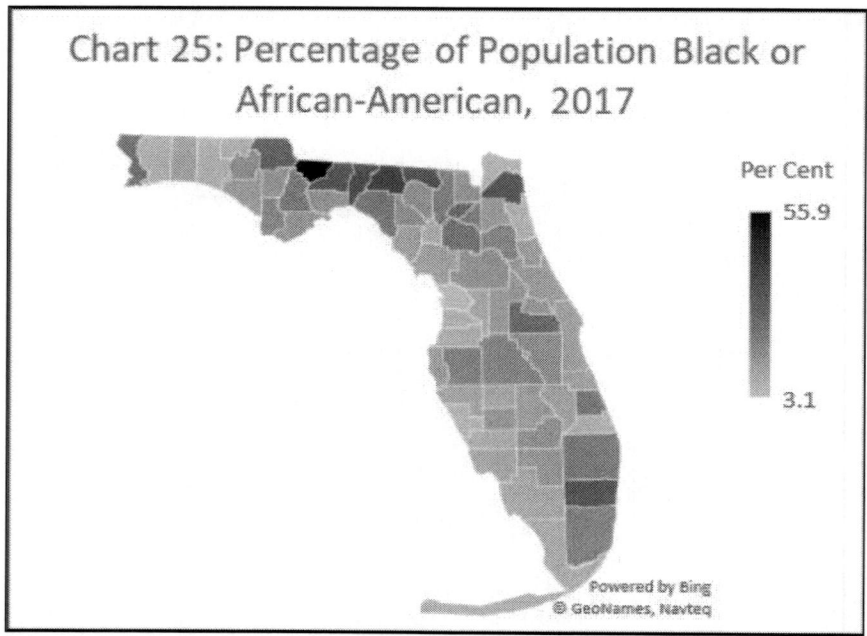

Chart 25: Percentage of Population Black or African-American, 2017

Per Cent
55.9
3.1

Source: U.S. Census Bureau, QuickFacts, 2018.

8
THE INDIANS NEVER GAVE UP ON THEIR FLORIDA DREAMS

The emblematic Indians of Florida are the Seminoles. Made up of other Indian tribes, including Creeks and other Muscogee speakers living in southern Georgia and northern Florida, they moved south into Spanish Florida in the 18th century seeking refuge from the aggressive expansion of American settlements. At that time, Florida was an unsettled wilderness of pristine forests, prairies, rivers and swamps. Its earlier Indian inhabitants, like the Timucua, Tequesta, and the Calusa, had already been wiped out by disease like smallpox and measles and skirmishes with the Europeans.

The life the Seminole found in Florida did not remain peaceful for long, despite their idyllic natural surroundings. In what came to be called the First Seminole War (1817-1821), General Andrew Jackson and his army marched into Spanish Florida and attacked the Seminoles. The *casus belli* was twofold: protecting the U.S. settlers moving into Florida from Indian attacks; and grievances over the harboring of escaped slaves who had joined the Seminoles. The Spanish, who were unable to resist militarily, reluctantly accepted the inevitable, and agreed to allow the Americans to take over Florida in 1821. According to the 1823 Treaty of Moultrie Creek, the Seminole were supposed to move to a reservation.

Once in control of the Florida territory, the U.S. Government tried to get the Seminoles to relocate to what was then Indian Territory, and today is Oklahoma. A small group of Seminoles were persuaded to sign the 1832 Treaty of Payne's Landing agreeing to move in three years. When the Army came back to force the move, the Second (and most bloody) Seminole War (1835-42) erupted. Though outnumbered and outgunned, the Seminoles, under the intrepid leadership of Osceola, fought a very effective and costly guerrilla war against the U.S. Army, until their leader was tricked by a flag of truce and captured. By its end, most Seminoles had been removed to Oklahoma, but no peace treaty was signed, and a group of around 500 Seminoles managed to slip away and to find refuge in the unsettled wild country of South Florida.

The Third Seminole War (1855-1858) was not very much of a war. It started over a clash between Seminole Chief Billy Bowlegs and a military team surveying (trespassing on according to Bowlegs) his banana plantation in Collier County near Big

Cyprus. Another small-scale guerrilla war ensued, and the Army recommenced its efforts to round up Indians. Finally, recognizing the futility of resistance, Billy Bowlegs surrendered. For a modest bounty, he was convinced to take his small band of 165 followers to Oklahoma. The U.S. declared the war over, even without a treaty, and gave up on its efforts to remove Indians. By this time, only a couple of hundred Seminoles remained in the Everglades and other swamps of South Florida to pursue their Florida Dreams. Over the years, though, others trickled back from Oklahoma to join them, adding to their numbers.

The Seminoles take great pride in their valiant struggle against the superior forces of the U.S. Army and the fact that they never signed a formal treaty with the U.S. Government. They call themselves the "Unconquered."

The Florida State University three-time national champion football team is called the Seminoles, proudly reflecting this heritage. Since the Seminoles that were consulted didn't have any problem with that, the NCAA gave FSU a pass from the sanctions it was considering as part of its politically-correct campaign to expunge references to Indians from college sports. (Tierney, 2013).

For many years, the Seminoles eked out a subsistence living for themselves hunting, fishing and trapping and trading skins and hides in posts on the outskirts of the Everglades. Their meager livelihoods were threatened, however, by the water diversions that were begun by Hamilton Disston in the 1880s to drain the swamp in South Florida (Grunwald, 2006). The always-enterprising Seminoles responded by developing roadside attractions for tourists to showcase Indian life and to sell native arts and crafts. Alligator wrestling, which showcased traditional hunting techniques, was a feature attraction.

Alligator wrestling at the Miccosukee Village on the Tamiami Trail.

The Seminoles Go After Their Own Florida Dream

The Federal Government's antagonistic approach to Indians slowly changed in the 20th Century. Land was set aside for the Seminole around Big Cyprus, Hollywood and Brighton so they could make a living in agriculture. Congress established a new framework for Indian self-government in the Indian Reorganization Act of 1934.

The largest group of Seminoles finally took advantage of this opportunity and established the Seminole Tribe of Florida, which was officially recognized as a tribe by the U.S. Government in 1957 and which is democratically governed by a tribal council and board. Today it has approximately 4,100 enrolled members living on 90,000 acres of land on six reservations. It is headquartered in Hollywood, Florida, where the venerable Council Oak stands, near the Hard Rock Casino. The largest part of its population resides in Big Cypress. The other four reservations are in Brighton, Immokalee, Fort Pierce and Tampa.

A smaller group of more traditional Seminoles, who speak the Mikasuki language, established the Miccosukee Tribe of Indians, which was officially recognized in 1962. It has around 640 members. who live along the Tamiami Trail, Alligator Alley, and Krome Avenue in Miami.

And there is an even smaller group of "Independent" Seminoles that is not formally recognized by the Government. They have an even bigger Florida Dream, an open land claim covering much of Florida.

The Seminoles have used their lands, and the $11.5 million they received in 1992 from the Federal Government in settlement of a claim, to create large cattle ranches and other remunerative agricultural businesses, including citrus groves. Starting small with roadside tourist attractions, they moved into gasoline stations, tobacco shops and other tourism activities, cannily taking advantage of their on-reserve tax breaks. Under the shrewd leadership of the larger-than-life, alligator-wrestling, country singing, Chief Jim Billies (Sortal, 2016), they moved into high-stakes bingo, which readied them for the casino gambling business when it was opened up by the passage of the 1988 Indian Gaming Regulation Act and the subsequent 1996 U.S. Supreme Court decision in the Seminole Tribe of Florida v. Florida, which ordered the state government to respect the Seminoles' right to enter the casino gambling business.

The Seminole Tribe of Florida now owns six casinos: the Hard Rock Hotel and Casinos in Hollywood and Tampa; the Seminole Casino Hotel in Immokalee, and Seminole Casinos in Hollywood, Brighton, and Coconut Creek. In 2007, they purchased, for $965 million, Hard Rock International, which franchises rock-themed restaurants, hotels and casinos worldwide (Herrera, 2016). The spectacular guitar-shaped Hard Rock Hotel & Casino now being completed in Hollywood at a cost of $1.5 billion will be their new feature attraction. It will have over a thousand rooms, a 10-acre swimming pool, and 30 restaurants and bars. Its 3,000 slot machines, and 193 gaming tables will expand the existing Hard Rock's gaming capacity by 30 per cent (Herrera, 2017).

New Seminole Hard Rock Hotel & Casino going up
and scheduled for completion in 2019.

The Miccosukees also have the Miccosukee Indian Resort and Gaming Facility at the intersection of Krome Avenue and U.S. 41 in Miami. While it is much smaller than the Hard Rock, it's still a money machine for the tribe.

Miccosukee Casino on a more modest scale, but still brings in the money.

Spending the Gambling Winnings

Gambling certainly turned on the money tap for the Seminoles. The tribe reportedly took in $2.3 billion in the fiscal year ending June 30, 2016 (Beckett, 2017). And Florida hasn't done so badly from the business either. Since Governor Rick Scott took office in 2011, the Seminoles have paid the state over $1.75 billion in payments under the revenue sharing agreement, which has been extended till April 2019. This includes more than $290 million in the fiscal year ending June 30, 2017 (Rosica, 2018).

The bonanza from gambling is enabling the Seminole Tribe to achieve the Florida Dream of financial independence for its members. Each receives a dividend of $128,000 per year (as of 2016). In addition, they are entitled to free education, university scholarships, housing and healthcare (Debter, 2016). The tribe also makes jobs available for those who want them and employs over 300 members. The tribal government provides members with the usual array of municipal services on the reserve including police, fire, waste disposal, water, and schools. With so much money at stake, it should not be surprising that many would like to join the tribe and tribal rolls have to be closely controlled. To qualify as a member, a person must be at least one quarter Seminole with direct lineage to a grandparent on the 1957 Florida Seminole Tribal Roll.

Tribal leaders like the recently deposed Chief Jim Billies (Sortal, 2016) have been conspicuously extravagant, flying around in their fleet of private planes and helicopters, all decked out in Seminole red, yellow and white colors. But the members are willing to overlook this and continue to vote them in, so long as they continue to bring home the bacon.

What About All the Rest of the Indians?

The Seminoles' rags to riches story only applies to the members of the two officially recognized Seminole tribes, which only account for a very small proportion of the 129,074 Indians living in Florida in 2017 (Bureau of Census, American Community Survey, 2017). The vast majority of Florida Indians are far from millionaires. However, neither have they been totally left behind by Florida's growing prosperity. They have been getting good educations. While not quite as many of them proportionally have gotten bachelor's degrees as whites (28.4 per cent versus 31.2 per cent), they have done better than Hispanics (24.1 per cent) and blacks (18.8 per cent). This pattern of higher education is mirrored in their incomes. Indians had a mean household income of $49,893 in 2017 compared to $47,257 for Hispanics, $40,104 for blacks, and $58,110 for whites (Bureau of Census, ACS, 2017). Given the adversity that Florida Indians have had to overcome, they've done an amazing job of realizing their Florida Dreams.

9
SNOWBIRDS: MORE THAN TOURISTS, BUT NOT QUITE RESIDENTS

Every year now a million snowbirds migrate to Florida for the winter (and many fewer sunbirds go north in the summer, but that's another story). The term snowbird here is used loosely to include seasonal residents coming down any time from October to April, which, of course, depends on how long they are able to stand the miserable weather back home. Snowbirds differ from tourists in the annual regularity of their visits and the length of their usual stay. The cut-off often chosen is a month, but most snowbirds stay much longer, perhaps even for the whole "season" which runs roughly from October to April. (Smith and House, 2006).

Being able to be away from their home states so long is another key characteristic of snowbirds. It precludes having a regular 9-5 jobs where they are required to show up and hang around every day. Most snowbirds tend to be older and retired (or, less frequently, independently wealthy or telecommuters).

Because of the duration and regularity of their stays, many own properties in Florida, running the gamut from expensive estate homes, to condos, to mobile homes. Others come down in RVs bringing their housing along. Or they might just bring suitcases and rent property or stay with friends or relatives.

Snowbirds are few compared to tourists, but each makes a much larger contribution to the Florida economy than the typical tourist because of the length of their stay. While in Florida, they spend as much money as Florida residents, on food, clothing, housing, entertainment, dining and hospitality, gas, electricity, water, insurance, car licenses and registrations, financial services, and a whole wide range of other goods and services. While they pay no income taxes, just like other Floridians, they pay their share of other taxes, except for property taxes which they pay more of because they don't benefit from the homestead exemption (the working of which is explained in Chapter 4).

The debt of gratitude owed to the snowbirds for their contribution to the Florida economy, and the state government's coffers, however, does not stop the locals, when the season arrives, from grousing about the overcrowding and congestion the snowbirds bring. Indeed, that is often a favorite topic of conversation of Floridians while waiting in lines to get a table at a restaurant or stuck in traffic.

Being a snowbird is also often a step on the road to living full time in Florida. Many snowbirds find they enjoy living in Florida so much, even in the hot and humid summers when they have to come down to check on their properties, that they take the leap into full time residency. The reasons for doing so are usually to economize on the expenses of having two underutilized residences. But the lack of income and estate taxes provides an added inducement, particularly for those coming down from high tax states in the Northeast. (See Chapter 4). For instance, someone coming down from New York and making over $21,400 could avoid paying a marginal rate of at least 6.33 per cent, and someone coming from New Jersey and making over $40,000 could avoid paying a marginal rate of at least 5.525 per cent. That's quite an incentive even for snowbirds with lower incomes to take out Florida residence.

Some high-tax Frost Belt States try to make it difficult for residents to give up their residency status and consequently pursue aggressive residency audits. The key factors in determining the residency status of a person for state income tax purposes is "whether he or she is domiciled or maintains an abode in the state and are [*sic*] 'present' in the state for 183 days or more (one-half of the tax year)" (Baker Tilley, 2011). Proving this to the satisfaction of state tax authorities can be a tedious affair, requiring extensive documentation. If the stakes are high, professional tax advice and representation might be a good idea.

Snowbirds by the Numbers

The *Palm Beach Post* guestimates that 900 thousand to a million snowbirds (defined as seasonal residents staying more than a month) flocked to Florida in the 2016-17 season, raising the state's population by 5 per cent (Marshall, 2017). The reason no hard data are available is that the U.S. Census Bureau, which is the source of much of the data in this book, doesn't separately count snowbirds like they do the other groups. But the concept of "usual residence," which the Bureau uses in determining state of residence, excludes those who do not live in the state "most of the time" and should thus exclude snowbirds from the state's population count (U.S. Census Bureau, 2018a).

The *Palm Beach Post's* figures are supported by a somewhat dated study of snowbirds by Stanley K. Smith and Mark House of the Bureau of Economic and Business Research at the University of Florida (Smith and House, 2006). Based on data collected from a relatively small survey, they estimated that there were 818,000 snowbirds (temporary residents 55 and older) in Florida at the peak of the 2005 winter season and only 62,000 remaining in the summer. Scaling this up for the increase in population since then, it would be consistent with the *Palm Beach Post's* estimate.

Smith and House (2006) also found many other interesting facts. For instance, 78 per cent of snowbirds came from the Northeast or Midwest. Snowbirds were disproportionately Non-Hispanic whites, with higher educations and incomes. A high 92 per cent owned their homes up north. And 30 per cent told the interviewers that it was likely or very likely they would move permanently to Florida sometime in the future. The most expected result of all was that 83 per cent said they came to Florida because of the weather. And you can believe it.

Canadian Snowbirds Too, Eh?

The bone-chilling cold that grips Canada for almost half the year inexorably drives Canadians southward towards Florida every winter. Some of them are snowbirds, others tourists. But exactly how many of each, nobody knows for sure, as, surprise, no data are again collected. However, there is an estimate available from Smith and House (2006) that Canadian snowbirds would comprise about 8 per cent of the total. So, if the total number of snowbirds was a million, then it can be deduced that the number of Canadians would be 80,000. Other sources suggest the number could be much higher. *The Economist* wrote, offhandedly in 2014, that a half a million Canadians owned homes in Florida (*Economist*, 2014). Where they got this number is anybody's guess. Florida Tax Watch said in a study of international homebuyers in Florida that Canadians accounted for 27 per cent of international housing purchases from 2009 to 2013, but that the total of international purchases over the period was only just over 140 thousand units (Florida Tax Watch, 2014).

Canadian snowbirds are admitted to the United States on a B-2 tourist visa, which allows them to stay for six months (180 days) in any 12-month period and to make multiple entries, although no paper visa is issued. The accounting for the stay can get complicated as even part days count as a day and some Canadian snowbirds like to push the limit. There are a couple of bills in Congress, including the Snowbird Act formerly sponsored jointly by Florida Senators Bill Nelson and Marco Rubio, but these bills never seem to get passed as they are a low priority for most non-Florida legislators.

Like the migratory Canadian goose, the Canadian snowbirds' time in the United States is not without its perils, not the least of which is being caught in the net by the IRS and having to pay U.S. income and/or estate taxes. This will happen if the Canadian snowbird triggers the substantial presence test, which involves being in the U.S. for even much less than the prima facie allowed six months, and imprudently neglecting to file the IRS Form 8840 establishing a "Closer Connection" to Canada to the IRS's satisfaction. Getting U.S. source income, such as from a rental, is another way of ending up in the IRS net. And last, but not least, the ownership of U.S. property such as a seasonal home can subject the Canadian snowbird to withholding tax on sale or to estate tax (on the amount over $60,000) on death (Chevreau, 2017; Deloitte, 2016). Canadian snowbirds, like Americans from other states seeking to establish Florida residency, can benefit from professional tax advice to avoid running afoul of the IRS.

Healthcare is another major pitfall for Canadian snowbirds. Their provincial healthcare plans are not much use in the case of a health emergency while in Florida. It does not take long to run up a mega-bill in any U.S. hospital that can bankrupt most people. Good travel insurance with medevac coverage is needed to avoid a Florida Dream turning into a medical and financial nightmare. Canadians also must be careful to not stay out of their province of residence beyond the period allowed by their provincial healthcare plans or they can lose coverage from their provincial plans. This is helped by the fact that they are only supposed to stay in the U.S. for half a year, which is equal to or less than the time allowed by most, if not all, of their plans.

10
THE RICH SHARE IN THE DREAMS

It's not only those living in cinder block houses, condos, mobile homes and RV parks that have been living their Florida Dreams. Large numbers of the super-rich have also migrated to Florida for all or part of the year. Indeed, because they had the money to do it even back in the old days, they were the very first to start the trend early around the turn of the last century, when they began their annual pilgrimages to Palm Beach. There they spent the "Season" in Henry Flagler's Royal Poinciana Hotel or Palm Beach Inn enjoying, all the lavish parties, social and cultural events and charity galas that only the rich can afford to throw and attend.

To paraphrase a fictitious, but insightful, exchange between F. Scott Fitzgerald and Ernest Hemingway, the rich are not all that different from everyone else, they just have more money. Like seniors, Hispanics, African-Americans, Haitians, and Indians, they like to live together in secure little enclaves where they feel more at home and can socialize with others like themselves.

Where might the rich's exclusive hideaways be? Everybody, of course, knows that they include Palm Beach and Naples, but since this is a work of social science, it's necessary to be scientific and demonstrate the obvious with some data. Fortunately, or unfortunately depending on your point of view, the Internal Revenue Service conveniently makes everyone fill out a form every year listing their income and then publishes the results on their website. This provides a useful compilation of the tax information on the form broken down by income levels and even by zip code. It can be used, for instance, to spy on your neighbors. But let's leave that for another time. The purpose here is to identify the hideouts of the wealthy.

Fisher Island, Miami Beach

The zip code in Florida with the highest average adjusted gross income (AGI) reported to the IRS in 2016 was 33109. It's located in Miami Beach and called Fisher Island, after Carl Fisher, the developer of Miami Beach. He also was the promoter of the Lincoln and Dixie Highways connecting the country east-west and, most importantly for Florida, north-south. The 200 tax filers who filed from that tiny island, which is only accessible by helicopter or ferry, had an average AGI of $2,212,450. While it's impossible to say exactly who is included in tax filings from the island, the average AGI is not really so high given the small number of people filing from the island and the fact that there are at least a couple of billionaires living in their midst. For instance, couple Bharat Desai and Neerja Sethi, who founded Syntel, received $2 billion for their share of the proceeds from its sale (Das, 2018). And billionaire Oprah Winfrey has one of her six residences there. Either some of the richest people living on the island file their taxes somewhere else or they all must have wizards for tax advisers.

As exclusive as Fisher Island is, it's too minuscule to harbor more than a small number of the Miami rich. And the real Miami story, which is being saved for a later chapter, is one of Hispanic wealth. But, if you can't wait, skip ahead to Chapter 13.

Not such a bad house on Star Island, Miami Beach.

Palm Beach

The second highest income zip code in Florida was 33480, which is, of course, Palm Beach, the traditional wintering place of the Eastern American elite, on an 18-mile long barrier island off the Atlantic Coast, north of Fort Lauderdale. It's the locale of the Mar-a-Lago Club, President Trump's home away from home. The 5,200 people filing there, which excludes many seasonal residents like probably the President, reported an average AGI of only $1,064,842.

Palm Beach has been the winter playground of America's eastern old money families since Henry Flagler opened his hotels for business. The aristocratic Palm Beach sojourners built their own snooty clubs like the Bath and Tennis and the Everglades Club (designed by Addison Mizner, the much sought-after architect whose Mediterranean Revival styles defined the Palm Beach look and indeed much of south Florida, even now including assisted living residences). The clubs were both very WASPy and were notorious for excluding newcomers, including, particularly, wealthy

Jewish families, who in turn, not to be outdone by the haughty gentiles, founded their own equally exclusive Palm Beach Country Club. By the way, if you ever visit it and don't want to upset any of the club members, don't ask them if Bernie Madoff is still a member (Dargan, 2015).

Now the delicate social equilibrium has been further disturbed by the Mar-a-Lago Club, which was created by Donald Trump in 1995 out of the sumptuous estate of Marjorie Merriweather Post, that he had earlier acquired along Billionaires Row, facing the ocean. While membership is expensive ($200,000 plus tax for the initiation fee and $14,000 plus tax annual dues), it is not so exclusive that you can't get in provided you have the money. The old money crowd is thus not impressed with such lax standards that ignore pedigrees. And the discontent has only grown in the tight upper-class world of Palm Beach, now that President Donald J. Trump has set up shop at the Florida White House aka the Mar-a-Lago Club. Many sanctimonious liberal charities and socialites have been shunning him like a skunk at a party by moving their charity events away from his venue to register their disapproval (the 25 events scheduled for the 2017-18 season had dropped to 3 by September 21, 2017 according to Helen Brown [2017]). However, hate him or love him, Trump's larger than life presence in their smug little community is hard to ignore when their limousines and private jets are being constantly diverted and delayed so as not to interfere with the Donald's frequent comings and goings.

The tranquility in the clubby little community has also been disturbed by a nasty dispute between Canadian businessman Harold Peerenboom and Marvel Comic billionaire Ike Perlmutter over, of all things, the management of tennis courts in a gated community called Sloan's Curve, which is on Ocean Boulevard, just down the road from Mar-a-Lago. Specifically, Peerenboom wanted to put out a tender for a tennis pro, even though, for 25 years, they already had had one that everybody liked. Well, it escalated from there, to a bitter feud with law suits and counter suits for slander, malicious prosecution and even DNA theft. Fueling the litigation, and providing juicy fare for the tabloid press, were alleged letters sent to friends, neighbors, and prisoners making preposterous allegations against Peerenboom involving sexual perversion, homicide, racism and even, of all things, Nazism (Gollom, 2017; Castaldo, 2017) The first suit is supposed to be on the docket for the fall of 2018 (Gardner, 2018), but so far, according to Google, which knows everything, no word. Ironically, in the end, the legal expenses may turn out to be enough to have engaged Serena Williams as the club pro. That's what happens when the egos of the ultra-rich clash in the courts, and not on the courts.

Naples

The third highest income zip code in Florida is 34102, which covers most of Naples on the Southwest Gulf Coast. Its 4,870 filers, again excluding many seasonal residents, reported average AGI of $572,585. While this includes the uber-rich area of Port Royal, it obviously is not representative of their real incomes, as PortRoyalistas represent only a small part of the zip code area and many file their taxes elsewhere.

Naples was developed by Barron Collier who had purchased 1.3 million acres of Southwest Florida land in the early 20th century. It is more low key than Palm Beach, but has attracted more than its share of the rich and famous, including 5 billionaires and, naturally, has very swanky homes. The richest, number 217 on the Forbe's 2018 list of billionaires, Shahid Khan, the founder of Flex-N-Gate, an automotive products company, and owner of the Jacksonville Jaguars, lives there. Others, in descending order of wealth on the Forbe's list, residing in Naples are: Reinhold Schmieding who owns 95 per cent of Arthrex, a medical device company; Tom Golisano, the man behind Paychex, the payroll company; William Stone, founder of SS&C Technologies; and Catherine Lozick, the Swagelok (gas and fluid system components) heiress (Layden, 2017a).

Dick Portillo, the founder of Portillo's and Chicago's hot dog king, has a home in Naples where he docks his yacht, Top Dog (Wohl, 2015). John Schnatter, the Papa John of the pizza company, whose mouth recently managed to get him the boot from his own company, owns a North Naples condo. On the market now are 2750 Gordon Drive for $42.5 million and 3100 Gordon Drive for $49.5 million (Zillow).

The anchor of the super-rich Port Royal community is the Port Royal Club, which is only open for membership to residents of the area and offers dining, fitness and a spa, tennis and a Gulf Beach Club with beachside pool. It's not cheap, if you were wondering. The membership fee on acquiring a membership eligible property in Port Royal is $100,000 and annual dues are $8,900. If, heaven forbid, the property's membership eligibility has been allowed to lapse, an additional reinstatement fee of 75 per cent of the membership fee must be paid on top of the $100,000.

Naples is another nice little clubby place where the run-of-the-mill billionaire can get away from the cold without getting caught up in all the *sturm und drang* of Palm Beach.

The Naples home of recently deceased John F. Donahue, founder of Federated Investors, at the end of Gordon Drive on Bay Road (Layden, 2017b). Senator Rick Scott is a neighbor and could pop by for a coffee.

11
OPENING THE DREAM TO THE YOUNG

Not everyone in Florida lives in gated 55 plus communities that ban children, but welcome dogs. In fact, almost 6 million young people under 24 lived in Florida in 2017 (American Community Survey, 2017). This represented 28.4 per cent of the state's population, a larger share than the elderly 65 and over. Like young people everywhere, they have their dreams for the future. And to fulfill these dreams in today's ultra-competitive world, they and their parents know that they need to get a first-rate, world-class education.

Florida is currently in the middle of the American pack in the race to educate its population to be competitive in the more technologically sophisticated economy of the future. With only 29.7 per cent of its population 25 and over with a bachelor's degree or higher, Florida ranks 28th among the states (Chart 26). This is well behind the 10th ranking New York with 36 per cent and the 16th ranking California with 33.6 per cent, not to mention Massachusetts, the most highly educated state with 43.4 per cent of its population with a bachelor's or better. Moreover, Florida can take little consolation from its miniscule lead over Texas the 29th ranking state, with 29.6 per cent with degrees. Florida has some ground to make up in education if it wants to give its young the level of education they are going to need in today's world.

The Numbers of Students Enrolled

In 2017, 4,770,596 Floridians age 3 and over were enrolled in school at all levels (American Community Survey, 2017). Of these, 1.9 million were enrolled in elementary school, one million in high school, and almost 1.4 million in college or graduate school (Chart 27). Florida runs the third largest system of public education for students up through high school, which is not bad for a state that is supposed to be full of old people. It is administered decentrally by school boards at the county level.

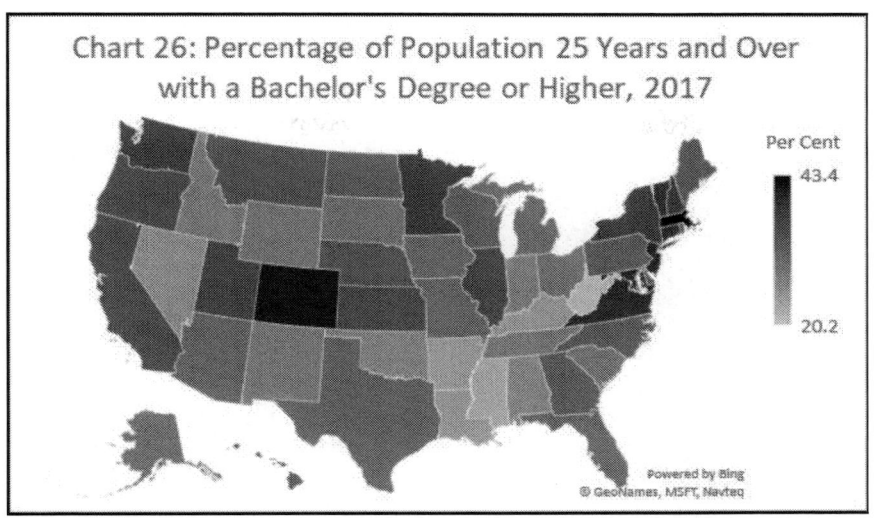

Chart 26: Percentage of Population 25 Years and Over with a Bachelor's Degree or Higher, 2017

Per Cent 43.4 – 20.2

Source: U.S. Census Bureau, American Community Survey, 2017.

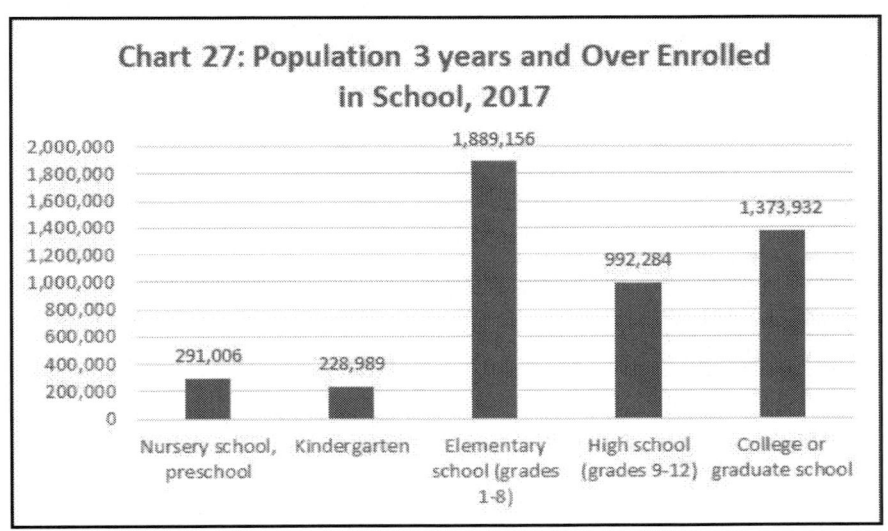

Chart 27: Population 3 years and Over Enrolled in School, 2017

- Nursery school, preschool: 291,006
- Kindergarten: 228,989
- Elementary school (grades 1-8): 1,889,156
- High school (grades 9-12): 992,284
- College or graduate school: 1,373,932

Source: U.S. Census Bureau, American Community Survey, 2017.

The Florida College System has 28 colleges and 800,000 students. The Miami-Dade College alone has 165,000 students making it the second largest undergraduate college or university in the country and the one with the most Hispanic students.

The Florida University System has 12 universities and more than 345,000 students. It's the 2nd largest public university system in the United States, after the State University of New York System (SUNY), and ahead of the University of California System.

Charter Schools

Charter schools have been an important part of the public-school system in Florida since the Charter School Law was passed in 1996. They have become very popular and have almost doubled in size over the last decade, since they provide parents with school choice options for their children, not offered in the traditional public schools. Charter schools are an important instrument of the Florida School Choice Program, which also offers scholarships and the Florida Tax Credit Scholarship Program aimed at disadvantaged students who are predominantly from lower income minorities (Kisa, 2018). Ex-Governor Jeb Bush started this program and is a great proponent of school choice and for improving the quality of education through his foundation ExcelinEd.

In 2015, 270,920 Florida students attended charter schools or 10 per cent of all public-school students. This is significantly higher than the U.S. average of 6 per cent. While it's not much higher than the 9 per cent in California, it's much higher than the 5 per cent in Texas, 4 per cent in New York, and 3 per cent in Illinois (National Center for Educational Statistics, 2018).

A study by the Florida Department of Education (2017) found that charter school students outperformed those in traditional public schools and that, consequently, 35 per cent of charter schools were graded A compared to only 21 per cent of traditional public schools. In addition, learning gaps for Hispanic and African-American students were found to be smaller in charter schools. Hispanic students are substantially overrepresented in charter schools, whereas African-American students are slightly underrepresented.

Charter schools are not popular with many older teachers and teachers' unions who have a large stake in keeping traditional public schools just as they are. They resent charter schools for diverting resources from the traditional public-school system. Critics also don't like the additional flexibility accorded to charter school principals and administrators to manage the schools. Charter school supporters, on the other hand, attribute the better performance of charter schools to just this flexibility to hire and reward good teachers and to fire underperformers, and to be more selective about the students enrolled. In addition, charter schools can require more active parental involvement as a precondition of acceptance, and this helps to boost student performance. This is something traditional public schools can't do as they are required to accept all students who want to attend even if their parents take no interest whatsoever in their children's schooling and the school.

How Do the Elementary and Secondary Schools Stack Up?

In a nutshell, not so well. Florida only provided public schools $9,562 per student in 2017. This was a very low level of resources, leading to the state being ranked 44th out of 50 states and the District of Columbia (National Education Association, 2018, p.2).

Florida is also one of the states with the lowest teachers' salaries. Florida ranked 45th with an average salary of $47,267 in 2017 (National Education Association, 2018, p.29). A poll in Jacksonville found that three-quarters of respondents would support a tax increase for education, and most agreed that a pay raise was needed (Campbell, 2018). So, there is some support in Florida for higher teacher salaries. My daughter, who teaches in Lee County, was glad to hear this.

Florida's overall rating in the U.S. News and World Report's Pre-K to 12 Educational Ranking was a disappointing 40th. The six elements making up this ranking were: 14th in college readiness, 43rd in the high school graduation rate, 42nd on the National Assessment of Educational Progress (NAEP) math score, 31st on the NAEP reading score, 41st on Pre-K quality, and 16th on preschool enrollment (U.S. News, 2018c).

However, there is some good news hidden here. Florida does well on college readiness. This is probably the best indicator of how well Florida graduates are prepared to succeed in colleges and universities. It's measured by the proportion of students taking the ACT and SAT who score above the SAT and ACT benchmarks. For instance, according to the CollegeBoard, "The SAT benchmark scores represent a 75% likelihood of a student achieving at least a C grade in a first-semester, credit-bearing college course in a related subject." (CollegeBoard, 2016). Thus, at least the Florida students who do graduate from high school appear to be in relatively good shape to start college or university.

Another indicator where Florida ranks right up at the top of the state rankings, ahead of California, New York, Illinois and Texas, is in the number of Advance Placement tests taken per student in 2018 (CollegeBoard, 2018). Students, who do well on these examinations, which are administered by the CollegeBoard, can get advanced placement or course credits from most colleges and universities. This helps them to graduate sooner and to save on tuition and living expenses at university.

All things considered, Florida's public-school system actually does fairly well given the low level of funding provided. And it could, of course, do much better if more money was made available.

Florida's Colleges and Universities are Becoming World Class

Many people might find it hard to believe, but, in 2018, *U.S. News and World Report* ranked Florida 1st in the country in Higher Education. You ask, how can this possibly be? Very simple, the metric used to compare states gives Florida high marks for 2-year and 4-year college graduation rates, low student debt, and low tuition. But for educational attainment, which is based on the proportion of a state's residents holding associate degrees or higher, not so much. (*U.S. News*, 2018c). However, this does not necessarily point to a problem with the current system of higher education. Rather, it reflects more on the past deficiencies of the system, and the resulting low levels of educational achievement of the population back when they were in school.

The Florida higher educational system is well designed to meet the state's needs. The Florida College System is a very good and inexpensive way of introducing almost two-thirds of Florida students to higher education and preparing them for entry to one of the State University System's twelve universities or the state's many private 4-year colleges and universities. One of the reasons it's so cheap is that it relies on a high proportion of underpaid adjuncts, like I used to be, with no benefits to teach the students. On the more positive side, the shared curriculum for introductory courses and the seamlessness with which credits can be transferred make it easier for students to earn their degrees without having to redo earlier courses.

Florida Southwestern State College, Charlotte Campus in Punta Gorda where I taught for a couple of years.

The high quality of the Florida University System is being increasingly recognized both nationally and internationally (Table 5). Last year $232 million in additional funding was provided to state universities, a large chunk of which went to the flagship of the System, the University of Florida. It was ranked 8th among U.S. state colleges in 2018 by *U.S. News and World Report*. And Florida State University was ranked 26th. In addition, other state universities like the University of South Florida, the University of Central Florida (once dubbed Space U for its work with NASA), and Florida International University are being recognized in the rankings. The University of Florida was also covered in the World University rankings produced in the *Times Higher Education Supplement* and the QS World University rankings, both of which are widely respected and closely followed by those in higher education.

It's important for Florida to have world-class public universities because, as a relatively new state (the 27th, which was only admitted to the Union in 1845), it doesn't have the prestigious private (and more expensive) universities found in older or richer states like the Ivy League schools, Stanford, the University of Chicago, Northwestern, Duke, and Vanderbilt. The only private universities in Florida that were ranked by *U.S. News* in its National Universities category, which includes private as well as public universities, were the University of Miami (53rd), which was ranked between the University of Florida (35th) and Florida State (70th), and the Florida Institute of Technology (177th), which fell between the University of Central Florida {165th) and the Florida International University (197th).

Florida Gulf Coast University in Fort Myers.

And, for the price, no one can beat the deal offered by the Florida University System. It only charges in-state students tuition and fees of $6,380 in the 2018-19 academic year. All the other highly ranked state universities charge much more in 2018-19 (Table 6). The most expensive are almost three times as much, and most are almost twice as high. If an affordable, good-quality higher education is part of your dream, Florida is the place to be.

An area where Florida universities may be getting ahead of themselves, however, is in the generosity of the compensation they pay their presidents. Three of the top 10 highest paid public university presidents in the country in the 2016-17 academic year were at Florida universities according to the *Chronicle of Higher Education's* salary survey. These are: John Hitt, University of Central Florida (No. 6) $1,278,371; Judy Genshaftk, University of South Florida (No. 7) $1,184,520; and W. Kent Fuchs, University of Florida (No. 9) $1,099,975 (Wurth, 2018). Surely, it should be possible to recruit the high-quality leaders required to make Florida universities competitive without paying such outsized compensation premiums. After all, they're not football coaches.

Table 5: Ranking of Florida Universities in 2018-19

	US News US Public Universities	THE World University Rankings	QS World University Ranking
University of Florida	8	156	180
Florida State University	26	251-300	472
University of South Florida	58	251-300	521-530
University of Central Florida	87		751-800
Florida International University	100		801-1000

Source: *U.S. News* (2018c); *Times Higher Education*, World University Rankings 2019; and QS World University Rankings, 2019.

Table 6: Tuition and Fees at Large Public Universities in 2018-19

	Tuition and Fees	US News Rank
Pennsylvania State University	$18,436	20
University of Illinois	$17,293	13
University of Virginia	$16,520	3
University of Michigan	$15,265	4
University of California Berkeley	$13,900	2
Rutgers University	$11,886	17
University of Georgia	$11,830	13
University of Washington	$10,955	20
Ohio State University	$10,726	17
University of Wisconsin	$10,556	15
University of Texas	$10,112	15
Purdue University	$9,982	17
University of North Carolina Chapel Hill	$8,987	5
State University of New York	$8,480	32
University of Florida	$6,380	8

Note: These are tuition and fees for the academic year for freshmen in arts and sciences.

Source: University websites and *U.S. News and World Report*, 2018.

12
THE TOURISM JUGGERNAUT

The warm sunny weather was what drew the early tourists to Florida. They came to bask like gators in the warm winter sun and discovered a beautiful subtropical environment with clear springs and ocean beaches and abundant wildlife. Hunting and fishing, especially for the Silver King Tarpons, became the rage.

Don't forget to stop at the Welcome Center for your free orange juice.

Roadside Attractions and More

It didn't take long before entrepreneurs – big and small – began to see the business opportunities presented by the affluent, and even the not so well-heeled, tourists wandering around Florida with money jingling in their pockets, eagerly looking for things to do. The old Florida roadside attractions were soon set up all along the state's highways and byways like tents in a carnival. Lacking the grandeur and stateliness of the castles, estates and galleries of Europe to draw in the crowds, the roadway impresarios took advantage of what was unique and exotic in Florida's semitropical environment, and most likely to titillate visitors looking for something different to write about on the post cards they so avidly sent home. The early attractions were built around local springs, swamps and wilderness areas with other standout features. They started small but grew in number and magnitude. Jungle parks featured Florida's lush tropical flora and fauna like monkeys and parrots, crystal springs offered glass bottom boat rides. Alligators, living and stuffed, were always a good draw. They were on display at many roadside orange stands where their taxidermized body parts could be purchased as macabre souvenirs to serve as ashtrays or table decorations and boggle the folks up north. An early attraction was the Fountain of Youth in St. Augustine, which, unfortunately, didn't work, and consequently is not of so much interest to the expanding population of retirees streaming into Florida.

Cypress Gardens, established by Dick Pope Sr. in Winter Haven in 1936, with its spectacular water-skiing spectacles, Southern Belles in hooped skirts, and Florida-shaped swimming pool, became, for a time, a signature Florida attraction. Another more modest attraction founded before the war was the Shell Factory in Fort Myers. Its promotors figured out how to sell the worthless shells that washed up on the local beaches at a tidy profit. The City of Mermaids, which opened at Weeki Wachee Springs in 1949, was another Florida icon. Tourists of all ages, but especially little girls and dirty old men, have been enchanted by the synchronized swim routines of the beautiful "mermaids."

The fascination of tourists with alligators has spawned larger, and ever-more spectacular, gator attractions. Gatorland in Orlando was founded in 1949, and Gatorama in Palmdale near Lake Okeechobee in 1958. The Jungle Adventure in Christmas, a Florida town east of Orlando, has Swampy the World's Largest Gator. At least that's what they call their 200-foot long gator-shaped gift shop. The Animal Planet's hit show Gator Boys has turned the Everglades Holiday Park in Fort Lauderdale into a top attraction where visitors hope to schmooze with Paul and the boys as well as see plenty of alligators. Are you starting to see a pattern in what tourists will pay to see? Strange, but since I've moved to Florida, I too have become captivated by alligators.

Grander theme parks like Busch Gardens in Tampa which combined a jungle zoo with a state-of-the art amusement park also cropped up after the war. At around the same time, aquariums also proliferated around the state from the initial Marineland south of St. Augustine, to the Aquartarium in St. Petersburg Beach, Sea-Orama, Ocean World, Seaquarium, and the Gulfarium. Of late, though, Blackfish has been a bit of a downer for the aquarium business.

FLORIDA DREAMS

The John F. Kennedy Space Center

For those more intrigued by outer space than underwater, NASA brought an ambitious new space program to Florida where it soon became an out-of-this-world attraction drawing visitors from all over the globe. They came to Cape Canaveral to watch the first sub-orbital flight of Mercury astronaut Alan Shepherd, to see John Glenn orbit the earth, and to cheer on Apollo astronauts Neil Armstrong and Buzz Aldrin as they blasted off for the moon.

Again, Florida was a beneficiary of its location. No, it wasn't necessarily the weather as Florida has too many seasonal lightning storms and hurricanes offsetting the advantages of its warm year-around climate. It was Cape Canaveral's position near the southernmost point of the United States in a sparsely populated area with the vast expanse of the ocean on its east. This enabled NASA to shoot rockets off in an eastward direction taking advantage of the earth's rotation to gain additional speed without fear of crashing on people living underneath. And nearby Patrick Air Force Base had already established itself as a missile testing ground in use since 1947.

In 1963, a temporary visitor center was set up around the same time as the John F. Kennedy Space Center (KSC) was established. It was replaced by a much more elaborate Visitor Information Center in 1967 to accommodate an ever-growing stream of visitors. This was enhanced over the years as the program evolved. Some of the most popular activities are: the Kennedy Space Center bus tour to see the launch complexes and Vehicle Assembly Building; the Apollo Saturn V Center portraying the moon race; and the space shuttle training simulators and Shuttle Launch Experience® (Kennedy Space Center).

The region around the Kennedy Space Center has been dubbed the "Space Coast." Some high-tech manufacturing companies that supply the KSC are located there. And some entrepreneurial engineers working on the space program have also established spin-off companies nearby. Others, less scientifically inclined, have also taken advantage of the proximity to the Cape to market kitschy space-themed hotels like the Polaris, and restaurants such as the Moon Hut. Near the KSC, it's all about space.

The Kennedy Space Center has been listed as Florida's number 2 tourist attraction according to Touropia. But its estimated 1.5 million visitors a year falls far short of those received by the state's major theme parks. Maybe that's because the KSC is more scientific and educational and puts more strain on the brain than other less intellectually demanding, but more entertaining, attractions. Nevertheless, the NASA astronauts created new Florida Dreams of space travel shared by all Americans and the world.

Mickey Takes Over Orlando

The granddaddy of all attractions, you know, the one that made Orlando the Tourism Capital of the World, was the one that Walt Disney unveiled at a press conference in October 1965. The Walt Disney Company had already been stealthily buying up land, ultimately acquiring over 40 square miles of it in Lake Buena Vista, 14 miles southwest of Orlando. The company had also used the political leverage from its proposed $400 million development project to negotiate a nice sweetheart deal with the state government. It established the Reedy Creek Improvement District, which gave the company free rein over its new domain by granting municipal-like powers to borrow tax free and immunity from state and county land use laws. Disney World, in effect, became a government unto itself in a big piece of Central Florida.

Space Shuttle Atlantis on display at Kennedy Space Center. Courtesy of Dan Felton.

After Walt Disney World's Magic Kingdom opened on October 1, 1971, Mickey welcomed an ever-growing crowd of visitors to this mega-attraction whose parking lot alone had room for Anaheim's Disneyland with enough space still left to park over 3,800 cars. In 1982, EPCOT, the Experimental Prototype Community of Tomorrow, was added. In 1989, came Disney-MGM Studios. Its competitor Universal Studios soon followed. Then, in 1998, Animal World opened. Water parks and resort facilities completed the package and Disney became the world's most comprehensive tourist destination, especially for families with children, and the largest single-site employer in the U.S. with more than 70,000 cast members in central Florida. Nearby is Celebration, the town (really an unincorporated community) that Disney built to celebrate a theme-park vision of small-town America of yore, which probably, and not coincidently, was the same thing that seniors were seeking in communities like The Villages.

Because of Disney, Orlando (including Lake Buena Vista) has seven theme parks out of the first eleven in the list of the country's top 20 in 2017 as ranked by the Themed Entertainment Association (Table 7). Orlando also has 5 of the top 10 in the TEA's worldwide rankings. The only Florida theme park outside of Orlando included in the listing is Busch Gardens in Tampa, which is ranked 12th in the country. Nowhere else in the world comes anywhere close to Orlando when it comes to theme parks. It is every child's Florida dream vacation spot, and many adults' too.

The Commercialization Carries on at Disney Springs.

Sports are Part of the Florida Experience

Sports are another tourist attraction. Florida has a full complement of professional teams for all sports and seasons: for football, there are the Miami Dolphins, Tampa Bay Buccaneers and the Jacksonville Jaguars; for basketball, the Miami Heat and Orlando Magic; for baseball, the Miami Marlins and Tampa Bay Rays; for ice hockey, the Tampa Bay Lightning, and Florida Panthers. And the Grapefruit League teams bring many baseball fans to Florida for an economical preview of their home team's prospects for the upcoming season.

The World's Cruise Ship Port

The modern Florida cruise industry was started when Israeli citizen Ted Arison followed his dream to Miami in 1966 to co-found Norwegian Cruise Line (taking the name from his Norwegian partner's nationality instead of his own for marketing reasons). It wasn't long, however, before he split off to set up his own Carnival Cruise Line in 1972. This is now the cruise industry's largest player, which his son Micky, another Florida billionaire, still chairs today. From such a beginning, the Florida cruise industry blossomed into the world's leader and Miami into the globe's largest cruise port (Wilde, 2016).

Table 7: Florida Theme Parks in the Top 20 in the U.S., 2017

Rank	Attraction	Visitors
1	Disney's Magic Kingdom	20,450,000
3	Disney's Animal Kingdom	12,500,000
4	Disney's EPCOT	12,200,000
5	Disney's Hollywood Studios	10,722,000
6	Universal Studios	10,198,000
8	Islands of Adventure at Universal	9,549,000
11	SeaWorld	3,962,000
12	Busch Gardens	3,961,000

Source: TEA/AECOM, 2018.

Celebrity Equinox queued up loading passengers behind five other cruise ships at Port Miami.

With the Caribbean and Latin America next door, that's where most Florida cruises head, but some do sail all over the world. And like everything else Florida, cruises have tended to get more over-the-top with time. The Royal Caribbean's latest mega-ship, the Symphony of the Seas, is as large as a Nimitz Class Aircraft Carrier and will hold 6,800 passengers. And people don't just sit around on deck chairs, and dine with the captain in formal eveningwear anymore. The latest ships have water parks, skydive simulators, go-cart racetracks, surfing machines, not to mention casino gambling, which makes a pile of money for cruise ship companies as well as the Indians. (Radcliff, 2017).

The numbers speak for themselves. In 2016, Florida accounted for 7,079,000 passenger embarkations or 60.7 per cent of the U.S. total. Florida's share of the expenditures of all the cruise ship passengers was almost $8 billion or 37 per cent of the U.S total. And there were almost 150,000 jobs provided in the industry or 38 per cent of the U.S. total. (BREA, 2017)

Miami remained the top Florida cruise port in 2016 with most of the major lines sailing from there (Table 8). Carnival, Royal Caribbean and Norwegian (the top two and 4th largest cruise companies) also have their headquarters in Miami. Port Canaveral is slowly moving up, capitalizing on its proximity to Orlando and Celebration, the landlocked town where Disney Cruise Lines is headquartered. And Port Everglades in Fort Lauderdale, which offers a wide range of cruise ship departures, is firmly in 3rd place with Tampa and Jacksonville bringing up the rear. Key West, always popular with tourists looking to experience Florida at its most outlandish, like at Fantasy Fest where wild partyers prance around in nothing but body paint, has emerged as a cruise destination in its own right, expecting in 2018 to host 812,800 visitors, who'll arrive by boat rather than the Overseas Highway. The largest Florida cruise ports have all either undergone or are undergoing expansions in their facilities to meet growing demand.

Table 8: U.S. Embarkations by Port, 2016

	Number	Per Cent Share
Miami	2,551,000	21.9
Port Canaveral	2,088,000	17.9
Port Everglades	1,840,000	15.8
Tampa	405,000	3.5
Jacksonville	195,000	1.7
All Florida Ports	7,079,000	60.7
Other U.S. Ports	4,579,000	39.3
U.S. Total	11,658,000	100.0

Source: BREA (2017, p.11).

Florida is the Tourism State

More than 118 million visitors came to Florida in 2017, many probably to enjoy the attractions highlighted above. And the state is on track to welcome another 125 million in 2018. Between the end of the recession in 2009 and 2017, the number of visitors increased over 46 per cent. While it's difficult to get a handle on the impact of visitors, their spending in 2016 reached $112 billion or more than 12 per cent of GDP, $45 billion of which was on value created in Florida. This activity in turn employed

875,722 workers accounting for over 10 per cent of total employment (Oxford Economics, 2018). Tourism is clearly Florida's largest and leading growth industry, far outpacing agriculture and creating many better-paying jobs.

Tourists come to Florida from all over the country, Canada and oversees. The largest share of U.S. visitors came from neighboring Georgia, but large shares also came from New York, Texas, Ohio and Pennsylvania (Table 9).

The top country for international visitors is Canada, the home of many of the snowbirds. The United Kingdom is the source of the largest number of European visitors (Table 10). The two other European countries on the list, Germany and France, provide far fewer. Latin American countries like Brazil, Argentina, Columbia, Venezuela, and Mexico are also a large source of visitors, as they are of immigrants. More surprisingly, China makes the top 10 list, albeit in last place. Florida ranked 2nd in 2016 among all the states in terms of overseas visitors (which excludes Canadians and Mexicans). This is a little behind New York and ahead of California. But it's an even better performance than it looks as a larger proportion of overseas visitors must pass through either New York or California on their way through to other destinations in the United States (U.S. Department of Commerce, National Travel and Tourism Office, 2017).

Tourism is making Florida a national leader in the accommodation sector of the new "sharing economy". On the basis of its booking data for the first half of 2018, Airbnb ranked Orlando and Miami 7th and 8th as the top global travel destinations. In the United States., only New York City ranked higher (Airbnb, 2018).

Table 9: Top Origin States by Percentage of Domestic Visitors in 2017

	Per Cent		Per Cent
Georgia	9.6	Missouri	3.8
New York	8.5	Illinois	3.8
Texas	5.5	Alabama	3.5
Ohio	5.3	Maryland	3.4
Pennsylvania	5.3	Michigan	3.3
Tennessee	4.5	Virginia	2.9
New Jersey	4.4	Indiana	2.8
North Carolina	3.9		

Source: VisitFlorida, 2018.

Table 10: Top 10 Countries for International Visitors, 2017	
Country	Number
Canada	3,447,000
United Kingdom	1,438,000
Brazil	993,000
Argentina	649,000
Columbia	528,000
Germany	472,000
Mexico	415,000
France	311,000
Venezuela	310,000
China	286,000
Source: VisitFlorida, 2018.	

13
MIAMI: THE EMERGING CAPITAL OF LATIN AMERICA AND THE CARIBBEAN

Coming down to Miami through the clouds. Courtesy of Dan Felton.

Miami is an American city unlike any other. Its clubs and discos pulsate to a Latin beat. It's set apart by its art deco buildings and lush semitropical setting, amidst blue-green waters, and white sand beaches. The city is even recognizable to migrating Bedouin tribes in the Sahara who have seen it on cassette reruns of Miami Vice and marveled at Crockett and Tubbs' prowess in zigging and zagging their overpowered speedboat through its narrow canals in pursuit of fleeing "narcotraficantes." Hollywood's obsession with Miami has familiarized moviegoers worldwide with the city's cosmopolitan Latin ambience (albeit while creating a false impression of the sinister omnipresence of drug lords).

The Clevelander on Ocean Drive in South Beach.

Miami has morphed over the years from being a small resort and retirement city to its current flashier status as the largest Latin American city, not actually in Latin America. In 2017, there were 1,887,266 people of Hispanic or Latino origin living in Miami-Dade County, or almost 69 per cent of the total population (U.S. Census Bureau, 2017, American Community Survey, 1-Year Estimates). That's a lot of people, but even the whole Miami Metropolitan Area of 6.2 million is not large enough to win a very high place among overpopulated Latin American cities. Fortunately for Miami, however, it's the excessive size and poor quality of life offered by large Latin American cities that makes Miami look so good in comparison. Consequently, according to an admittedly unscientific survey, many, particularly affluent, Latin Americans would chose Miami as their favorite place to live (Moreno, 2013).

Miami's magnetism for affluent Latin Americans is affirmed by their purchases of residential real estate in Miami. According to a survey conducted for Florida Realtors, foreign buyers accounted for 21 per cent of the residential dollar volume of sales in 2017, and 53 per cent of these foreign sales, which were mostly in cash, were concentrated in the Miami-Fort Lauderdale-West Palm Beach Metropolitan Statistical Area. Not surprisingly, 46 per cent of the foreign buyers came from Latin America with the largest numbers from Brazil, Argentina, Venezuela, and Columbia. Latin American buyers bought mainly in Miami. The largest proportion were buying the homes as vacation and/or rental properties (National Association of Realtors, 2017).

Miami's sprouting downtown skyline.

Miami started its transition to be the Gateway to Latin America and as Latin America's most admired city with the arrival of so many Cubans fleeing Castro, and gained momentum as other Latin Americans, both rich and poor, rushed to join them, sending word back home about the wonders of Miami. Unlike other cities with large Hispanic populations, Cubans predominated with 1,000,518 people in 2017 or 53 per cent of the Hispanic population and South Americans, largely Columbians and Venezuelans, followed with 352,862 or 18.7 per cent of the Hispanic population (Chart 28). Central Americans, who number 240,586 or 12.8 per cent of the population, are reasonably well represented. But Puerto Ricans, who number only 93,190, and Mexicans, who number only 70,637, and who are the 2nd and 3rd largest groups of Hispanics state-wide in Florida, are very underrepresented in Miami. This is why Miami has such a different flavor from other cities with large Hispanic populations. It is dominated by Cubans and South Americans, many of whom have become quite affluent in contrast to so many of the Mexicans and Central Americans who are struggling more to get ahead.

Miami is also the American city with the largest proportion of the population that is foreign born. In 2017, 1,489,421, or over 54 per cent of the population of Miami-Dade was foreign born (ACS, 2017). By contrast, only 1,262,375, or 46 per cent of the population was native born. However, over 57 per cent of the foreign born have taken out U.S. citizenship and are now counted as full-fledged Americans.

Nevertheless, Miami has become a Spanish-speaking city. Three quarters of the population speaks a language other than English at home (most commonly Spanish) and over 35 per cent of the people speak English less than "very well" (ACS, 2017). On the bright side, Miami is also the city where most language learners are studying English on the widely used DuoLingo free app (Shammas, 2017).

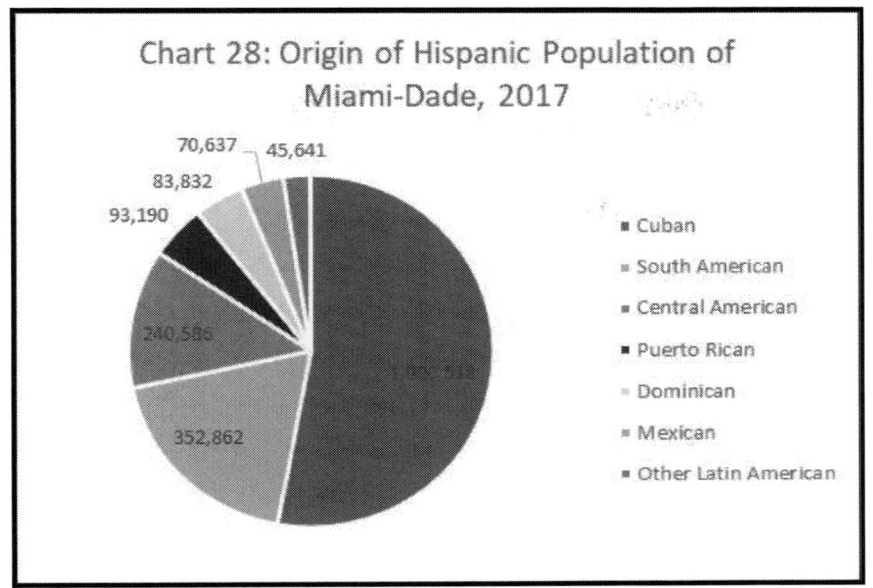

Chart 28: Origin of Hispanic Population of Miami-Dade, 2017

- Cuban
- South American
- Central American
- Puerto Rican
- Dominican
- Mexican
- Other Latin American

Values shown: 70,637; 45,641; 83,832; 93,190; 240,586; 352,862

Source: U.S. Census Bureau, American Community Survey, 2017.

The other side of the coin from the expanding Hispanic population of Miami is Anglo white flight. Since 1960, when the Latinos first started to arrive in Miami in large numbers, the Anglo white population of Dade County has fallen by a half. This is an indication that many English speakers don't feel comfortable living and working in a Spanish-speaking environment. And while it is illegal to discriminate against a job applicant because of their national origins under Title VII of the Civil Rights Act of 1964, an employer can require Spanish or bilingual Spanish/English fluency if it is required to do a job.

The U.S. Equal Employment Opportunity Commission (EEOC) is responsible for hearing complaints from employees about the legitimacy of the language requirement imposed and can sue an employer on the employee's behalf if it deems them not justified. Nevertheless, there is some evidence that English speakers are leaving Miami to find employment elsewhere (NBC, 2008). It is also evident from an inspection of advertisements for job openings in Miami on the internet that a significant proportion of the ads either list a Spanish language requirement or are written in Spanish. Consequentially, there is at least *prima facie* evidence that there isn't a level playing field between English and Spanish speakers in the Miami labor market and that English speakers are getting the short end of the stick.

Home of the World's Richest Latinos

Miami is home to a very large community of affluent Hispanics or Latinos. Many of the Cubans who came to Miami were doctors, lawyers, engineers and other professionals with a high level of education as were many of the other Latin Americans that followed them. They worked hard to learn English and to succeed in their professions or related activities. Many of them did quite well for themselves. Others did even better and became fabulously rich. Wealth is on display in Miami, and it's not mostly Anglo wealth.

Miami houses a good crop of Latino billionaires who made it big there, really big. Jorge Pérez, who built many of the high rise condominium towers making up the Miami skyline and was a leading benefactor of the Pérez Art Museum Miami, came as an immigrant born of Cuban parents and now has a net worth of $2.6 billion (Forbes, 2018). Adriana Cisneros, the current CEA of the Cisneros media and entertainment empire, lives in Miami. Her father Gustavo, who owns the Grupo Cisneros and was born in Venezuela, has a net worth of $1.1 billion (Forbes, 2018). The other two Cuban-American billionaires are the Fanjul Brothers, Alfonso and José, who own the Fanjul Corp., which controls a large share of the world's sugar in Florida and abroad including Florida Crystals (see Chapter 24). While they don't live in Miami, but instead in Palm Beach, that's close enough. Another Cuban American who became rich in South Florida is Mike Fernandez. Through his firm MBF Healthcare Partners, he owns stakes in a portfolio of healthcare companies and is said to be worth $200 million (Seemuth, 2014). And don't forget "Beto" Perez the Columbian-American Zumba King from Miami. He has managed to make a fortune parlaying Zumba from instructional videos into clothing, shoes and more.

Broadcasting in Spanish to the Nation and the World

Miami has capitalized on its comparative advantage as a predominantly Spanish-speaking city to dominate the Spanish-speaking radio and television airwaves (and cable) in the United States. While headquartered in New York City, Univision, the largest Spanish network in the United States with 120 local TV and radio stations and the country's biggest Hispanic audience, has its studios and production in Doral, a predominantly Hispanic suburb of Miami. Telemundo, the second largest Spanish language network, which is owned by Comcast, is in Hialeah, another Hispanic Miami suburb. The broadcasting of this American programming in Spanish throughout Latin America will inspire many a future Florida Dream.

It's not only the broadcasting industry that finds Miami to be the ideal place for servicing Spanish speakers. The U.S. State Department has chosen Miami as the location of its "Media Hub of the Americas." This is its propaganda arm whose aim is to communicate U.S. policies in Spanish throughout Latin America and the Caribbean to journalists, academics, civil society groups, and the public more broadly.

Communications Hub of Latin America

An indication of the key role that Miami plays as a communications channel between Latin America and the Caribbean and the rest of the world is the existence of the Century Link MI1 Communications Data Center for Latin America right in the heart of the city. It is the Network Access Point of the Americas where all the submarine fiber optic cables from the data centers in the major cities across Latin America and the Caribbean connect their national networks to the U.S. and global networks in Europe, Asia, Africa, and the Pacific. Voice, data, video, internet communications, all funnel through this access point in Miami into all the U.S. networks of AT&T,

Century Link, and Verizon. The structure containing the center is built like a fortress with reinforced concrete walls capable of withstanding a Category 5 hurricane 32 feet above sea level and is classified as critical infrastructure by FEMA (Garcia, 2018).

The Miami Sound

Miami has been the epicenter of the Latin music industry since the 1970s when Julio Iglesias came over from Spain to set up shop. The Miami Sound Machine soon burst on the scene with its spectacular young schoolgirl singer Gloria Estefan, who went on to become a superstar. Miami became a hotbed of Latin talent spawning singers like Marc Anthony, Enrique Iglesias, Ricky Martin, and Pit Bull.

The Latin music industry has had some major triumphs of late. In 2017, Louis Fonsi and Daddy Yankee's remix of their Latin reggaeton mega-hit, "Despacito," with Justin Bieber, topped the Pop Charts. Cuban-American Camila Cabello's hit "Havana" made number one on the Billboard 100 in early 2018. While it's mostly in English, it certainly sounds very Latin to most Anglos like me.

The three major music companies – Warner, Sony and Universal – all have studios in Miami to take advantage of the local talent pool and its links to Latin American artists. Each produces under two labels, one for the U.S. Hispanic Market, and the other for Latin America and Spain, which, apparently, don't have the same tastes in music as U.S. Latinos. Several minor labels are also based in Miami. The Latin Recording Academy, which awards the Latin Grammy, is there as well. (Rodriguez, 2016).

The U.S Latin Music business grew spectacularly in the first half of 2018 reaching $135 million as it finally began to take advantage of paid subscriptions on the services like Apple Music and Amazon Unlimited.

Miami Takes Over the Art World

For one week in December each year, Miami becomes the global art cynosure drawing over 70 thousand, mostly affluent, art connoisseurs to the city from all over the country, Latin America and the world. Since 2002, it has hosted Art Basel Miami, an offshoot of the Swiss Art Basel, that has come to rival its parent. It's known for its celebrities in attendance and glamorous parties taking place in venues all over the town during Miami's Art Week. But the real serious business is selling art, $3.5 billion of which was on sale in December 2017 from over 250 participating galleries. Artsy, the art collecting website, reports that hundreds of sales in the six-figure range took place and even more activity in "the five-figure range."(Forbes, 2017). Leo DiCaprio was reportedly spotted sneaking around in a hooded sweatshirt bargaining for a Basquiat (Cohen, 2017). Many come to town to spot the celebrities as much as to view the art, some of which is quite outrageous, but always interesting. This year, in 2018, the show attracted its usual quota of A-list celebrities; Leo was back and even Bill Gates made a cameo appearance. The feature art offerings up for sale were a Mark Rothko for $50 million and a Jean-Michel Basquiat for $16.5 million (Munzenrieder, 2018).

Crowding in to see Art Basel Miami.

The Darker Side of Miami

Not all Florida Dreams have been beneficial for society. Unfortunately, and probably unavoidably, Miami has undergone a phenomenon that can only be called Latinamericanization. This mouthful of a word means that, in addition to the good characteristics of a vibrant Latino language and culture that links it to that dynamic region, it has acquired some of the nastier and less desirable characteristics of large overgrown Latin American cities, namely crime and inequality.

The Economic Policy Institute revealed in a study that Miami has the largest income gap of any major U.S. Metropolitan Area (Sommeiller and Price, 2018). The top 1 per cent of income earners in Miami-Fort Lauderdale-West Palm Beach, who earn on average $2,345,381 per year, make 54 times as much as the other 99 per cent. While this is not as much as the lofty level of 90 times reached in the much smaller Naples-Immokalee-Marco Island, it's enough to earn the Miami Metropolitan Area the title as the most unequal major city in the country. And inequality as well as high crime are two of the key characteristics of Latinamericanization.

In 2016, Miamians were aghast to read that their beloved city was the worst city in the country to live in according to a study by 24/7 Wall St. of the 50 worst cities, worse even than Detroit (Kaufman, 2016). Fortunately, this fake, or at least misleading, news has been corrected in 24/7 Wall St.'s updated study this year, which demotes Miami to 42nd worst and restores Detroit to its well-deserved 1st position (Stebbins and Comen, 2018). Nevertheless, the study still underlines some unpleasant facts about Miami that got it on the 2016 list, namely that it has relatively high poverty, inequality, house prices, and crime.

According the FBI's Crime Statistics for 2016, the Miami Metropolitan Statistical Area (MSA) ranked 6th highest in violent crime and 4th in property crime in comparison to the other 24 MSAs that provided data. The violent crime rate was 486.1 per 100,000. While this wasn't so much higher than the 397.1 national average, the 887.5 for Miami city proper was more than two times the national average, which, however, again is not that unusual for a large U.S. city. Specifically, it was much lower than the 1,105.5 in Chicago, 1,780.4 in Baltimore, 1,913.2 in St. Louis, and 2,046.5 in Detroit, which are all cities notorious for their high violent crime rates.

The City of Miami also has the highest rate of violent crimes among the Florida's four largest cities. It is higher than the 507.0 in Tampa, the 625.1 in Jacksonville, and the 838.3 in Orlando. It is even slightly higher than the 880.1 in Tallahassee, which, by the way, is a shamefully high rate for a city with a population of only 190 thousand. So, even if the drug wars haven't broken out again, Miami is still a dangerous city. If you visit, maybe you should consider bringing your gun.

It may seem that Miami is still a city with lots of crime. However, Miami has made extraordinary progress since the infamous days of the Drug Wars. Crime, including especially murder rates have plummeted drastically.

Forty years ago, starting with the Cocaine Cowboys shoot-out with Mac-10 machine pistols at the Dadeland's Mall in 1979 and continuing through the early 1980s, there were a record 573 murders in 1980, and an even greater 621 in 1981. So many dead bodies were piling up that an ice truck had to be rented to serve as a temporary morgue. (Alvarado, 2011). And the police were too corrupt to do much to stop it, and worse even participated in killings over drugs, as evidenced by the notorious Miami River Cops Case (Miller, 2009).

The U.S. Government, however, didn't put up with Miami becoming the nation's shooting gallery for long, and sent in everything it had, including the DEA, FBI, Coast Guard and the military, to clean things up. Now, years later in 2016, there were only 55 murders, which wasn't even enough to place Miami on the list of the top 30 cities with the highest murder rates (*Lincoln Journal Star*, 2018). Oh, how times change! But the condo towers financed with the drug money still stand.

While public concern has shifted to opioids, there is evidence that cocaine is coming back in South Florida. Seizures by Customs and Border Protection are way up. And overdose deaths in Florida from cocaine are at their highest level since 2007. Columbian criminals still control the inflow, but their organizations are smaller, and less prone to resort to public displays of violence than the infamous Medellin Cartel, whose hubris had made it a target for the U.S. and Columbian governments (Van Velzer, 2017). Even though, with full legalization on the horizon, the marijuana trade is booming, the main front in the drug wars has shifted to the Mexico border, making life easier for Miami law enforcement and the streets safer. Hollywood is the only loser. It will have to look elsewhere than Miami for future material.

14
WALL STREET JOINS IN THE DREAM

The Masters of the Universe from Manhattan and Greenwich have, like the retirees and the Latinos, been thronging to Florida to pursue their dreams. It's not the weather that's been luring them either, although that hasn't hurt. It's the low taxes and operating costs. And they've come in such numbers that Palm Beach and Miami are being referred to as "Wall Street South" by some. Unlike Bernie Madoff whose forays to Palm Beach were predatory and left many of his coreligionists at the Palm Beach Country Club impoverished, the financiers moving to Florida are bringing down wealth and creating thousands of jobs.

The financial firms are locating in two clusters in Southeast Florida. The largest is Brickell Avenue in Miami and the other is in and around the Flagler Financial District in West Palm Beach. The two cities are just a little further apart than Greenwich and Manhattan and are similarly linked by a train.

Tax Motivations for Coming to Florida

The tax advantages of moving to Florida for footloose financial service firms like hedge funds and private equity that don't need to be near their clients are huge. By moving to Florida, they can eliminate state income tax paid by their principals and employees, as well as state estate tax, since income and estate taxes are not allowed under the Florida constitution. This results in no small savings as taxes are high in their home states. Remember that the top income tax rate is 8.82 per cent in New York and 6.99 per cent in Connecticut. The rates apply to capital gains as well as income. Moreover, in New York City, there is a city individual income tax rate with a top rate of 3.88 per cent levied in addition to the state rate that can be escaped as well. There are also high estate tax rates with a top rate of 16 per cent in New York and 12 per cent in Connecticut.

The Business Development Board of Palm Beach County is not bashful about publicizing some eye-popping illustrative examples of the possible reduction in taxes from pulling up stakes and moving to Florida. For instance, an individual with an income of $1 million would cut income taxes by $105,395 by moving from New York

City and $63,100 moving from Greenwich. And these reductions could even be greater as a result of the SALT cap in the 2017 Tax Cut and Jobs Act, which limits the deduction of state and local taxes from Federal Income Tax to a maximum of $10,000. If the same individual were to die with an estate of $25 million, he/she would pay $3,466,800 less in Florida than in New York and $2,526,300 less than in Connecticut. And if the same individual were to sell a business or property and make a $100,000,000 gain, they would save $8,814,720 relative to New York and $4,750,000 relative to Connecticut in capital gains tax. With numbers like this, it shouldn't take long for the light to go on in even the dimmest financial wizard's brain. (BDB of Palm Beach County, 2018).

There are also corporate income tax advantages to sweeten the pot more. For one, the Florida corporate income tax at 5.5 per cent is lower than the 6.5 per cent charged in New York and 7.5 per cent in Connecticut. For another, there is no corporate income tax on limited partnerships or Subchapter S corporations, which can be used to reduce tax liabilities. (BDB of Palm Beach County, 2018).

Connecticut has moved to curtail the increased taxes resulting from the SALT cap by passing a new law in June 2018 which will directly assess taxes on individuals for the profits of limited liability companies and partnerships, including as an added balance, their carried interest profits in order to avoid double taxation (Soule, 2018). This shows that the Connecticut government realizes that it's in danger of losing many hedge funds and private equity firms because of high taxes, but it is constrained by its own weak fiscal position and need for revenue, in how much it can do to lower them.

Hedge Fund Refuge in Palm Beach

The hedge funds and private equity firms are attracted to Palm Beach by its similarity to their natural habitat in posh Fairfield County, Connecticut. Greenwich, which is located there on the Long Island Sound east of New York City, has ritzy mansions, beaches, marinas for yachts, and is very horsey. Not coincidently, so does Palm Beach where many hedge funders already have their winter getaway homes, not too far from the International Equestrian Center.

The Business Development Board of Palm Beach County estimates that "60 to 70 asset management firms, including hedge funds, have opened offices in Palm Beach County within the past four years." Also it looks like Palm Beach might have caught some financial whales. Paul Tudor Jones whose Tudor Investments manages $7 billion, sold his home in Greenwich and bought Casa Apava on Billionaires Row for $71 million two years ago, and is now making renovations that could cost as much as $6.4 million (Hofheinz, 2017). Other executives of Tudor Investments have also purchased property in Palm Beach. Another billionaire, Thomas Peterffy, who owns discount brokerage, Interactive Brokers, has moved to Palm Beach (Fortado, 2018).

Brickell Avenue, Miami's Wall Street

Brickell Avenue in downtown Miami, with its shiny glass financial temples reaching to the sky, is becoming a symbol of Miami's new status as the Hemispheric Financial Center. Money pours in from all over the world attracted by Florida's favorable tax and business climate. But Miami's special edge is its Spanish language and culture, which makes it the first choice of Latin Americans as the place they feel most comfortable stashing their hard-earned, as well as not so legally obtained, wealth. The political instability in many of the countries in the region like Maduro's Venezuela and Ortega's Nicaragua makes many anxious to squirrel away their money outside the reach of greedy socialist governments looking to confiscate wealth to fill their empty coffers.

Brickell Avenue, Miami's Financial District.

Miami's position, as a Latin American and international financial center, is built on a strong domestic base. All the major U.S. banks have branches there or at least in the metropolitan area. There is also a large group of smaller local and regional banks there, the biggest of which is BankUnited with $30 billion in consolidated deposits. Bauer Financial, which publishes independent credit ratings for banks, gave 21 of these Miami area banks its highest five-star rating for the year ending June 30, 2015. (Nehamas, 2015).

The thing that makes Miami different from all other regional financial centers is the large number of offices of foreign banks located there. There were 31 foreign bank offices (international and Edge Act banks) in the Miami Metropolitan Area as of March 31, 2018 that could be identified in the published quarterly data (FRB, 2018). The largest number of these foreign bank organizations in Miami came from Latin America and the Caribbean (with the number in parentheses after the country indicating the number of banks if more than one) - Argentina, Brazil (4), Chile (2), Ecuador, Honduras, Jamaica (2), Panama, Peru, Portugal, and Venezuela. Some also came from other areas of the world, including: Canada (4), France, Israel, Portugal, Spain (2), Switzerland (2) and the United Kingdom (3). The best-known banks on the list are the Bank of Nova Scotia from Canada, the Banco Espirito Santo, S.A. and Banco De Sabadell, S.A. from Spain, and UBS from Switzerland, and the HSBC and

Barclays from the United Kingdom.

While the type of banking organization listed includes agencies and representative offices, which typically don't hold large assets, the foreign banking organizations on the list collectively held $28 billion in assets in Miami. The largest asset holder with $10.8 billion in assets was the City National Bank of Florida, which was owned by the Banco De Credito E Inversiones S.A. from Chile and functioned as a national bank for that country. The Mercantil Bank, which was owned by Mercantil Servicios Financieros, C.A. from Venezuela, held $8.4 billion, and also functioned as a national bank. The Banco Santander International and the Banco De Sabadell SA Miami Branch held $6.1 and $5.4 billion, respectively. Banco Do Brasil SA Miami Branch held $1.4 billion in assets, and the Banco De Bogota SA Miami Agency from Columbia $1.2 billion.

The foreign bank organizations are much more important than suggested by their relatively small asset bases as they can draw on their foreign parents for funds if needed, and thus play a key role in financing trade and investment between the United States and their home countries and can serve as conduits bringing money from Latin America into Miami.

Like Palm Beach, Miami has also attracted and is attracting major hedge funds, mutual funds and private equity firms. In recent years, ESL Investments, Everest Capital, Fairholme Capital Management and H.I.G. Capital have all come. In 2014, Mark Spitznagel transplanted his edgy black swan style investing firm Universa from California. (Dahlberg, 2014). Barry Sternlicht moved his $55 billion real estate fund, the Starwood Capital Group, to Miami Beach. (Browning and Tan, 2018). Sadek Wahba and Adil Rahmathulla are going to be moving their private equity firm I Squared Capital in 2019 (Tan, 2018).

15
THE REAL ESTATE BUST ONLY TEMPORARILY SPOOKED THE DREAM

Florida land has always been characterized by colossal cycles of boom and bust. The 1920s saw a boom when unusable or inaccessible land was sold, sight unseen, using "binders," describing the properties, to gullible northerners. The subsequent humungous bust at the end of the decade, precipitated by cold weather and hurricanes scared the bejesus out of potential northern home buyers and killed the market for many a year. A widely repeated punch line that became part of the pop culture repertoire and could always get a laugh was: "Don't buy any swampland in Florida."

In the early years of the 21st Century, it looked to everyone like housing prices always went up and never down. It became the conventional wisdom that there was no better investment than owning a home, even if it was a vacation property or a rental in Florida (Chart 29). The Florida housing market was hotter than in most of the rest of the country. This was because of the large inflow of people into the state, including snowbirds, that stoked the demand for housing. In addition, the same factors fueling the national housing market were in play in Florida. Interest rates had been lowered following the September 11, 2001 terrorist attacks to prop up the economy. And the same institutional innovations, such as mortgage backed securities and credit default swaps, that increased the availability and lowered the cost of mortgages, further fueled the demand for housing. The same as elsewhere in the country, there were no shortages of mortgage brokers and banks willing to originate questionable mortgage loans and distribute them for a fee to securities firms able to package them into mortgage backed securities, get an artificially good rating on the securities from accommodating credit agencies, and sell them to naïve investors across the country and the world. Indeed, the whole process was encouraged by the Federal Government, and its alphabet soup of housing agencies like Fannie Mae and Freddie Mac, to spur home ownership. This all worked very well for as long as the housing market was going up.

But, of course, nothing goes straight up forever, even the housing market. In Florida, it peaked in the fourth quarter of 2006, and, after a few quarters, experienced a stomach-churning decline that lasted until the second quarter of 2012 (Chart 29). By the fourth quarter of 2009, the drop has reached 36 per cent, and by the second quarter of 2012, the housing price fall bottomed out at heart-stopping 45 per cent (FRED, 2018). This was a housing price decrease like no other, that even worldly-wise senior citizens like me had never seen in our lifetimes. Many had their Florida Dreams crushed by falling housing prices.

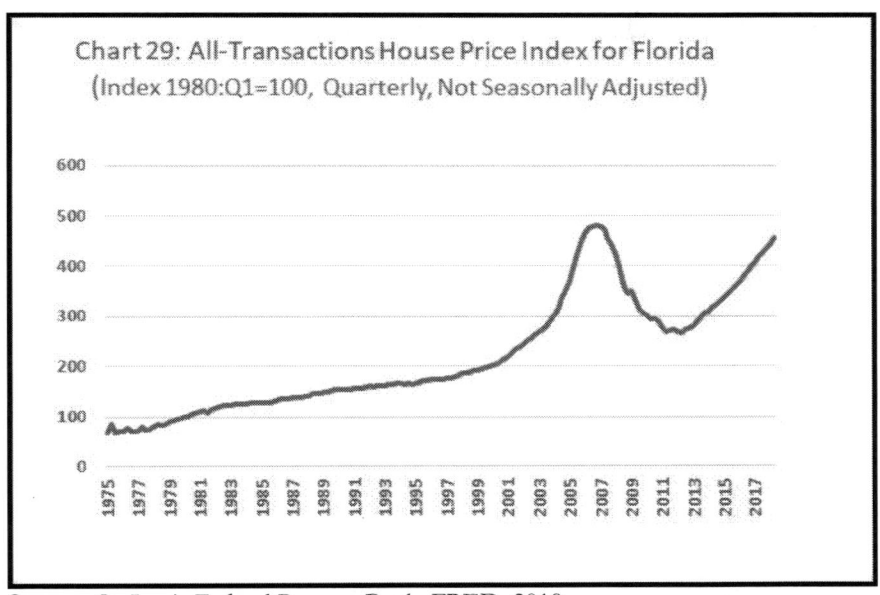

Chart 29: All-Transactions House Price Index for Florida
(Index 1980:Q1=100, Quarterly, Not Seasonally Adjusted)

Source: St. Louis Federal Reserve Bank, FRED, 2018.

Florida (along with Nevada) became ground zero for the national housing market meltdown that featured so prominently in the 2008-09 Financial Crisis. You know, the one that almost toppled the U.S. financial system and the global economy. While policy makers, central bankers, financiers and economists, wrestled with the big questions of too big to fail, the appropriate fiscal and monetary policy response, and needed regulatory reforms to stabilize the economy and financial markets (such as the Dodd–Frank Wall Street Reform and Consumer Protection Act and stress tests), individual Floridians had to deal with the personal consequence of the crisis on their own finances, not the least of which was the collapse in value of their biggest (and in some cases only) asset, their home.

Many people lost their jobs as the economy tanked. The downturn in the Florida economy mirrored the decline in the housing market because of the contraction in construction (see Chapter 3). Others lost money in the market either directly or through their retirement investments. Their reduced circumstances, combined with the decline in the value of their homes, left many people under water with their mortgages, and led many to consider actions that had previously been unthinkable. Many stopped paying their mortgages and eventually defaulted. Financial institutions holding the mortgages began to foreclose on homes in default, and to approve short sales for those who could demonstrate financial hardship. In case you're not from Florida and don't know what a short sale is, it's a listing where the lender agrees to accept the proceeds of the sale as full payment of the outstanding mortgage balance, even though it is "short" of the amount. A short sale can be a very complicated and lengthy process, as it requires approval for the sale by both the seller and the lender and can involve additional side payments from the seller to the lender.

The Fort Myers, Cape Coral areas, and especially Lehigh Acres, all in Lee County, were some of the worst hit parts of the state. In Lehigh Acres, where many people work in the construction trades, unemployment hit 25 per cent and a large proportion of the homes were in various stages of foreclosure. Properties were abandoned or neglected and neighborhoods that had been well kept quickly became rundown with uncut lawns and weeds replacing grass. Distress sales and urban blight drove prices down as much as 80 per cent in many cases. It was so bad that one of the first things President Obama did after being sworn in was to come down to Lee County to see with his own eyes the housing devastation and the hardship it was causing, which was also good PR (Toadvine and Shea, 2009).

While there are no studies looking specifically at the Cape Coral-Fort Myers Metropolitan Area, there are studies that survey and document the many adverse effects that foreclosure can have on people (Tsai and Coyne, 2015; Kingsley, Smith and Price, 2011; Kizito, 2015). These include a deterioration of the physical and mental health of the individuals impacted, and an increased incidence of depression and suicide. There is also the resulting breakup of families and divorces, which can harm the children. And some, who lose their home and can't get accommodation, can even become homeless.

The real estate bust has had lingering effects on the Florida economy. In the wake of all the foreclosures, home ownership has decreased from over 72 per cent of households in 2006 to around 64 per cent in 2016 (FRED, 2018). Housing starts have only recently climbed back to the level of 10 to 15 thousand per month that used to be considered normal before the boom and are still way below the 30 thousand level reached at the peak of the boom (Chart 30). While foreclosures have fallen sharply from the stratospheric altitudes reached at the height of the housing bust, legacy foreclosures in Florida that were initiated earlier are still proceeding at quite a clip and are elevated in relation to other states. Consequently, foreclosures in Florida are still much higher than the national average; 60 per cent higher as of October 2018 to be more precise (RealtyTrac, 2018). Moreover, in 2018 there has been something of a run-up of foreclosures in South Florida.(Breakstone, 2018).

But at least in terms of direction and the mood of the market, a strong recovery has gotten underway, although, admittedly, it still has a way to go to reach past peak prices in real terms and levels of housing starts. Nevertheless, throughout the state, the state's biggest home builders like D. R. Horton, Lennar, Pulte and Mattamy are again busy filling out their planned communities with new houses (Carruth, 2018).

After already spending $3 billion over the last 10 years, the Tavistock Lake Nona Development is ramping up. It recently opened USTA's new tennis facility, which is the largest in the world, as well as a new Medical City and two major universities offering medicine and pharmacy programs. When finished, it will accommodate more than 25,000 residents and offer the whole range of goods and services expected of a full-fledged city. Construction is also beginning in other brand-new, planned communities including the Avenir Development in Palm Beach Gardens (Peters,

2018), and Babcock Ranch, a new solar-powered city, where a population of 50,000 is expected at build-out.

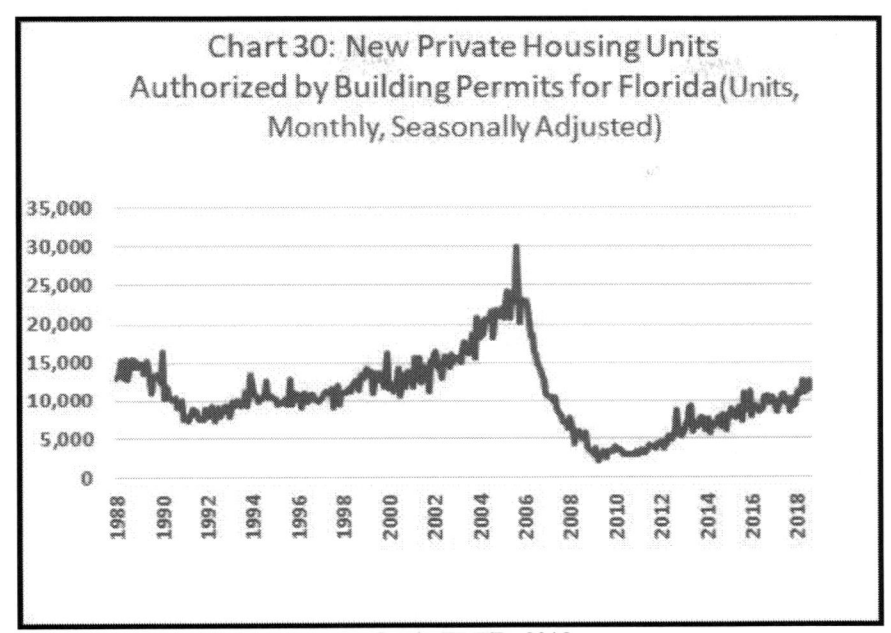

Chart 30: New Private Housing Units Authorized by Building Permits for Florida (Units, Monthly, Seasonally Adjusted)

Source: St. Louis Federal Reserve Bank, FRED, 2018.

The good news is that those who stuck it out and held on to their properties through the downturn have seen their property values recover. And those who managed to strategically default through foreclosures or short sales, as well as those who have bought up distressed properties at a fraction of their previous values, have made out like bandits. But that's the way it is in Florida. It's not for the faint of heart. Florida has always had its share of pirates and swashbucklers, especially in real estate.

16
FLORIDA DEVELOPERS DREAM BIG

The real estate crash has not stopped developers from dreaming big. Cranes are again being erected all around Florida's cities and new construction sites are cropping up everywhere. Big plans are on the drawing boards. Nothing yet quite on the scale of Disney World, but big, nevertheless, even by Texas standards.

While there is an abundance of major projects to choose from, two stand out for their scale and audacity: American Dream Miami Mega-Mall; and Water Street Tampa.

American Dream Miami Mega-Mall

The American Dream Mall, planned to be built in Miami off the Florida Turnpike, is expected to cost $4 billion. Its developers, the Triple Five Group (controlled by the Ghermezian family from Edmonton), also developed the Mall of America, the largest mall in the United States, and the West Edmonton Mall, the largest mall in North America.

If built, and it does still lack some final approvals and financing, the American Dream Mall will be the largest and most expensive mall in the United States. At 6 million square feet, it will be twice as big as the current two largest in the United States: the Mall of America in Minnesota; and the King of Prussia Mall outside of Philadelphia. It will even be larger than the West Edmonton Mall in Alberta, Canada. Only the New China Mall in Dongguan, China will be able to boast of being larger (Touropia, 2017).

Like these other mega-malls, the American Dream Mall will be a destination mall designed to bring in tourists from all over the country and the world. Its developers expect it to draw 30 million visitors, about the same as their West Edmonton Mall, but given that it is in Florida, will have Florida-style over-the-top attractions, and can appeal to Florida's larger number of tourists, this estimate may very well turn out to be very conservative.

In addition to the customary water park and "submarine" rides, the Mall will have an ice-skating rink, and a ski hill for the amusement of those Floridians not turned off by ice and snow. Shoppers will also not be disappointed by the variety offered by its up-to-1,200 stores and dozens of restaurants (Garfield, 2018).

Visitors may also come simply to gawk at the space-age architecture of the American Dream Mall. The architectural rendering of the project provided to the press eerily resembles Tipoca, you know, the Capital City of the watery planet Kamino in Star Wars.

A modest suggestion: the Florida Dream Mall would be a better name.

Water Street Tampa

Tampa Bay Lightning owner Jeff Vinik has an innovative vision to turn the faded downtown waterfront of Tampa into a brand-new modern pedestrian-friendly city (Guttman, 2016). To realize his dream, he has teamed up with none other than Bill Gates of Microsoft fame and his Cascade Investments to create a firm named Strategic Property Partners. The new $3 billion mixed-use development that it's building on 50 acres of former industrial land in the heart of Tampa is called Water Street Tampa (Danielson, 2018). It will be one of the largest downtown redevelopment projects in the United States.

During the first phase of the project, two new towers will be added to the Tampa skyline – the 20-story 1001 Water and the 19-story 400 Channelside. Pedestrians will have access to a million square feet of street-level space devoted to satisfying all their retail, educational, and entertainment needs. In addition, they will be able to stroll around 13 acres of parks and other public spaces. The development is designed to bring people back downtown by adding 3,500 residential units, which will almost double the existing supply of housing in the area. Finally, in the future, the University of South Florida's College of Medicine and Heart Institute will be added to the complex, along with a building for health-related businesses (Griffen, 2017).

Sunseeker Resort Charlotte Harbor

In today's Florida, it's not even possible to escape development in my sleepy little hometown of Punta Gorda. Across Charlotte Harbor, a big $420 million project called the Sunseeker Resort is being launched by Allegiant Airlines to corral some of the millions of passengers they fly to Florida to spend money in other people's resorts. While its name may sound like a nudist colony, it's actually a huge resort complex with 500 hotel rooms, a thousand-foot swimming pool, and dozens of restaurants, cafes and bars where clothing may be informal, but not optional (Gilbertson, 2018). It's expected to employ 500 people and accommodate 300 thousand tourists a year when, and if, it gets finished (Kimmel, 2018).

Construction Rebounding, but Still Down

While there are some big projects getting underway, construction has a long way to go before it gets back to the lofty levels reached before the 2007-09 recession (Chart 31). From its peak in 2005, construction in real terms had decreased 47 per cent by 2009 and 58 per cent by 2013. But since bottoming out in 2013, it has rebounded by 46 per cent by 2017 to almost $41 billion 2009 dollars.

Construction is reviving all over Florida, but in no other place as obviously as Orlando, aka boom city. Cranes and congestion around Disney World, and throughout the city core, make it impossible for even the most oblivious to ignore the ongoing burst of construction activity.

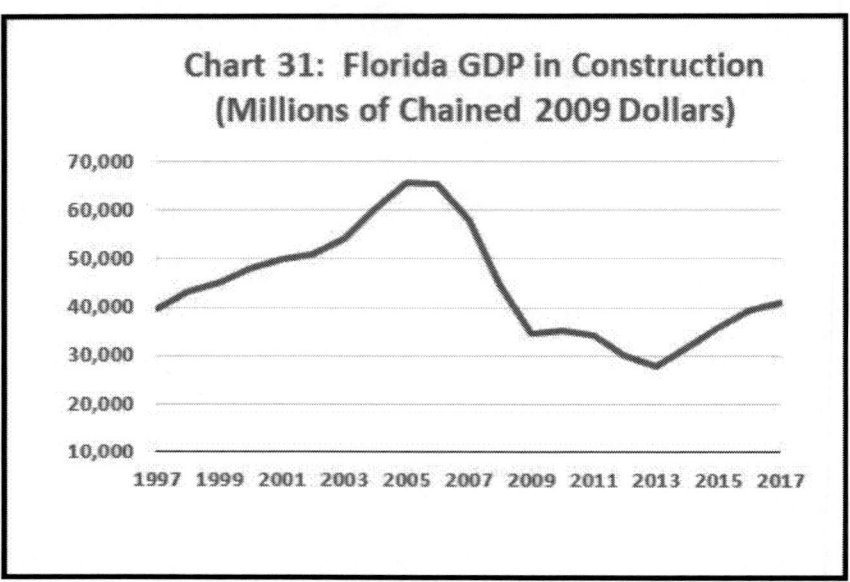

Chart 31: Florida GDP in Construction (Millions of Chained 2009 Dollars)

Source: Department of Commerce, Bureau of Economic Affairs, 2018.

17
THE DREAMS OF ENTREPRENEURS DRIVE DEVELOPMENT

At the beginning of the 20th century, the Florida economy was dominated by its resource and agricultural sector which included lumber, naval stores, phosphate mining, cattle, cotton, tobacco, sugar cane, rice, and fishing. Some of these industries had only thrived in Florida's antebellum economy under slavery, and were already in decline (Stronge, 2008, p.265).

After the Second World War, with the development of the technology to make concentrated frozen orange juice by a team commissioned by the Florida Citrus Commission (Copage, 2000), Minute Maid and Tropicana used the new technology to dominate the orange juice market. Florida's citrus industry expanded, becoming the largest part of the agricultural sector.

In more recent years, the Florida economy has increasingly turned away from agriculture to the new service, industrial and high-tech sectors as its main engines of growth. Tourism has become the biggest driver of the Florida economy. But other new industries have also developed in response to the demands of Florida's increasing population, the development of new technologies, and the opportunities presented by trade.

Florida's Leading Companies

Enterprise Florida, the state's main economic development organization, which brings business and government leaders together as partners to foster development, has prepared an instructive map (available on the web) that shows the corporate and regional or hemispheric headquarters of Florida's leading companies.

Eighteen of these Florida companies are large enough to be included in *Fortune's* 2018 ranking of America's biggest companies (*Fortune*, 2018). The elephant missing from both the map and the ranking of Florida companies is the Disney Corporation, which despite its high visibility and concentration of activity in Orlando, is headquartered in Burbank, California. If it were headquartered in Florida though, it would give the state the 55th largest company in the U.S. by revenue. (The important contribution of Walt Disney and of the Disney Corporation to the Florida economy is discussed in Chapter 12.)

Florida with only 18 *Fortune 500* companies does not have its proportional share of large companies on the list (Chart 32). New York with its long history as the financial and industrial capital of the country has the most with 58. California, the home of Silicon Valley, comes in 2nd with 49, and Texas, the energy state, a close 3rd with 48. Illinois, another old industrial state, also comes far ahead of Florida with 37. After that, the gap quickly shrinks, and Florida comes in 10th. Even though Florida may not rank as highly as might be expected based on the size of its economy, it does do well given its relatively late start after World War II on the road to development. The Florida companies on the *Fortune 500* consequently tend to be newer, and more entrepreneurial, than average in the old industrial states. Furthermore, an economy like Florida with tourism as its most important sector is not as likely to spawn such large companies as a more industrial-based economy.

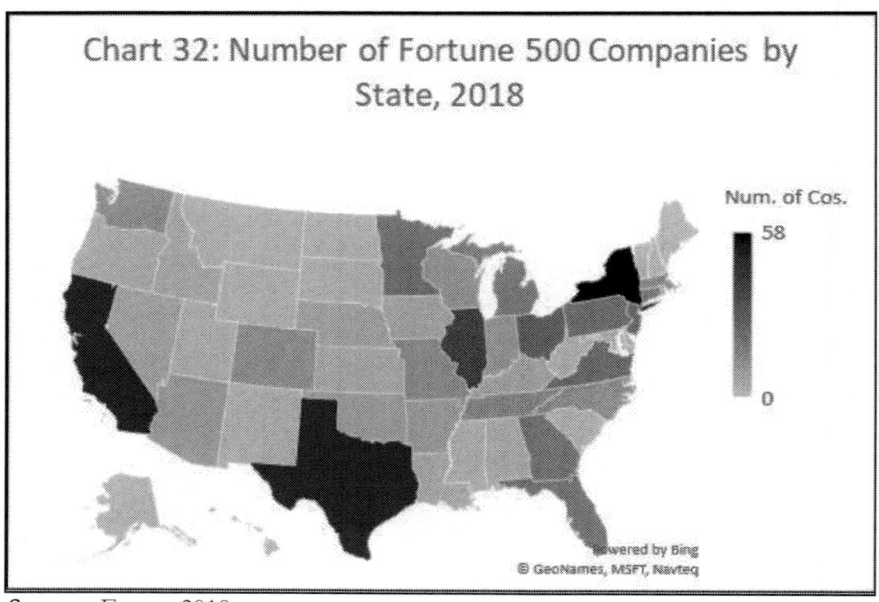

Chart 32: Number of Fortune 500 Companies by State, 2018

Source: *Fortune*, 2018.

Florida's Largest Companies Realize Entrepreneurs' Dreams

Some of the big Florida companies have been built by entrepreneurs over their lifetimes. Others, span generations and have become institutionalized. The creative power of a dream is most evident when a company has a founder (or founders) who takes their company from a start-up (most impressively from a workshop in the garage) to a large global corporation. There are some examples of these among the Florida companies in the *Fortune 500*. Maybe not the garage part. (Unless otherwise referenced, the source of information is company websites.)

FLORIDA DREAMS

Tech Data (No. 83), the largest corporation in Florida by revenues, which is in Clearwater, was started by Edmund Raymund in 1974. From a start, selling data processing supplies to mainframe and mini-computer users, it grew exponentially increasing its range of IT products and expanding geographically both organically and through acquisitions. Tech Data had revenue of $37 billion in the fiscal year ending January 31, 2018.

Publix (No. 88), the grocery and pharmaceutical chain based in Lakeland, Florida, began as a single store that George Jenkins, its founder, opened in 1936 in Winter Haven, after quitting his job as the manager of the local Piggly Wiggly grocery store. By 1940, he had mortgaged, what else could it be in Florida but an orange grove, and used the proceeds to open his "dream store, the first Publix Super Market....A 'food palace' of marble, glass and stucco." "Mr. George's" philosophy was to treat employees and customers as family. From this small beginning, Publix has become a chain of 1,100 supermarkets with a revenue of $34 billion in 2016. As of July of the same year, it was Florida's largest private sector employer with 133 thousand people on staff (Lemieux and Mize, 2018, p.198).

World Fuel (No. 92), which is headquartered in Miami, was founded in 1984 by Michael J. Kasbar, who remains its Chairman, CEO and President. It offers fuel supply and related services such as "logistics, financial, energy management, and technology-based services" to customers in air, water and surface transportation around the world. Its total revenue in 2017 was $33.7 billion.

AutoNation (No. 138) was founded by Wayne Huizenga, an entrepreneur with no shortage of dreams who passed away in March 2018. As well as AutoNation, he also founded Blockbusters, Waste Management, and Extended Care America, which is quite the eclectic list (Zhao, 2018). AutoNation brags that it is the first auto dealer in the nation to sell 10 million cars in a year at its over 300 dealerships. Its revenue for 2017 totaled $21.5 billion.

Jabil (No. 159) is a name made up of the first two letters of its founders' names, James Golden and Bill Morean. It was set up in St. Petersburg in 1966 to sell semiconductors and other electrical components, but now bills itself as a "product solutions company providing comprehensive design, manufacturing, supply chain and product management services" to its customers worldwide. Its revenue for the 2018 fiscal year ending August 31 was $22.1 billion.

NextEra Energy (No. 167) owns Florida Power & Light (FPL), the state's largest electric utility, and NextEra Energy Resources (NEER), the world's largest solar and wind operator among other things. It's headquartered in Juno Beach and had revenue of about $17.2 billion in 2017. (See Chapter 19 for more on its role in supplying electricity to Floridians).

WellCare Health Plans (No. 170) which is headquartered in Tampa, provides health insurance and managed care, mainly focusing on Medicaid, Medicare Advantage and Medicare Prescription Drug Plans, for all of which Florida provides an ample supply of customers. Its total revenue was $17 billion in 2017.

Lennar (No. 230) is a homebuilder that was founded in Miami in 1984 by Leonard Miller and Arnold Rosen. It has since grown to be the second largest homebuilder in the United States with revenue of $12.6 billion in 2017.

CSX Transportation (No. 265), which is headquartered in Jacksonville, was the result of two mergers. The first was the combination of the Chessie System and

Seaboard Coast Line Industries Inc. in 1980 as the CSX Corporation (C for Chessie, S for Seaboard, and X for the multiplication of their forces). The second was the merger with Sea-Land Service in 1986 to become CSX Transportation. The history of CSX is long and storied going back to the Baltimore and Ohio Railroad, America's first, and incorporating the railroad lines of Henry Plant's Plant System in Florida and Georgia. In 2017, CSX Transportation had consolidated revenue of $11.4 billion.

Office Depot (No. 281), which is based in Boca Raton, was founded in 1986 by F. Patrick Sher, Stephen Dougherty, and Jack Kopkin. The initial $2.5 million public offering and founders' seed money enabled them to open three stores in the Fort Lauderdale area selling office supplies and an eclectic range of household products also used in offices (Gale, 2015). While Home Depot wasn't happy to have the second part of its name borrowed by another company, the branding was good and Office Depot grew quickly taking advantage of the hot market for office technologies. Unlike other entrepreneurial start-ups, the founders faded into the background at an early stage and the company became institutionalized. Much of its growth came from mergers and acquisitions, including international expansion. On November 5, 2013 Office Depot completed a merger with Office Max. Then on February 4, 2015, Office Depot accepted a purchase offer from its main rival, Staples. But this takeover was not to be. It was subsequently blocked by the Federal Trade Commission (Office Depot, 2016). In Fiscal Year 2017, the latest year available, Office Depot had $10.24 billion in sales.

Fidelity National Financial (No. 302) is a venerable old property and casualty insurance company founded in Jacksonville in 1847 before the Civil War. It took a more aggressive approach to expansion, however, when it acquired, in 2003, a young firm named Systematics that was started in 1966. This firm was rebranded as Fidelity National Information Services. FIS (No. 326) also based in Jacksonville, provides financial information technology to financial institutions globally. Its claim to fame is that it has more than 20,000 clients in 130 countries and moves $9 trillion a year in financial transactions

Hertz Global Holdings (No. 335) is another corporation that's been around for a long time, having been founded in Chicago more than a hundred years ago. Its brand is universally recognized as one of the world's largest automotive rental companies. But the main thing of interest to Floridians is that it moved its head office from New Jersey down to Estero starting in 2013 to take advantage of some of opportunities discussed in this book like the favorable business climate and the importance of the tourism industry, the source of many of its customers. While there have been the usual teething problems with the move, Hertz seems to be working through them and has met its job creation requirements necessary to qualify for the state and local incentives negotiated. (Layden, 2017b). Hertz's revenue for 2017 was $8.8 billion.

Ryder Systems (No. 387) is a trucking and truck leasing company, headquartered in Miami. It was founded there in 1934 by James Ryder who started with a single Model A truck bought on credit with $35 down. Over the years, Ryder kept on buying more trucks and getting more and more delivery and fleet management contracts for bigger and bigger companies. The business just snowballed. Now it manages over 234,000 vehicles and has 50,000 customers, including more than half of the *Fortune 500*. Its revenue in 2017 was $7.3 billion.

Darden Restaurants (No. 396) is a restaurant chain that set out to distinguish itself from fast food outlets by offering its customers a fine dining experience at reasonable prices. It was founded in Orlando in 1968 by Bill Darden, when he opened the first Red Lobster. At that point, he already had had two decades of experience in the restaurant business, starting with a luncheonette called the Green Frog, which he had opened in Georgia at the age of 19 (Daszkowski, 2018), and with Gary's Duck Inn, a seafood restaurant he purchased in Orlando. By 1970, he had opened four more Red Lobster's in the Orlando area before selling out to General Mills. Not wanting to mess with a winning formula, they signed him up as well to run the restaurants (Shenot, 1994). Over the years, Red Lobster became less central to the company. And Bill Darden passed away in 1994. Darden Restaurant's Olive Garden became its most popular brand. To grow the company, it also introduced additional full-service dining brands such as the LongHorn Steak House, Cheddar's Scratch Kitchen, and Bahama Breeze (for those like me who have a taste for Floribbean cuisine). In the fiscal year ending May 27, 2017, its revenue reached $8.08 billion.

Harris (No. 407), which was founded as an automatic press company in 1895 in Niles, Ohio by Alfred Harris, became a complex firm specializing in aerospace and defense, including the production of specialized semiconductors. In 1975, it moved to Melbourne, to be near the NASA program in Cape Canaveral. By the dawn of the 21st century, it had completed its transformation into a global communications and information technology company. Harris has been involved in manned space flights, GPS satellites, military avionics, weather imagery, air traffic management, night vision goggles and military tactical radios. Revenue in the fiscal year 2018 ending July 31 was $6.182 billion. Harris will benefit from the ramping up of the Space Program and the establishment of a Space Force. It's Florida's number one Space Coast firm.

Mastec (No. 428) is an engineering, construction firm established by Jorge Mas Canosa in Coral Gables in 1994. For those of you who don't know him, Mas Canosa was a Cuban who fled Castro's Cuba and became the high-profile leader of the exiled anti-Castro opposition in Miami, founding the Cuban American Association. In that capacity, he had a big hand in shaping American policy towards Cuba under both Republican and Democratic Administrations. But he didn't let this distract him from having a successful business career that put his engineering expertise to productive use. In 1971, he acquired a Puerto Rican engineering firm which became Church & Tower, and by 1994 went public as Mastec making Mas Canosa and his sons, who joined their father in the business, very wealthy men (Rohternov, 1997; Marquis, 1997). Under Jorge's son José, Mastec has continued to grow becoming one of the largest engineering construction firms in the country. In 2017 its revenue was $6.6 billion.

Raymond James Financial (No. 431) is a securities firm that was founded by Robert James as Robert A. James Investments in 1962. Two years later it was renamed Raymond James by agreement after acquiring Raymond and Associates. While it has raised a few eye-brows in the financial community by having had a relatively high percentage of its financial advisors disciplined for financial misconduct (Trigaux, 2016), it has still managed to grow its client assets to over $750 billion with its 7,700 financial advisors located in 3,000 locations in North America and overseas.

Florida has clusters of important companies in key industries, which are shown on the maps prepared by Enterprise Florida. While all these companies are not as large as the *Fortune 500* companies, they are all still very large and constitute the next tier of important Florida companies. They include: professional services; manufacturing; logistics and distribution; life sciences; information technology; defense and homeland security; cleantech; and aviation and aerospace.

The entrepreneurs who built the largest companies in Florida are only the tip of the iceberg. Across the state were a multitude of others who, albeit on a smaller scale, built businesses to meet the needs of Floridians and to provide them with jobs. They include: retail shop owners; franchisees; restaurateurs; real estate agents; insurance brokers; doctors; dentists; chiropractors; lawyers; accountants; fishing guides; tour operators; plumbers; electricians; contractors; financial advisors; and bar owners. All the medium and small businesses that dot the landscape have an entrepreneur of one sort or another behind them. A few of them may make it to the next level. And even fewer may come up with a new idea that will create a giant out of a small business and revolutionize an industry like some of the founders of Florida's *Fortune 500* companies did. It's not a common event, but it does happen. And when it does, it makes for a very dynamic and competitive economy, which Schumpeter (1942) described as "creative destruction."

The Lost Opportunity of Silicon Swamp

On March 31, 1970 IBM Chairman Thomas J. Watson Jr. cut the ribbon on a mammoth new 1.7-million-square-foot IBM manufacturing facility located on 550 acres of scrubland west of Boca Raton (Clough, 2017). In this building, which was as big as one of those built in the Soviet Union, but not as ugly, and was under tight security rivalling the Pentagon, the most revolutionary development of the information age took place. A small team of a dozen engineers, led by Don Estridge, built the first IBM PC, which was internally called the Acorn. From the time of the initial proposal to the unveiling of the finished product at a press conference in New York on August 12, 1981 was scarcely a year, proving that, at least sometimes, an elephant can dance. With a price tag of $1,565 and the IBM imprimatur, the new IBM PCs sold like hotcakes and production and employment in Boca Raton took off (IBM).

For a while, it looked like Florida would become Silicon Swamp. But, alas, that was not to be. IBM gradually lost out in the PC market that it had created. By 1987, the PC division was moved to North Carolina, and by 1996, the Boca Raton campus was shuttered, only to be eventually sold. The largest office building in Florida was first marketed as a corporate innovation center, but now all other options, including housing, are being explored for this white elephant by the latest owners (Clough, 2018). Moving did not save the PC Division. In 2005, IBM produced its last PC.

What went wrong? Obviously, lots of things. Dancing is not easy for an elephant. The biggest mistake was not making the operating system and the CPU chip proprietary like Apple did with its products and instead going open architecture. That more than anything else explains why Apple is now 4th on the *Fortune 500* with a market value of $851 billion (as of March 29, 2018) and IBM has fallen to 34th with a market value of only $141 billion (*Fortune*, 2018). Everything Apple sells is proprietary, and its intellectual property is defended ferociously. IBM, on the other hand, built its PC using the Intel 8088, which was available off the shelf to anybody wanting to produce a clone. As for the PC-DOS operating system, well, IBM got it from Microsoft, who in turn had bought it under the name of 86-DOS from Seattle Computer Products (who may or may not have derived it from Digital Research's

CP/M, but that's another story). IBM was reportedly offered the choice of purchasing the operating system directly but instead decided to go through an intermediary, namely Microsoft. The final mistake was that rather than acquiring complete ownership of the operating system, IBM chose to save a little money and pay less by agreeing to let Microsoft sell a rebranded version of the DOS called MS-DOS to other computer companies to bundle with their machines (competing, of course, directly with IBM) (Miller, 2011; Maher, 2017). Penny wise and pound foolish was what this turned out to be for IBM.

These strategic blunders provided the opportunity for a highly competitive PC clone industry to spring up and undersell IBM, eventually capturing the whole PC market. They also allowed Microsoft to use its partnership with IBM to establish its own dominant position in the industry as the effectively monopolistic supplier of the operating system. This opportunity transformed Microsoft over time from a small start-up to the colossus that now dwarfs IBM in market value ($688 billion at end of March 2018 compared to $141 billion for IBM).

So much for what went wrong. The other question is why IBM didn't seem to want to take control over the PC industry that it was creating. One possibility is that they didn't think the PC industry was going to be worth the effort and the risk. In their view, it might not have looked like a very important segment in the whole computer industry, which ran the gamut from supercomputers, to mainframes and mini-computers, and in which IBM was the dominant player. Another is that they were gun-shy from their antitrust battles with the U.S. Justice Department. A consent decree issued in 1956 had imposed constraints on IBM's ability to market their products. And IBM had been the subject of an ongoing antitrust prosecution (some would say persecution) beginning in 1969 for monopolizing the computer industry. As a defensive strategy, IBM unbundled sales of its software and services from its hardware in 1969. (Passell, 1994). This largely self-imposed constraint on its business practices may have determined its ill-fated strategy with respect to the PC and its operating system.

But the Justice Department certainly deserves a big share of the blame for what happened. The United States shot its own economy in the foot with its overly aggressive antitrust policy. That's why most PCs are now produced by foreign companies in Asia and not in the United States, where they were born.

Such is the sad tale of how the behemoth IBM botched the strategic aspects of the PC rollout and let the PC industry slip through its fingers leaving behind only a partially-occupied jumbo office building in Boca Raton as a monument to what might have been. It's hard to imagine that an entrepreneur who dreams big like Bill Gates or Steve Jobs would have given up so easily on such a revolutionary product. And if Florida wants a Silicon Swamp, some new visionary entrepreneurs are going to have to build it again, but Floridians need to know that it was almost here once and could be again.

18
TRANSPORTATION MOVES THE DREAM

Florida's transportation network is large and growing. It connects Florida to the other states and the world. Like almost everywhere else, it includes roads, rail, air and water.

Superhighways Criss-Cross the State

The backbone of Florida's road system is the interstate highway system, which is all linked up. Interstate-95 comes down the East Coast from Maine to Florida. On the way, it goes by or through such major cities as Boston, New York, Philadelphia, Baltimore, Washington, Richmond and Savanah. In Florida, it passes through Jacksonville and down the east coast of Florida to Miami. Then there's Interstate-4 that goes from Daytona to Tampa through Orlando, and Interstate-10, which extends the length of northern Florida from Jacksonville by Tallahassee to Pensacola and on across the south of the United States to New Orleans, Houston, Phoenix, and Los Angeles. Interstate-75, which, in sections, follows the path of the Old Dixie highway connecting the Mid-west to the South, starts in Miami and runs over to and up the west coast of Florida by Tampa all the way to northern Michigan passing through Atlanta, Cincinnati, and Detroit.

Toll roads are also run by the state. The Florida Turnpike System provides almost 500 miles of superhighways. The longest line runs from Miami to central Florida, but it also incorporates several shorter roads such as the Suncoast Parkway, the Homestead Extension and the Sawgrass Expressway as well as some toll bridges. It also offers a pre-paid program using transponders called SunPass that collects the tolls more conveniently and doesn't impede the traffic as much.

Railroads Remain Important

Railroads played a key role in opening Florida to visitors from up north. Many of these people liked what they saw and decided to stay. David Levy Yulee's Florida Railway was completed just before the Civil War. It linked Fernandina on the East Coast to Cedar Key on the west, and mainly carried freight. Before the turn of the last century, Henry Flagler merged several small railroads and went on to build the East Coast

Railway down the coast to Palm Beach and Miami. His Overseas Railroad, which was an engineering exploit in its time, eventually reached Key West in 1912. Henry Plant opened up the state's west coast with the Plant System, which later joined the Atlantic Coast Line, also building hotels as he went to accommodate his passengers. The Seaboard Air Line Railway, which was established in 1900, consolidating many of the smaller railroads, and, despite its name, didn't fly, merged with the Atlantic Coast Line in 1968, before finally being acquired by CSX in 1986. CSX Transportation, based in Jacksonville and providing rail service in the eastern states, is now the country's 3rd largest railroad by operating revenue. (Kay, 2015).

Amtrak, which took over responsibility for passenger service in the U.S. in 1971, still provides daily service between New York City and Miami, on the Silver Meteor, which passes through Jacksonville and Orlando with a spur to Tampa. Passenger rail service connecting the four largest Florida cities is thus available.

All Aboard Florida's Brightline is a newer railroad that provides daily higher-speed (79 miles per hour qualifies as "higher") rail service from Miami to West Palm Beach. It's now the only privately owned and operated intercity passenger railroad in the United States. Originating at Government Center in downtown Miami with connections to local transportation links Metrorail and Metromover, it goes to West Palm Beach with a stop in Fort Lauderdale. There are plans to extend the service by 2021 to Orlando (Danielson, 2018), which also has SunRail providing local commuter rail service. Brightline has submitted a bid to the state to extend its line on to Tampa (O'Donnell, 2018) and a possible run to Jacksonville has been bruited. Most recently, it is partnering with British billionaire Richard Branson, who has taken a minority interest, and it's being rebranded as, you guessed it, Virgin Trains USA (Cordeiro, 2018).

One of the innovative ways that Brightline can manage to make money out of intercity railroad service is to combine it with real estate development. Its MiamiCentral rail terminal includes two office towers, two apartment buildings, and shops and restaurants. While Ex-Governor Rick Scott turned down $2.4 billion in Federal money in 2011 for a Tampa-Orlando rail link, he supports the proposed extension of Brightline. His justification for the turnaround is that this new private-sector-owned plan does not put taxpayer money at risk (Mower, Johnston and Contorno, 2018). The California experience with large unexpected cost overruns on publicly-owned high-speed rail suggests that the risk is not just a figment of Scott's imagination (Vartabedian, 2018).

For those more inclined to the futuristic, there is the proposal submitted by some Florida dreamers for a transit tube taking passengers from Miami to Orlando at 700 miles per hour in 26 minutes. Now that's high speed, putting even the Japanese bullet train to shame. This technology was named hyperloop by visionary Elon Musk, who is also behind SpaceX. The Florida proposal was one of ten chosen in response to a solicitation by Hyperloop One, a company trying to develop and commercialize the technology (Dahlberg, 2017).

Metromover is a free people mover in a loop around the
Miami City Center connected to Metrorail.

Air Gateway to Latin America

Florida has been the air gateway to the Americas since Pan American Airways expanded its operations in the 1920s and 1930s. Its signature Clipper service delivered by flying boats was based out of an Art Deco terminal on Miami's Dinner Key, which now has been turned into the Miami city hall.

Currently, Florida has four large hubs – Orlando, Miami, Fort Lauderdale, and Tampa – and two medium hubs – Palm Beach and Jacksonville. They all provide air service and connections to other airports including hubs in the United States and overseas. Fort Lauderdale now even has the headquarters of the 7th largest North American commercial airway, Spirit Airlines (Statista, 2018).

Miami and Orlando are ranked 12th and 14th in the United States in 2017 in terms of FAA data on passenger boardings. As befits its new status as the undeclared capital of Latin America and the Caribbean, Miami ranked 3rd in terms of international passengers in 2016 behind only JFK, and LAX and ahead of O'Hare according to data published by the Office of Aviation Analysis of the USDOT (2016, Table 6). Miami International Airport also was ranked 4th nationally in cargo landed in 2017 with landings of almost 8 billion pounds (FAA data on cargo landings). The only airports with much larger cargo landings were Memphis (24 billion pounds) and Anchorage (17 billion pounds), both of which specialize in cargo including refueling cargo flights. In Florida, the only other airports with substantial freight were Orlando and Tampa, which had cargo landings approaching only a billion pounds.

Ocean Ports

While Florida only handles a fraction of the water traffic going through Los Angeles, Long Beach and New York/New Jersey, it does have major seaports handling containers, which are higher value, than bulk shipments like grain, fuel and ores. Port Everglades, Miami, Jacksonville, and West Palm Beach ranked 11th, 12th, 16th and 20th respectively in North America in 2016 in terms of Twenty-Foot Equivalent Units (TEU) containers, the standard by which container shipments are measured. Port Everglades handled 687 thousand TEU, Miami 528 thousand, Jacksonville 238 thousand, and West Palm Beach 139 thousand (Burnson, 2017). Miami is expecting to ramp up its container traffic significantly in the future because it is the only port that can handle the larger new Panamax vessels now permitted by the enlargement of the Panama Canal's capability to accommodate ships. And, speaking of water transportation, don't forget that Florida and Miami are the cruise ship center of the world (see Chapter 12).

Even though Florida is not the transportation hub of the universe or even the United States, it has built up a world-class transportation system capable of meeting its needs, one of the most important of which is making it easy for tourists to come down to enjoy the attractions like Disney World and Miami Beach and to make connections with their cruise ships. That's pretty impressive for a 500-mile long peninsula that used to be in the country's boondocks.

19
ENERGY REQUIRED TO POWER DREAMS

An adequate and reliable supply of electricity is necessary for a rapidly growing and competitive economy like Florida's. And Florida produced 238,262,150 Megawatt hours (MWh) in 2016, making it the 2nd largest electricity generating state in the country. It was only behind energy powerhouse Texas which produced 454,047,591 Megawatt hours, and it was ahead of California (196,963,215 MWh) and New York (134,417,107 MWh) (Chart 33).

Florida consumed 235,721,822 MWh of electricity in 2016, making it the 3rd state in electricity consumption behind Texas and California. It used almost all the electricity it produced, which makes it self-sufficient in electricity unlike two of the other mega-states: California, which used 256,846,635 MWh; and New York, which used 147,803,038 MWh. Both mega-states had to import electricity over the grid from other states to meet their consumers' needs. California has found it difficult to expand energy supply because of resistance from environmentalists, which has subjected it to power shortages (Schlink, 2012, p.261). It has been criticized for reducing its production of greenhouse gasses by outsourcing its production of electricity (Schulz, 2008). On the other hand, even though Florida did not need to draw electricity from the grid net, it was not a big contributor to the national grid like Texas, which exported almost as much into the grid as California took out (Chart 34).

The competitiveness of a state's industry and the living standard of its consumers depend on the cost of its electricity supplies. While Florida's average retail price of electricity, at 9.91 cents per kilowatt hour (kWh), is not the lowest in the country, it is below the national average of 10.27 cents per kWh (Chart 35). It is also much lower than the 15.23 cents per kWh in California and 14.47 cents per kWh in New York, but above the 8.43 cents per kWh in Texas. Overall, Florida's electricity costs make it competitive with most other states and much more competitive than California and New York.

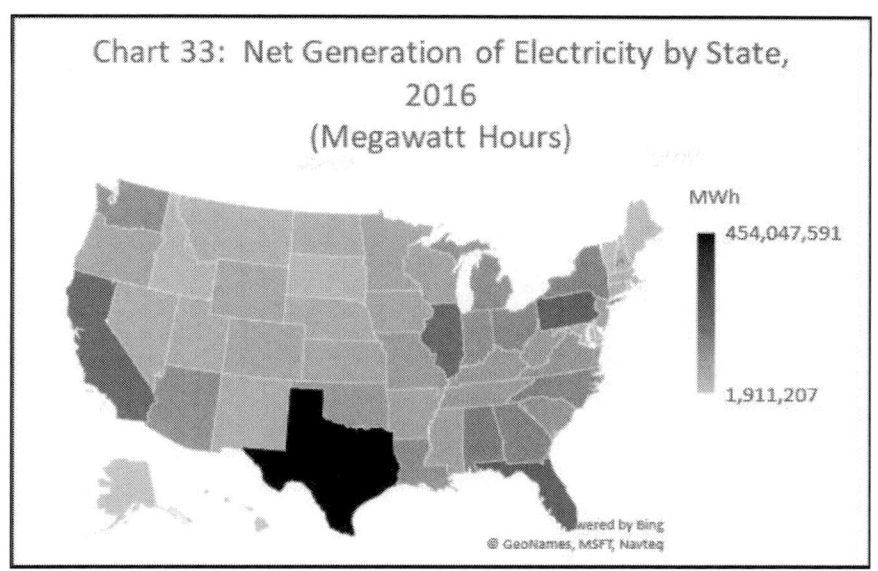

Chart 33: Net Generation of Electricity by State, 2016 (Megawatt Hours)

MWh
454,047,591

1,911,207

Source: U.S. Energy Information Agency, October 2018.

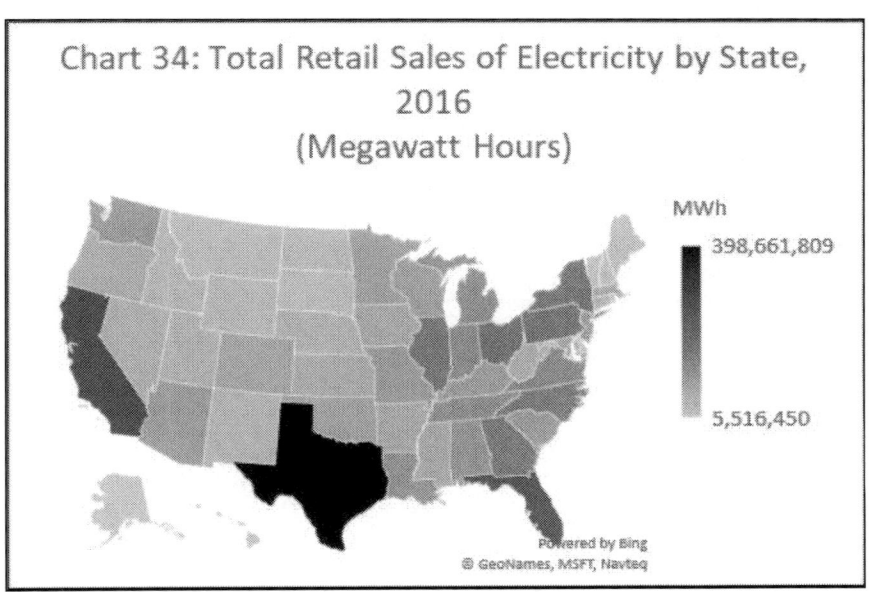

Chart 34: Total Retail Sales of Electricity by State, 2016 (Megawatt Hours)

MWh
398,661,809

5,516,450

Source: U.S. Energy Information Agency, October 2018.

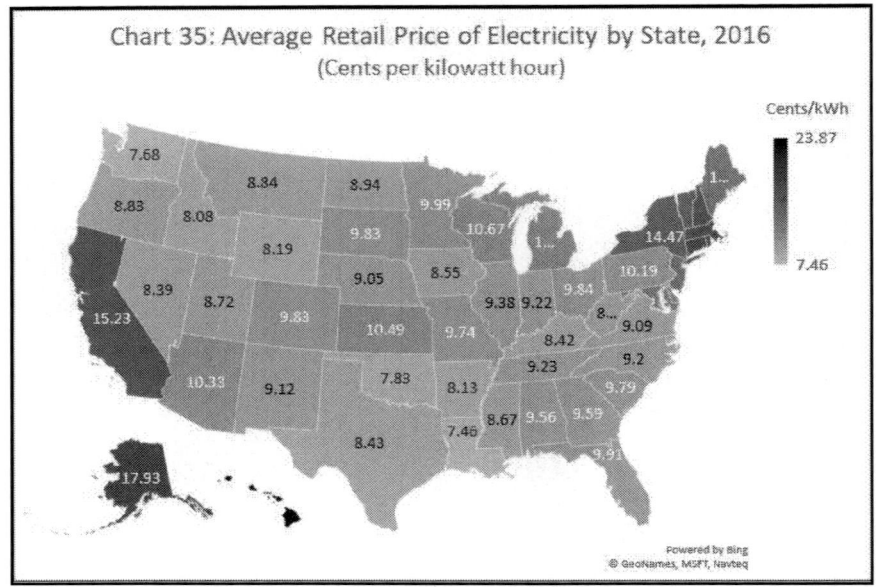

Chart 35: Average Retail Price of Electricity by State, 2016
(Cents per kilowatt hour)

Source: U.S. Energy Information Agency, October 2018.

How Florida Generates its Electricity

Florida produces its electricity in many power plants from a variety of energy sources (Chart 36). The ten largest power plants by generation in 2016 are listed in Table 11. They produce electricity using energy from natural gas, coal, and nuclear power. The largest proportion of electricity is produced using natural gas (73.9 per cent). Coal, which accounts for 11.9 per cent of electricity production, is slightly more important than nuclear, which produces 11.3 per cent of electricity generated. Florida also generates 2.6 per cent of its electricity from biomass. Most of this comes from bagasse produced by the sugar industry. While biomass accounts for only a small proportion of total electricity produced, it is a larger share than in any state except for California.

The largest of Florida's power plants is the nuclear facility at Turkey Point south of Miami near Homestead. It is not entirely nuclear, however, as it also has natural gas-fired units that generate about 1,100 MW in addition to its two nuclear units that each generate about 850 MW, making for a total nuclear capacity of 1,700 MW. Thus, if both its nuclear and gas generators are operating at the same rate, the plant would generate around 60 per cent of its output from nuclear fission, with the remaining 40 per cent from gas.

The 3rd largest power plant is also a nuclear plant at St. Lucie, north of Miami. The 2nd is the West County Energy Center in Palm Beach County. All of these three largest facilities are run by Florida Power & Light, which is the third largest electrical utility in the country and which provides electricity to over 10 million people across almost half of Florida. Duke Energy Florida provides power in central and north Florida since taking over Progress Energy in 2012. The Tampa Electric Company supplies electricity in the Tampa area and elsewhere in Central Florida.

FLORIDA DREAMS

Chart 36: Florida Energy Map from U.S. Energy Information Administration

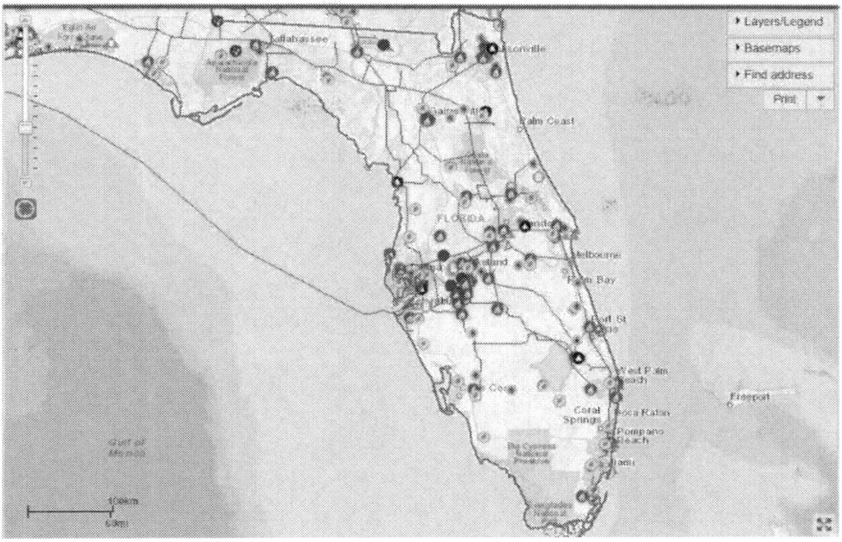

Source: U.S. Energy Information Agency, October 2018.

While Florida has two large nuclear power plants and produces 11.3 per cent of its electricity from nuclear, it only ranks 25th among the states in the proportion of its power that is nuclear. The states at the top of the list, like South Carolina, New Hampshire, and Illinois, produce over half of their power using nuclear fuel (Nuclear Energy Institute, 2018). Mega-state New York generates 33 per cent of its power with nuclear. Even Pennsylvania, which was traumatized by the Three Mile Island partial meltdown, still produces 41.6 per cent nuclear electrical power. Florida does, however, generate more power using nuclear than energy-rich Texas (8.5 per cent) and nuclear-phobic California (8.7 per cent) whose regulators have voted to close their last nuclear power plant at Diablo Canyon by 2025, reducing the state's reliance on nuclear power to zero (Nikolewski, 2018).

Florida has been reducing its dependence on nuclear since the Crystal River nuclear plant was decommissioned starting in 2013 (Thompson, 2018). The advantage of a well-managed nuclear plant is that it is clean and doesn't produce greenhouse gasses. However, incidents like Chernobyl and Fukushima have made many people leery of nuclear power plants and made efforts to build them politically unpopular and difficult. Nevertheless, FPL has obtained a construction and operating license from the Nuclear Regulatory Commission for two new nuclear units at Turkey Point, which have commissioning and start-up dates in 2032 and 2033 (World Nuclear News, 2018). These units will each have generating capacity of 1,100 MW and will increase the capacity of Turkey Point, provided FPL's request to the NRC to continue operating the two existing units past the end of their current 2032 and 2033 operating licenses is granted (FPL, 2018).

Table 11: Ten Largest Florida Plants by Generation, 2016

	Plant Name	Primary energy source	Operating company	Generation (MWh)
1	Turkey Point	Nuclear	Florida Power & Light Co	20,506,630
2	West County Energy Center	Natural gas	Florida Power & Light Co	20,297,460
3	St Lucie	Nuclear	Florida Power & Light Co	15,586,562
4	Hines Energy Complex	Natural gas	Duke Energy Florida, LLC	12,300,686
5	Martin	Natural gas	Florida Power & Light Co	10,884,521
6	Fort Myers	Natural gas	Florida Power & Light Co	9,370,286
7	Crystal River	Coal	Duke Energy Florida, LLC	8,885,472
8	Sanford	Natural gas	Florida Power & Light Co	8,486,154
9	Manatee	Natural gas	Florida Power & Light Co	8,383,457
10	H L Culbreath Bayside Power Station	Natural gas	Tampa Electric Co	7,881,817
	Total of 10			122,583,045
	Other Plants			115,679,105
	Grand Total			238,262,150

Source: U.S. Energy Information Administration, October 2018.

FLORIDA DREAMS

Turkey Point Nuclear Power Station 2 miles east of Homestead south of Miami next to the Biscayne National Park. Courtesy of Florida Power & Light Company.

Natural Gas to Generate Electricity Comes through Pipelines

The natural gas that Florida has been using to produce electricity has been replacing coal, and is also much cleaner, but, unlike nuclear, still does produce greenhouse gasses since it also burns a carbon-based fuel. Florida gets its natural gas through two important pipeline systems (Chart 36). One is the Sabal Trail Pipeline, which extends 517 miles, coming down from Georgia to a hub south of Orlando. NextEra has built a 126-mile extension called the Florida Southeast Connection Pipeline that connects the hub with the FPL Martin plant. Additional extensions are underway but are encountering the traditional resistance from environmentalists (Bonogofsky, 2017). Another pipeline is the Gulfstream Natural Gas Pipeline, which stretches 754 miles under the Gulf of Mexico from Mobile County Alabama to Port Manatee on the south side of Tampa Bay and then runs onshore through Polk, Martin and Pinellas Counties.

While Florida is well supplied with gas through pipelines, it has no oil pipelines. Tankers and barges bring Florida the bulk of the petroleum products it needs to terminals in its seaports. This exposes Florida more to the risk of an oil spill.

NextEra

NextEra Energy, the parent of Florida Power & Light and NextEra Energy Resources, is an innovator in the green energy area. It was selected as 21st on *Fortune's* fourth annual "Change the World" list of global corporations that are "pursuing core business strategies in ways that are good for people and the planet" (Fry and Heimer, 2018). No, it's not for safely managing two large nuclear plants that generate clean power, as important as that may be. It's because of the big bet NextEra is making on solar energy. *Fortune* reports that, to this end, NextEra has agreed to buy 7 million solar panels over the next four years from JinkoSolar, the world's largest supplier. These modules will be capable of generating 2,750 MW of electricity, which is sufficient to power hundreds of thousands of homes (Fry and Heimer, 2018). NextEra is working with communities and individual home owners to install panels and to enable them to sell surplus power back into the FPL grid. Babcock Ranch, southeast of Punta Gorda, which bills itself as the "the first solar powered town in America," is an example of such a community. The FPL Babcock Ranch Solar Energy Center intended to service the community has already installed, on a 440-acre plot north of town, 343,000 solar panels capable of generating 74.5 MW of power as well as a solar-plus-battery storage system billed as the country's largest. It is only one of many solar energy centers established by NextEra.

FPL solar panels at Babcock Ranch.

While *Fortune* doesn't mention it, NextEra is also a leader in wind technology operating 120 wind projects across the country and in Canada. In 2017, it was by far the largest generator of wind and solar power in the country.

Greenhouse Gas Emissions

Florida is a low emitter of greenhouse gasses (GHG) relative to the size of its economy, only ranking 34th out of the 50 states with its emissions of 292.4 metric tons of energy-related carbon dioxide per chained 2009 million dollars of GDP (Chart 37). However, this is greater than the 162.6 emitted in California and 133.0 in New York, both of which are at the bottom of the list of GHG emitters, in part because they import a significant share of their electricity consumption, especially California. But it is lower than the 419.3 emitted by Texas, which, even at that, is quite low compared to the other petroleum and coal producing states.

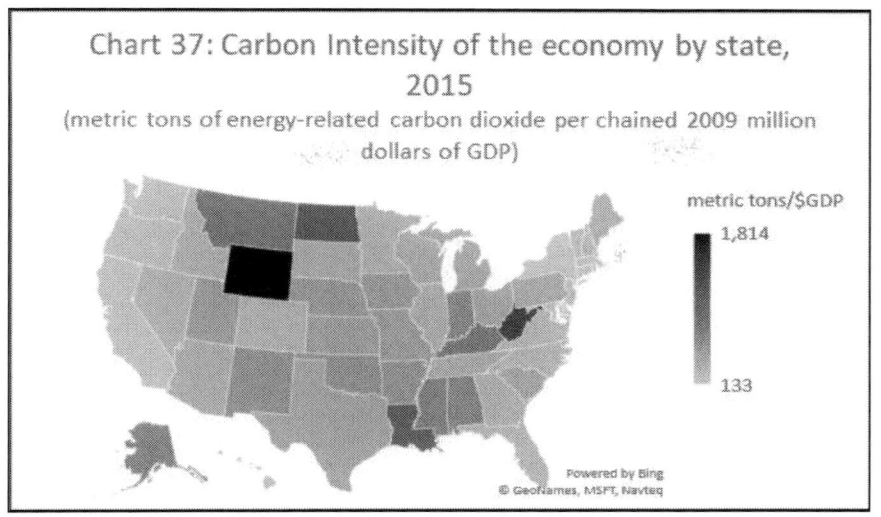

Chart 37: Carbon Intensity of the economy by state, 2015
(metric tons of energy-related carbon dioxide per chained 2009 million dollars of GDP)

Source: U.S. Energy Information Agency, October 2018.

A Mickey Mouse power pole near Disney World which generates about a quarter of its electricity.

20
THE MILITARY HAS BROUGHT MANY DREAMERS TO FLORIDA AND CREATED COUNTLESS JOBS

The military was the midwife of Florida. And it has had an important role in the Sunshine State's development ever since. A large military presence continues to this day and supports many businesses and jobs, including in high-tech industries like aviation, and aerospace and defense systems.

The Military over the Years

La Florida was colonized and christened by Spanish conquistadors. Spanish forts were constructed and manned to defend it from other predatory colonial powers, like France and Britain, looking to expand their domains. The most formidable of these fortresses was the Castillo de San Marcos, which was finished in 1695. It was a massive structure built of coquina (a soft limestone composite containing shells) strategically overlooking the Matanzas River controlling the water access to St. Augustine.

The U.S. acquired Florida from the Spanish only after an 1817 military incursion by General Andrew Jackson convinced the Spanish Government that their Florida colony was indefensible against an expansive United States and that a treaty was their only option. The first provisional Governor of Florida became none other than Old Hickory himself. In Florida's early years as a territory and then a state, the U.S. Army sent troops to Florida to fight three small-scale wars against the dauntless Seminoles. The U.S. government also built forts across the state, from Fort Pickens in Pensacola on the west, to Fort Clinch on Amelia Island in the east, and Forts Jefferson and Taylor in the south, at the tip of the Keys. While the Confederate States of America were not able to defend their state of Florida during the Civil War, and Florida's main ports were occupied by the Union, Florida was still an active participant in the war, providing troops and supplies, especially cattle. There were several small skirmishes in Florida and one major Confederate victory at the Battle of Olustee west of Jacksonville. And it wasn't so long after the last shot was fired in the Civil War that the

1898 Spanish American War against Cuba was launched from and run out of Tampa.

During World War I, training facilities were set up in Florida. But the scale of this activity was dwarfed by World War II, when the military brought some 2 million Americans to Florida. Over 170 military bases and airfields were built largely to provide facilities for training. Florida's vast, sparsely populated terrain and warm climate made it an ideal training ground.

World War II served as a major catalyst in promoting the development of the state. Many of the armed services personnel who had been stationed in Florida liked what they saw and came back to live after the war. This was an important source of population growth in the early post war years. And at the end of the war, the military had built up an impressive infrastructure, which it continued to use, and which provided substantial economic benefits to Florida.

The Military in Florida Today

Florida now has 21 military bases all around the state (source of information on military bases is <https://militarybases.com/Florida> unless otherwise indicated). Thirteen of them, including the largest, are airbases either of the Air Force, Navy or Coast Guard. Airbases tend to be much smaller than the army bases, which can have hundreds of thousands of assigned armed service personnel and occupy hundreds of square miles. The airbases in Florida include:

- MacDill Air Force Base in Tampa with 3,000 air force and 12,000 service members;
- Eglin Air Force Base and Hurlburt Field near Fort Walton Beach with 15,604 air force combined;
- Patrick Air Force Base in Brevard near Cape Canaveral, the home of the 45th Space Wing and the Air Force Space Command;
- Tyndall Air Force Base in Panama City with 3,343 air force;
- Naval Air Station (NAS) Jacksonville Navy Base in Jacksonville with 23,000 employees, military and civilian, making it one of the biggest airbases in the country;
- NAS Pensacola Navy Base in Pensacola, the home of the Blue Angels, the Navy's celebrated aerobatic team.

The Navy installations include two important advanced military research centers, which have close links to cutting-edge hi-tech companies and can generate industrial spin-offs:

- The Atlantic Undersea Test and Evaluation Center (Autec) Complex Navy Base in West Palm Beach;
- The Naval Air Warfare Center Navy Base in Orlando, which has a budget of almost $1 billion and employs many scientists and engineers in addition to military personnel and civil servants.

There are also three Coast Guard bases, which play a key role in protecting the border and combatting the drug trade:

- Air Station Clearwater Coast Guard Base in Clearwater;
- District 7 Coast Guard Base in Miami;
- Miami Coast Guard Base in Miami Beach.

Florida also has three of the ten Unified Combatant Commands, which is more than any other state (information from website of Commands). These are: the Central Command (USCENTCOM) and the Special Operations Command both at MacDill Air Force Base in Tampa; and the Southern Command (USSOUTHCOM) in Doral, a suburb of Miami. The USCENTCOM is responsible for the Middle East and has been fighting never-ending wars in the region since the First Gulf War in 1991. USSOUTHCOM, which is a just a large office building and not a proper base, is responsible for Central and South America and the Caribbean, which is a natural fit for Miami.

According to data from *Governing the States and Localities*, with 92,249 active duty and reserve armed military personnel based in the state as of September 30, 2017, Florida was the 5th ranked state behind California (184,540), Texas (164,234), Virginia (115,280) and North Carolina (112,951) (Chart 38). Moreover, Florida ranked a much higher 2nd in air force personnel, with 21,088 based in the state, only behind Texas with 37,116 (Chart 39).

Chart 38: Total Active Duty and Reserve Military by State, 2017

Source: Governing the States and Localities, 2018.

The Space Force and NASA Redux

Following the first meeting in October 2017 of the National Space Council, which was revived by executive order in the summer of 2017 and chaired by Vice President Michael Pence, President Donald J. Trump signed Space Policy Directive One instructing NASA to undertake a renewed program of lunar exploration and to launch further manned and robotic missions onwards to Mars. NASA's Acting Administrator submitted the agency's 2019 budget for $19.9 billion based on a strategic plan to implement the directive by leveraging the agencies own resources with "new commercial and international partnerships" (NASA, 2018, p.ExC-1).

FLORIDA DREAMS

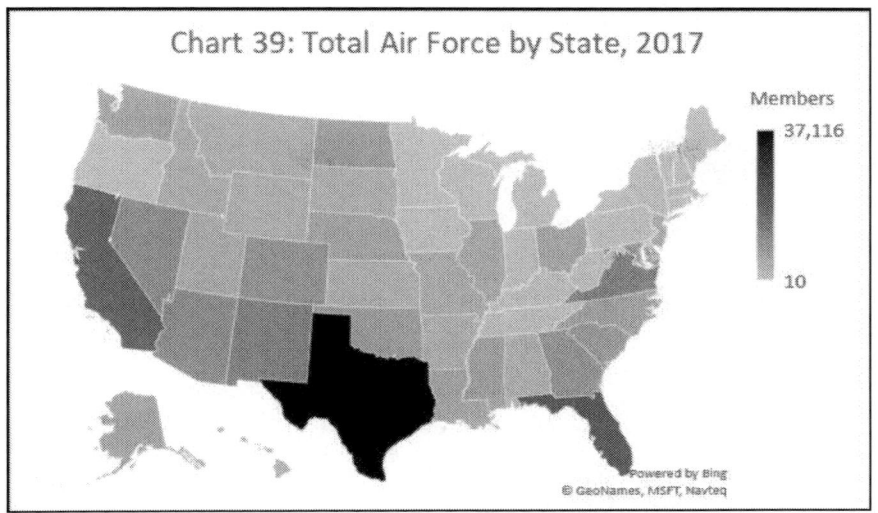

Chart 39: Total Air Force by State, 2017

Members: 37,116 to 10

Source: Governing the States and Localities, 2018.

In addition, the President announced in his June 2018 speech before the National Space Council that he was directing the Defense Department to establish a sixth branch of the military called the Space Force, which will be responsible for outer space (Katie Rogers, 2018). The Pentagon is working on the details of a legislative proposal and a budget for this, which it expects to have for Fiscal Year 2020 (Insinna, 2018).

While it's way too early to estimate the exact impact of the renewed effort on space exploration for Florida, it surely will be a boon for the Kennedy Space Center and the state. In Fiscal Year 2019, the Kennedy Space Center is budgeted to employ 1,926 Civil Service Full-Time Equivalents (and probably another 5 times this in contractors based on past ratios) (NASA, 2018, p.SD-6).

Crewed test flights on low-Earth-orbit missions by NASA partners Boeing Starliner and Elon Musk's SpaceX are scheduled to begin at Cape Canaveral for the first time since 2011, when the last space shuttle mission was flown by Atlantis. During this interval, the International Space Station was serviced by Russian Soyuz spacecraft shot up from the Baikanor Cosmodrome in Kazakhstan (Tribou, 2018). Unfortunately, Roscosmos, the Russian space agency, has been having problems with its launches, and a flight with two astronauts, on its way to the space-station had to be aborted, making for a hard emergency landing on October 31, 2018. This raised doubts about Russia's capacity to be a "reliable partner" in space (Chris Brown, 2018) that probably haven't been alleviated by the successful launch of three astronauts to the space station in December (Romo and Kim, 2018). Fortuitously, NASA may be getting back in the launch business just in the nick of time. It looks like man's dream to explore outer space is again becoming a priority and Florida will be the launch pad.

The Dream is for Man to blast off from here in Florida to Mars.
Courtesy of Dan Felton.

Military-Related Businesses and Spinoffs

Clusters of supporting companies, which have sprung up around air bases and NASA's Kennedy Space Center, have been mapped out by the Enterprise Florida (see maps on its website for defense and homeland security; and aviation and aerospace). Almost all the big aerospace and defense companies are represented on the maps including: Boeing; Lockheed Martin; General Dynamics; Northrop Grumman; Raytheon; L3 Technologies; Rockwell Collins; and SpaceX.

One of the most significant historic developments for the aerospace industry in Florida was when the Glen L. Martin Company came to Orlando to be close to the Kennedy Space Center. There it set up the Martin Company Orlando and built its large campus. Through its corporate transformations into Martin Marietta, and finally Lockheed Martin, the company built the large Vanguard Titan series of booster rockets for NASA and the Air Force that gave the space program the lifting power it needed.

Orlando has become a hub for defense industries. A little known esoteric fact is that the Central Florida Research Park, east of the city right next to the University of Central Florida, contains one of the largest collections of military simulation businesses in the country.

The Florida Chamber of Commerce estimated that direct defense expenditure in the state of Florida was $35 billion and that Florida received $10 billion in space and defense contracts, making it the 2nd highest among the states (Roberts, 2018). This provides substantial support for the Florida economy.

FLORIDA DREAMS

The Brazilian aircraft manufacturer Embraer, which produces more small planes than anyone else in the world, and more large planes than anybody but Boeing and Airbus, has also come to Florida. From a small start as a sales support office, the company has established its U.S. Headquarters in Fort Lauderdale. Its Florida operations have taken advantage of Florida's position in military and commercial aviation, and the available supporting suppliers and services, to employ 950 people in the state, making small and mid-sized jets in Melbourne, assembling military planes in Jacksonville, and doing research at its Space Coast Research Center. The latest planes to be added to its line are the Praetor 500 and 600, which are mid-sized jets capable of Trans-Atlantic flights. (Hemlock and Close, 2014; Price, 2018).

21
THE DREAM OF GOOD HEALTH

The health benefits of Florida living have, since the early days, been trumpeted by the state's boosters. In 1891, some early health enthusiasts from Orange Country made the ambitious claim that the Florida climate "invigorates the enfeebled body" (Mormino, 1987, p.10). This was not entirely an empty boast devoid of any scientific basis. A few years earlier, in 1885, a certain Dr. Van Bibber had given an address to an American Medical Association conference in New Orleans on the "benefits of the Gulf Coast climate and topography" (Sitler, 2006, p.41). Dr. Van Bibber was not the only doctor who held this view. Many people were sent to Florida by their physicians, hoping that the salubrious climate would cure their ills, particularly tuberculosis and other respiratory diseases. It was not long before the first sanitarium was established to accommodate them in Trilby, north of Tampa, in 1911 (Cannon, 2012), and more sanitariums followed as the misguided afflicted continued to arrive. Not only those with tuberculosis came down. Others came to Florida to "take the waters" from the mineral springs found in places like St. Augustine. Good health, whether real or imaginary, has always been part of the Florida Dream.

Health Benefits of Living in Florida

Those who claim health benefits from the Florida climate can find some support from the Center for Disease Control. Two of the most common infectious diseases in the United States that can cause death are influenza and pneumonia. The CDC data on influenza/pneumonia age-adjusted mortality by state for 2016 (age-adjusted mortality is used to eliminate the mortality attributable just to getting old) show that Florida is the 47th lowest state with a rate of 9.3 per 100,000 people, compared to the U.S. average of 13.5 (Chart 40). This is not just a one-year fluke. There is some evidence from scientific research that warmer weather is associated with a lower death rate (Moore, 1998). It also makes intuitive sense. If it is warmer, other things equal, people spend more time outside, away from other people hacking and coughing in confined germ-infected spaces and are less likely to catch contagious diseases like influenza and pneumonia.

Chart 40: Influenza/Pneumonia Mortality by State, 2016 (Age-Adjusted Rate per 100,000 People)

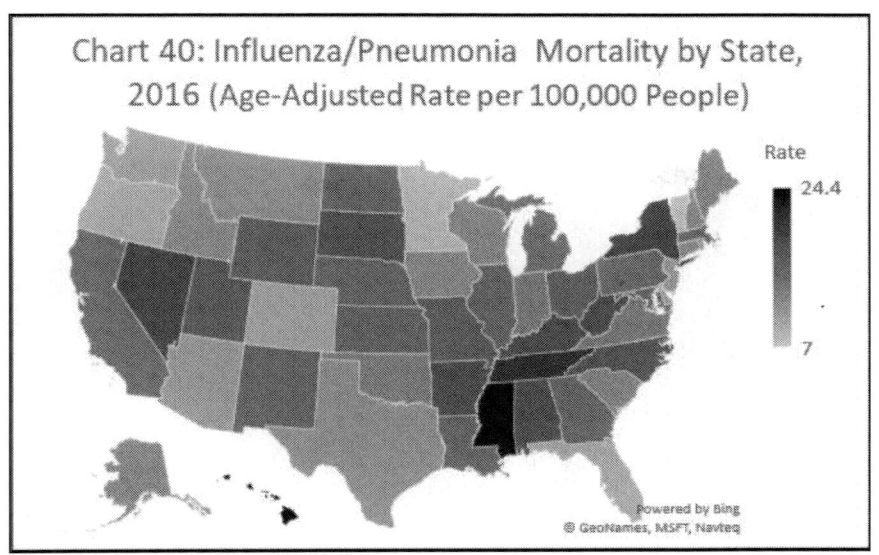

Source: Center for Disease Control, 2018.

The two leading causes of death in the United States are heart disease and cancer in that order. The mortality rate from heart disease in Florida in 2016, on an age-adjusted basis, was 146.2 per 100,000 people compared to a national average of 165.5. This made it the 38th lowest state slightly ahead of California with a 143.1 rate (Chart 41). The causes of heart disease are, of course, complex, but there does seem to be a suspiciously higher incidence of deaths due to heart disease along the Ohio and lower Mississippi rivers that warrants further examination by medical professionals.

Florida also has a relatively low age-adjusted cancer death rate of 150.1. This is well below the U.S. average of 159, and gives it a rank of 41st in the cancer death rate (Chart 42). On the other hand, it is slightly higher than the 148.4 in New York and 143.5 in California, which are also relatively low. The causes of cancer, like heart disease, are also complex, but similarly there is a higher cancer death rate along the Ohio and lower Mississippi rivers. Whether those rivers pose environmental health risks is a serious public health question that needs to be addressed.

Any overall conclusions on the health benefits of living in Florida are well outside my professional expertise as an economist (which doesn't usually stop me). However, there is a website prepared by a physician, Dr. T. Jared Bunch, that lists the health benefits to going south for the winter to get away from the cold, which should be equally applicable to people who live in Florida all the time. These include: the opportunity to do outside fitness and weight maintaining activities during the winter; greater mobility and reduced arthritis pain in the warmer weather; more oxygenated blood in warmer climates at lower altitudes putting less stress on the heart and lungs; more sun exposure and increased vitamin D (but that doesn't mean you don't need to wear sunscreen for protection from skin cancer); and reduced frequency of injury from falling on ice and snow (Bunch, 2018). Maybe the state's boosters back in the old days weren't just selling snake oil. Good health is part of the Florida Dream. It's what attracts many people to Florida.

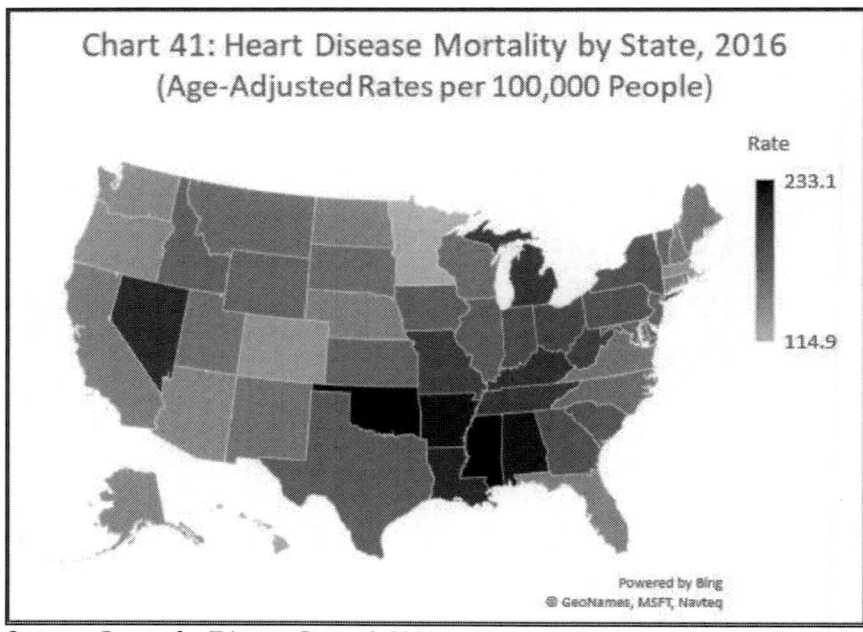

Chart 41: Heart Disease Mortality by State, 2016
(Age-Adjusted Rates per 100,000 People)

Source: Center for Disease Control, 2018

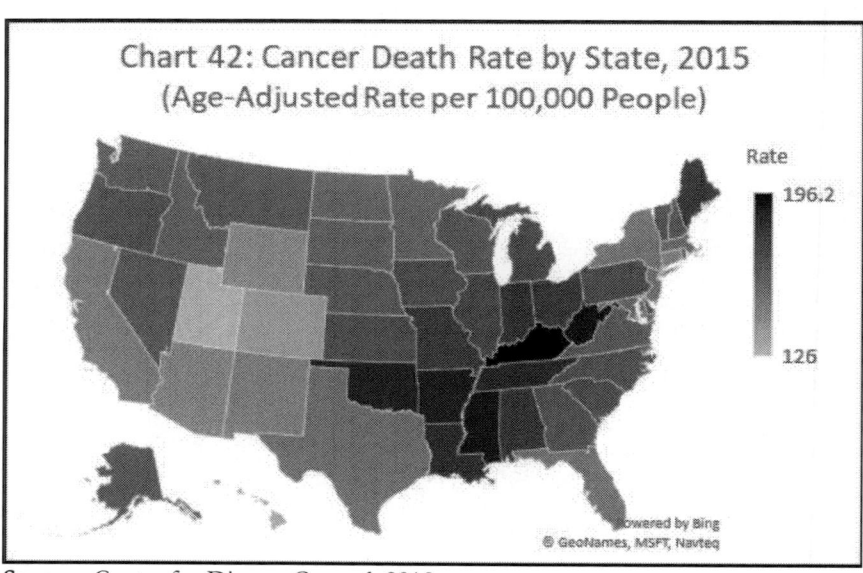

Chart 42: Cancer Death Rate by State, 2015
(Age-Adjusted Rate per 100,000 People)

Source: Center for Disease Control, 2018.

But the Florida Health System, Not So Much

Florida has not fared so well in recent studies of its health care system. In the *U.S. News and World Report* 2018 study of how well states were taking care of their residents' health-care needs, Florida ranked 34th lowest among the states. This was well below California (11th) and New York (15th). Floridians can take a small consolation, though, that it was, at least, ahead of all the other Southern States, an admittedly low bar. In the components of the ranking, Florida was ranked 48th in health care access, 34th in quality, and 18th in public health. (*U.S. News and World Report*, 2018b). Another study by the Commonwealth Fund (which included the District of Columbia) done in 2018 ranked Florida even worse, an appalling 48th, ahead only of Louisiana(49th), Oklahoma (50th) and Mississippi (51st) (Radley, McCarthy and Hayes, 2018). And a third study by the United Healthcare, which has been preparing such rankings annually for 30 years, ranked Florida a better 32nd (United Healthcare, 2018). Again, Florida was ahead of all the other Southern States, including Texas (34th).

The weaknesses in the Florida healthcare system that have been identified in the studies fall under the rubrics of health access and affordability, prevention and treatment, avoidable hospital use and cost, disparity (using the categories from Commonwealth Fund Study). They stem primarily from two factors: the relatively large number of uninsured people in the state; and the state's relatively low incomes.

With 12.5 per cent of the population not covered by health insurance in 2016, Florida had the 5th highest rate of uninsured people in the country (Chart 43). An important reason why this is the case is that Florida did not expand its Medicaid coverage, like in many other states, as allowed under the Affordable Care Act, to 138 per cent of the Federal poverty level. The non-expansion states like Texas (16.6 per cent uninsured) and most of the Southern States are those with the highest rates of uninsured. Interestingly, Massachusetts, home of Romneycare, is the state with the lowest uninsured rate (2.5 per cent).

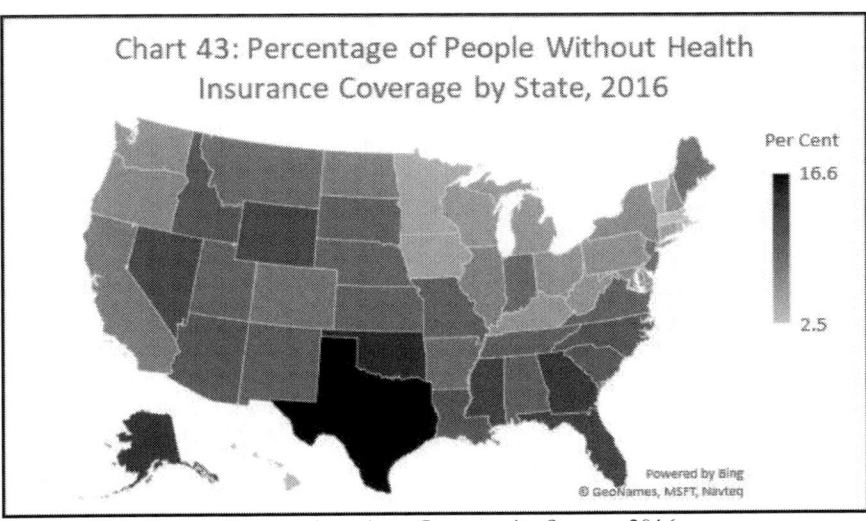

Chart 43: Percentage of People Without Health Insurance Coverage by State, 2016

Source: U.S. Census Bureau, American Community Survey, 2016.

Why would a state not take the money for Medicaid expansion offered by the Federal Government? The states, like Florida, that were reluctant to expand their Medicaid coverage, were concerned that they might get stuck with the bill if the Affordable Care Act were to be repealed and replaced as has been proposed and much debated. However, the longer the expansion of Medicaid is funded, the more unlikely it is that the Federal Government would suspend funding. Instead Medicaid for people with low income, but not poverty levels, is gradually morphing into an entitlement. That means that the President and Congress are going to be very reluctant to defund it. It's thus beginning to look like the Medicaid expansion money is going to be around for a long time. (Note: The Medicaid expansion could still continue under the doctrine of "severability," even if the rest of the Affordable Care Act were to be scrapped. A Texas Federal Court recently ruled that the ACA was unconstitutional now that the tax penalty has been abolished, but this decision still needs to be upheld on appeal. So, this is all speculative at this point. [Joshua Cohen, 2018]). Florida would be well-advised to take the money offered and expand its Medicaid program since it would cost Florida taxpayers very little and would benefit low-income Floridians with no health insurance who can't afford Obamacare. The old saying "don't look a gift horse in the mouth" may not be such bad advice.

The other main source of the weakness of the Florida health system is the relatively low level of income in Florida, which also applies to its Southern state neighbors. The fact that Florida ranks 38th in nominal GDP per capita means that its residents have lower incomes and are less able to afford quality healthcare, including preventive care, just like they can't afford to spend as much on everything else. It also means they are more likely to show up at the emergency rooms needing free treatment, that may turn out to be less than the highest standard of care. The much-bemoaned low ranking of the Florida healthcare system is just another manifestation of the relatively low level of Florida incomes.

Is High-Quality Health Care Available in Florida?

This is an important question, and maybe even a deal breaker, for people considering moving to Florida and concerned about Florida's low healthcare ranking. A related question is: how good are the hospitals in the state? Based on the *U.S. News and World Report* ranking of hospitals in the United States, the bad news is that none of the top 20 hospitals in the country are located in Florida (Comarow, 2018). On the brighter side, however, there are good nationally ranked hospitals in the state like the Mayo Clinic in Jacksonville, the Tampa General Hospital, the University of Florida Health Shands Hospital in Gainesville, the Cleveland Clinic Florida in Weston and Palm Beach Gardens, the Florida Hospital in Orlando, the Baptist Hospital of Miami , the Baptist Medical Center of Jacksonville, the Morton Plant Hospital in Clearwater, the Orlando Regional Medical Center and the Sarasota Memorial Hospital, just to name the top 10 of the 30 ranked in the state (*U.S. News and World Report*, 2018a).

If you have a serious health problem in Florida that you're worried is beyond the capabilities of your local hospital, and you have either good insurance or enough money, you can get the care you want at one of Florida's large urban nationally ranked hospitals. In addition, Florida's large hospitals are widely respected throughout Latin America and the Caribbean, and serve as tertiary care centers for some countries and as destinations of choice for medical tourism (Florida Chamber Foundation, 2015). The Florida health care system may not be very highly ranked in the United States, but it's much better than in most other countries in the region and can provide a very high level of care to discerning consumers of health services with adequate resources.

22
CRIME IS NOT PART OF THE DREAM

Florida has gotten a bad rap over several recent high-profile shootings that shocked the American public. The "Stand Your Ground" law has been unfairly portrayed as a license to kill rather than a right of legitimate self-defense. The principle behind the law was cast in an unfavorable light by the controversial killing of an African-American youth, Trayvon Martin, in Sanford on February 26, 2012, and the subsequent acquittal of George Zimmerman based on the SYG law.

More recently, there have been two very disturbing mass shootings. The first occurred at Pulse, an Orlando gay nightclub. At 2 am on June 11, 2016, a Muslim Afghan-American man, apparently sympathetic to ISIS, forced his way in and opened fire at the largely Hispanic crowd, slaughtering as many people as he could. By the time he was taken out by a SWAT team's bullets hours later, he had killed 49 innocent people and injured 53. The second recent mass shooting was the massacre at Marjorie Stoneman Douglas High School (MSD) in Parkland on February 14, 2018. A 19-year-old, mentally unstable, former student gained access to the school and started firing an AR-15 clone, killing 17 and wounding 17 others, including teachers as well as students, before walking out the door and ultimately being later apprehended by law enforcement.

The Parkland Massacre ignited public demands for tougher gun control led by MSD students who founded the "Never Again MSD" movement. Over NRA objections, the Florida government quickly responded with a new gun control law (CS/SB 7026). This law implemented wide-ranging new restrictions, which raised the age to buy a long gun to 21 from 18; extended the waiting period after purchase to 3 days; prohibited "bump stocks;" established "risk protection orders" to temporarily remove guns from people deemed by a judge to be a threat; imposed harsher penalties for making threats against a school, including on social media; and funded a "guardian program" that arms specially-trained teachers and school employees, to protect the students. Noticeably absent from the list of measures is the assault rifle ban demanded by the students. However, the seriousness of the government's intention to enforce these new laws is evidenced by the issuance of "risk protection orders" forcing hundreds of people to give up their guns (Darrah, 2018).

In addition to tightening the gun laws, the bill budgeted $400 million for new school security measures, including: $98 million to harden school buildings with such security features as metal detectors, steel doors and bullet-proof glass; $97 million for resource and safety officers; $67 million for the "guardian program"; and $25 million for mental health screening and other services such as counselling. The speed and strength of the Florida government's response, in a state known for jealously guarding its Second Amendment Rights, is evidence of how strongly everyone feels about the need to put an end to school shootings once and for all. The Marjory Stoneman Douglas High School Public Safety Commission was established to investigate the school shooting and other incidents and to make further recommendations to prevent such violence in the future.

Not the Gunpackingest State

People might be surprised to learn that the claim that everyone in Florida owns a gun, and that the state is filled with gun nuts, is not true. In fact, only 32.5 per cent of the adults in Florida owned a gun in 2015, according to a survey published in *Injury Prevention* (Kalesan, Villarreal, Keyes, and Galea, 2015). (Survey data must be used to make this estimate because no statistics are available.) While the rate in Florida is higher than the national average of 29.5 per cent, it still puts Florida in the middle of the pack, ranking 24th out of the 50 states and DC (Chart 44). This is well below the rate in the rural hunting states like Alaska, Arkansas, Idaho, and West Virginia, which all have rates in the mid 50s and above. And while it is well above the liberal coastal mega-states of New York (rate 10.3 per cent, rank 49th) and California (rate 19.8, rank 43rd), which more tightly control gun ownership, it is below the 35.7 per cent in Texas (rank 18th), another state often associated with guns.

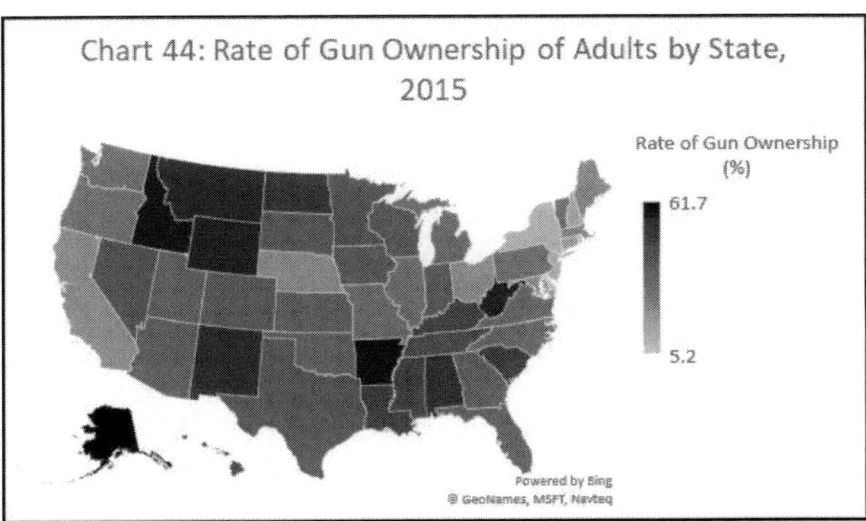

Chart 44: Rate of Gun Ownership of Adults by State, 2015

Source: Kalesan, Bindu, Marcos D Villarreal, Katherine M Keyes, and Sandro Galea. "Gun ownership and social gun culture" Injury Prevention. doi:10.1136. (2015).

Not So Violent

Violent crimes reported in the FBI statistics include: murder and nonnegligent manslaughter; rape; robbery; and aggravated assault. The violent crime rate of 430.3 per 100,000 people in Florida puts it a bit above the middle of the range of the states (Chart 45). However, it is much lower than the two highest violent crime states of Alaska (804.2) and New Mexico (702.5). And while Florida has a lot more guns, its violent crime rate is below California (445.3) and not that much higher than New York (376). But, even with less guns than Texas, it's only slightly below the rate there of 434.4 per 100,000 people.

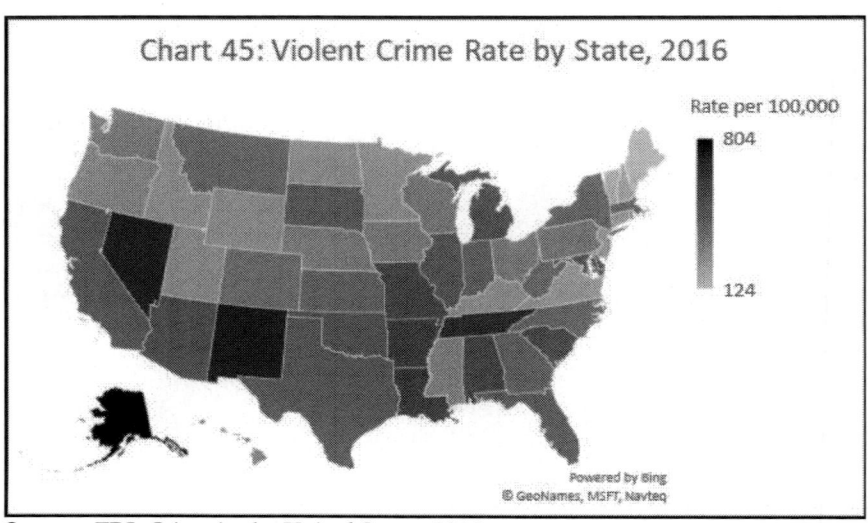

Chart 45: Violent Crime Rate by State, 2016

Rate per 100,000
804
124

Powered by Bing
© GeoNames, MSFT, Navteq

Source: FBI, Crime in the United States, 2016.

Property Crimes on the High Side

Florida's property crime rate, which includes burglary, larceny-theft and motor vehicle theft, was 2,686.8 per 100,000 people in 2016, earning it a rank of 22nd out of the 50 states (Chart 46). This is also a bit above the U.S. average of 2,450.7. The Florida rate is a little above California (rate 2,553.0, rank 27th) and well above New York (rate 1,545.6, rank 48th), the mega-state with the lowest property crime rate. Floridians can take small consolation from the fact that the property crime rate is slightly lower than in Texas (rate 2,759.8, rank 18th).

The conclusion is that Florida is neither a state with a particularly high violent crime rate, nor with an especially elevated level of property crimes. People retiring to Florida who will live outside the main cities have little to worry about. They can feel just as safe as in their home states. Moreover, Latin American immigrants coming to Florida from countries with sky-high murder rates will find even the largest cities like Miami and Orlando much safer than in their home countries (Lunhow, 2018). The people, who already live here in Florida, have gotten used to the risks of being a victim of crime, even if the risks are not so high, and have developed coping strategies. Many chose to live in gated communities, and to take advantage of the state's liberal concealed carry laws, to enhance their sense of security.

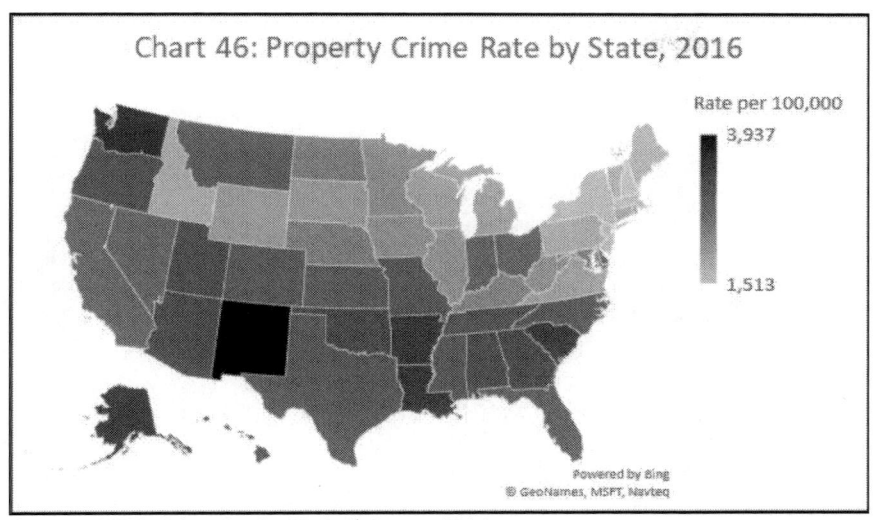

Chart 46: Property Crime Rate by State, 2016

Rate per 100,000
3,937
1,513

Source: FBI, Crime in the United States, 2016.

23
NEITHER IS POVERTY AND HOMELESSNESS

The Poverty Rate is Lower than Expected Given Income Levels

Poverty is nobody's dream. Yet some people still end up poor. If it's only a temporary spell between jobs or while going to school, it's not so bad because there's the hope of a brighter future. Like all the states, Florida has a significant proportion of the population with incomes below the poverty line. This is in relation to the official poverty income line that has been produced since the mid 1960s in the United States by the U.S. Census Bureau. The poverty line is a rough and ready measure that is calculated by tripling an inflation-adjusted food budget for the year 1963 and making further adjustments for the size and composition of the family, and the age of the head of household (U.S Census Bureau, 2018). The simplistic rationale behind this is that people are considered poor if they have to spend too large a share of their budget on food. While it's not very scientific, that's the way it's done.

The percentage of the population living under the official poverty line in Florida was 13.3 per cent, on average, over the two-year 2016-17 period giving it a rank of 15th highest among the states (Chart 47). This was worse than the U.S. average of 12.5 per cent, and higher than the 12.6 per cent in New York but almost the same as the 13.2 per cent in California, and better than the 13.6 per cent in Texas. On the bright side, it's better than would be expected given that the state's per capita income level was the 10th lowest from the bottom in 2017 (see Chart 8 above).

The population living below the poverty line in Florida resides in some of the agricultural counties in the north and in the center of the state, like Hardy, DeSoto, Hendry, Okeechobee and the counties along the Alabama-Georgia line, which have relatively large African-American populations (Chart 48). Miami-Dade, with its large population of Hispanic immigrants, also has a fairly high percentage living in poverty.

Chart 47: Percentage of People in Poverty by State, 2016-17 Average

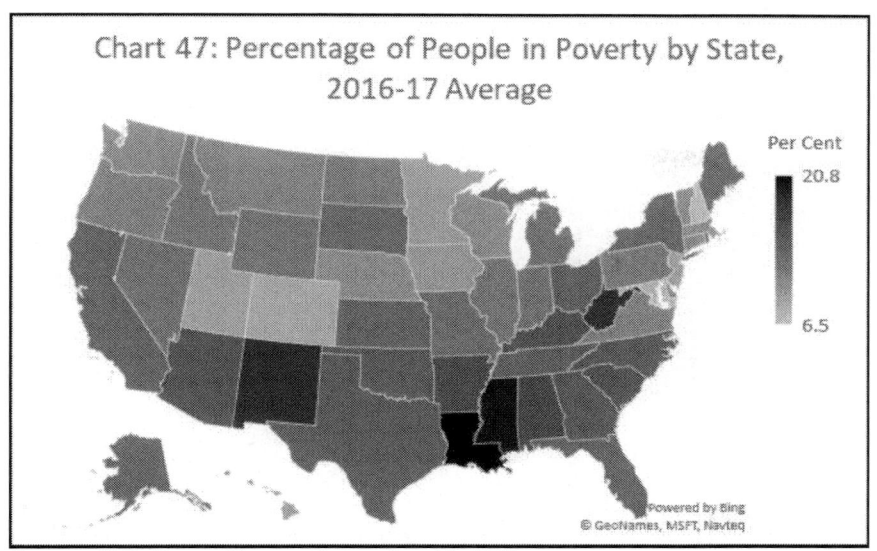

Source: U.S. Census Bureau, September 12, 2018.

Chart 48: Percentage of People Whose Income is Below the Poverty Line, 2016

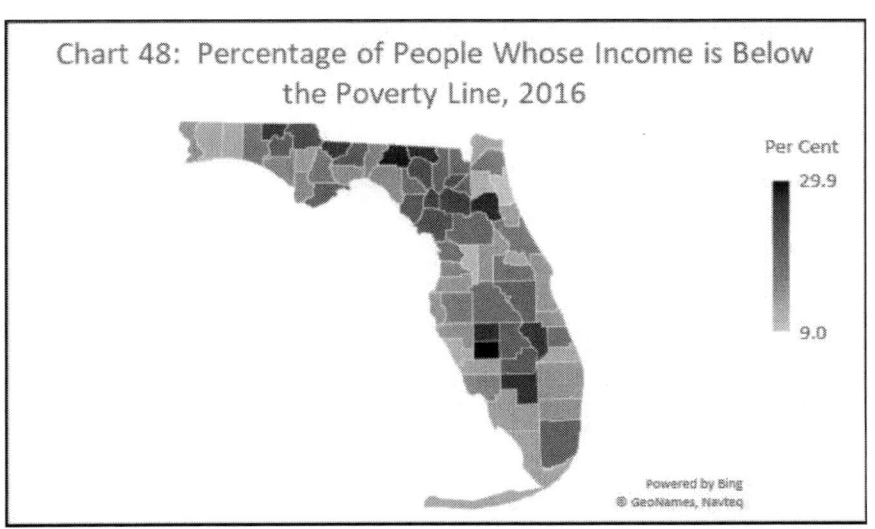

Note: These data are for 2016 and those in Chart 47 for an average of 2016-17, which is lower at the statewide level.
Source: US. Census Bureau, 2018.

Homelessness is Not So High Despite the Good Climate

Homelessness is an extreme form of poverty. It exists when people don't have adequate income to afford housing. This can be either because their incomes are too

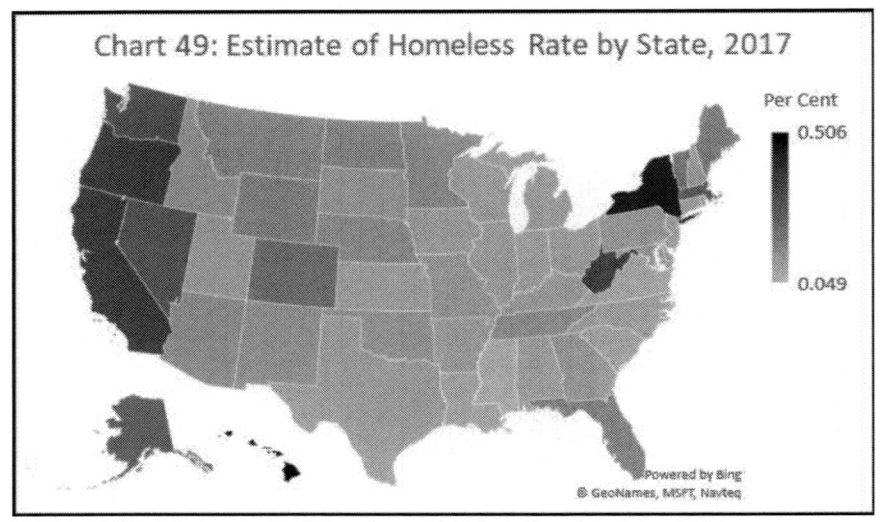

Chart 49: Estimate of Homeless Rate by State, 2017

Source: U.S. Department of Housing and Urban Development, 2017.

low, or housing is too expensive. The homeless can be living as families or as single individuals. Low incomes can result from lack of education or skills, or unemployment. Not having a job can be a temporary or permanent situation. People with mental problems or substance abuse issues often have trouble holding on to jobs and can become, in effect, unemployable. Single unattached individuals are more likely to be substance abusers than families. For women, and their children, domestic violence is an important cause of homelessness. These factors were identified in the U.S. Conference of Mayors' Report on Hunger and Homelessness (U.S Conference of Mayors, 2016). Homelessness is a complex issue with personal, family and societal aspects that cannot be adequately covered here, except in passing.

While the rate of homelessness in Florida, which is 0.156 per cent in 2017, putting it in 15th place among the states, is not low, it certainly could be higher given the appeal of Florida's climate for those who have to live outdoors. Moreover, it is barely over a third of that in much colder New York, which is 0.451 per cent (ranked 2nd), and only half that of California, which is 0.340 per cent (ranked 3rd) (Chart 49). It's also only a fraction of the District of Columbia, which at 1.077 per cent, is off-the-chart high. The higher levels of homelessness in these areas (and for that matter the whole West Coast) might reflect the higher cost of housing and the more tolerant attitudes towards vagrancy and panhandling of law enforcement, which results from a more permissive liberal political environment. Florida's lower level of homelessness is one of the reasons that tourists in Florida are not harassed as much as they are in cities like Washington, New York, and San Francisco. This makes Florida a more desirable destination for tourists and keeps them coming back to spend their money.

24
FADING DREAMS FOR AGRICULTURE AND THE FISHERIES

At one time Florida was an agricultural powerhouse, dependent on its farms and ranches to produce a large share of its income from its citrus fruit, sugar, horticulture and cattle. And, granted, it still produces a cornucopia of agricultural products ($4.1 billion in farm GDP in 2016, after subtracting the value of inputs from cash receipts), but their net value relative to the size of the economy has continued to shrink, falling from around 1 per cent of GDP in 1997 to a relatively small 0.4 per cent in 2016 (Chart 50). The prosperity of Florida has come to depend less and less on its agricultural sector. And this trend is not going to reverse.

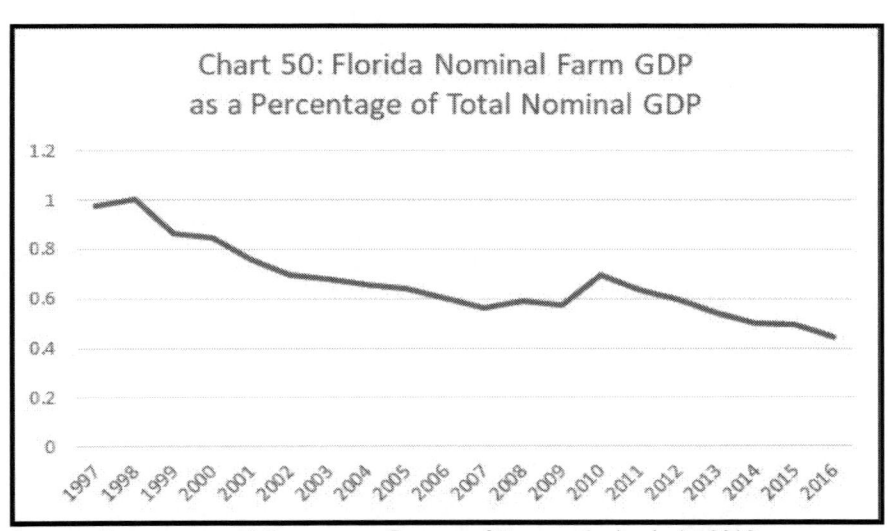

Chart 50: Florida Nominal Farm GDP as a Percentage of Total Nominal GDP

Source: Department of Commerce, Bureau of Economic Analysis, 2018.

The agricultural industry (narrowly defined so as not to include food processing and distribution) still directly employees 45,000 hired workers in 2017, but many only on a seasonal basis. Their pay is also relatively low in an $11.10 to $12.45 range in April 2017, which is the average for field and livestock work respectively. (Florida Department of Agriculture and Consumer Services, 2017, p.19). Even by a broader definition than just hired employees, including all the jobs involved on a full-time, part-time, and seasonal basis, direct employment in "crop, livestock, forestry, & fisheries production" was reported to only be 126,716 in 2014, according to a University of Florida IFAS study. Another 174,998 would be added if direct employment in "agricultural inputs & services" were included. (Hodges, Rahmani, 2015, p.5).

In 2015, cash receipts from farms were $8.4 billion, earning Florida a rank of 17th, well behind the leading states of California ($47 billion), Iowa ($27.7 billion), and Texas ($23.6 billion) (Fl DofA, 2017, p.14). This was also less than the estimated $9.5 billion in revenue Disney took in at its Orlando theme parks in the year ending October 1, 2016.

Florida has a lot of different crops including floriculture, vegetables, fruits and nuts, hay, and cotton. And it has poultry farms as well as cattle ranches and dairy farms. Floriculture had cash receipts of $1.04 billion in 2016, making it Florida's 2nd most remunerative agricultural commodity (Fl DofA, 2017, p.14). But Florida is, of course, still best known for its citrus fruit and sugar.

The value of agricultural products produced is highest in Palm Beach County where it was almost $1 billion in 2012 (the latest year data are available from the U.S. Department of Agriculture five-year census). The largest product there was sugar cane followed by vegetables, melons, potatoes, and sweet potatoes, and nursery, greenhouse, floriculture, and sod (USDA, County Profile Palm Beach County, 2012). More surprisingly, urbanized Miami-Dade is the 2nd largest agricultural county with a value of agricultural products of $604 million. This is because Miami-Dade has the biggest nursery industry in the state and second largest in the nation, producing ornamentals. Other large agriculture counties to the west and north of Palm Beach are Hendry County and Polk County, which produce large amounts of oranges.

Oranges Are Still the Biggest Crop

Nobody will be surprised to hear that Florida's biggest crop is oranges. They are, after all, Florida's most iconic product and the state fruit. Anyone who has driven through the center of the state has gone through miles of orange groves, but, if you haven't, you just need to read the label on the carton of juice in your refrigerator to see that it comes from Florida.

In 2016, Florida's 4,000 orange growers earned cash receipts of $1.17 billion and grapefruit earned $127 million. This was enough to make oranges Florida's most valuable single crop. Florida was the largest producer of oranges in the U.S. in 2016, supplying almost 60 per cent of the country's requirements (Fl DofA, 2017, p.16). And the total value of the citrus industry to the Florida economy is many times cash receipts if revenue from later stages of production such as processing, distribution, transportation, and the wholesale and retail trade are included.

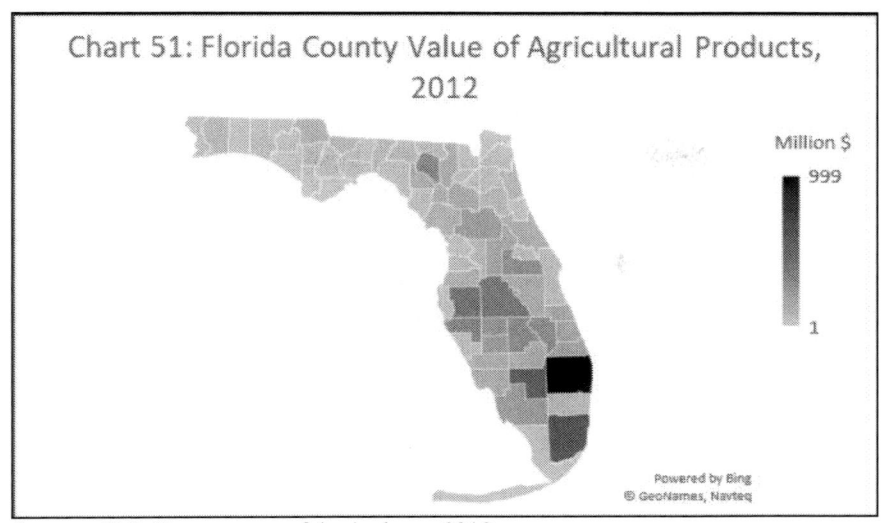

Chart 51: Florida County Value of Agricultural Products, 2012

Source: U.S. Department of Agriculture, 2012.

Palm trees in a nursery south of Miami near the Turkey Point Nuclear Plant in Miami-Dade County.

Citrus fruit (mostly orange) production is concentrated in the center of the state (Chart 52). The largest number of boxes (each weighing 90 pounds) are produced in Polk, Highlands, DeSoto, and Hardee counties and in Hendry County further south. There is also significant production in Indian River and St. Lucie on the east coast and in Collier County on the southwest Gulf Coast.

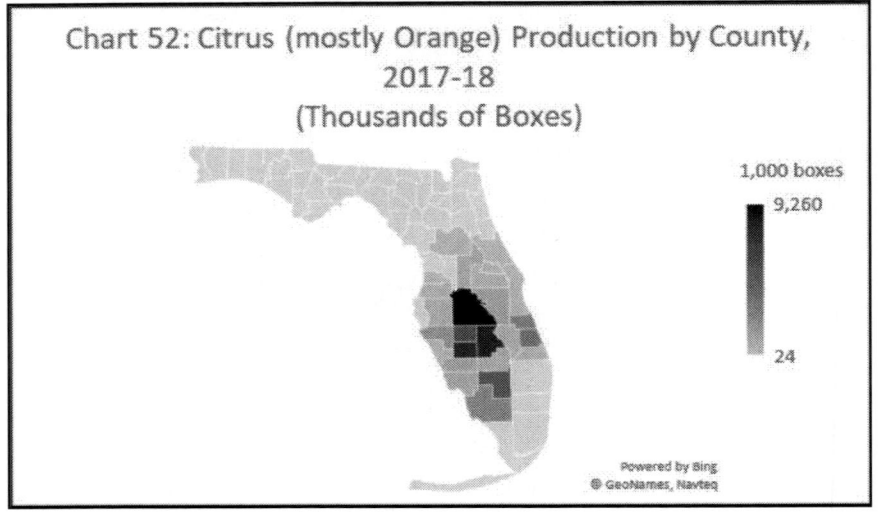

Chart 52: Citrus (mostly Orange) Production by County, 2017-18 (Thousands of Boxes)

[Map of Florida showing citrus production by county, with scale from 24 to 9,260 thousand boxes per 1,000 boxes unit. Powered by Bing, © GeoNames, Navteq]

Source: U.S. Department of Agriculture, 2018.

The bad news is that all has not been well in the citrus industry in recent years. Since producing the biggest crop ever in 1998, it has been downhill for the industry ever since. Historically, it has been subject to freezes and a canker blight, but, in 2005, first on a small scale, and then gradually spreading, a new affliction called "greening" began to emerge threatening the very future of the industry. (Williams, 2018).

Greening is a condition spread by the Asian citrus psyllid, an insect that infects the citrus trees with the greening bacteria. This causes the tree to produce a small fruit that has no commercial value instead of the juicy Florida orange that everyone associates with the industry. And once a tree is infected, it can't be cured.

The value and volume of production of citrus fruit has declined in recent years largely as a result of greening (Chart 53). In the ten years ending in 2018, the value of citrus production has decreased a staggering 61 per cent and the tonnage 76 per cent. In the 2017-18 crop year alone, the volume of production declined by 37 per cent, reflecting the damage done to citrus trees by Hurricane Irma as well as the ongoing impact of greening. The orange crop is now the lowest since World War II. Florida has lost much market share to Brazil, the number one in the global orange market.

Much research is being undertaken, by the government in cooperation with the industry, to find potential cures for citrus greening. It's been focusing on developing trees resistant to the bacteria causing the greening, and pesticides targeted to kill the Asian citrus psyllids spreading it. One novel solution, being tried, involves the free distribution to growers and subsequent release of wasps to kill the psyllids (Hobbs, 2017). Hopefully, something will be found soon that works, or the industry will continue to shrivel. In the meantime, however, growers have reportedly been spraying their trees more often with herbicides, pesticides and fertilizers to combat greening and other diseases including citrus canker (Williams, 2018). The run-off is contributing to the high level of pollutants in Lake Okeechobee, which is downstream from much of the industry.

An orange grove in Glades County.

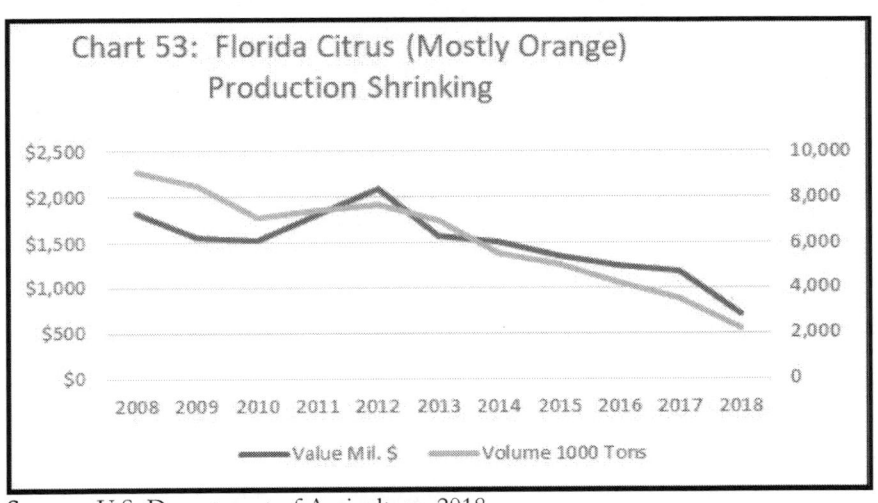

Chart 53: Florida Citrus (Mostly Orange) Production Shrinking

Year	Value Mil. $	Volume 1000 Tons

(Chart shows both Value Mil. $ and Volume 1000 Tons declining from 2008 to 2018)

Source: U.S. Department of Agriculture, 2018.

The Citrus Tower, which was built in 1956 in Clermont, east of Orlando, was meant to be a monument to Florida's premier industry. Tourists would come from all over and pay for an elevator ride to the observation deck atop the 226-foot structure simply to take in the panoramic view of orange groves stretching for miles. Now the few remaining visitors to the deck still get a spectacular view of hills and lakes in the distance, but the large groves of surrounding orange trees, which were hard hit by the freezes of the 1980s, have vanished. Moreover, the immediate vista has been transformed into one of urban sprawl created by the suburbanization of so much of Central Florida around Orlando. The Citrus Tower has become a monument to a citrus industry well past its prime.

Cattle and Calves

Cattle and calves and dairy products taken together accounted for $1.41 billion in cash receipts in 2016. (Fl DofA, 2017, p.16). This is more than the cash receipts of the citrus industry but combines two different commodities. Most of the receipts, or $859 million, came from cattle and calves.

The cattle ranches and inventory are concentrated in the south-central part of the state north of Lake Okeechobee (Chart 54). The phosphates and nitrogen in their manure is an important contributor to the pollution of the lake. The run-off from almost a half of the state's cattle ends up either in Lake Okeechobee or being dumped on the Southwest Gulf Coast or Atlantic Coast.

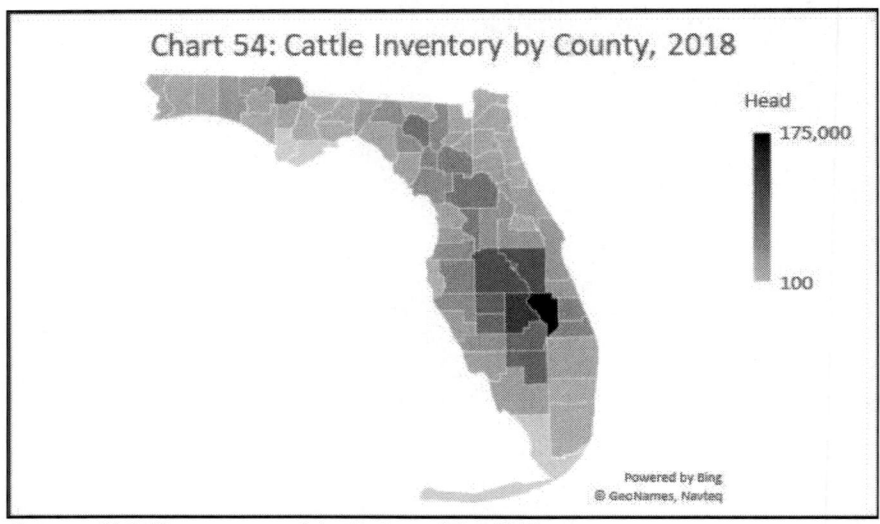

Chart 54: Cattle Inventory by County, 2018

Source: U.S. Department of Agriculture, May 2018.

Big Sugar

Sugar growers received $561 million in cash receipts for their harvest in 2016, making it the state's 4th leading commodity. This does not consider the amount they earned from the production of raw or refined sugar. It's just the amount received for the raw sugar cane.

FLORIDA DREAMS

Sugar cane growing south of Lake Okeechobee.

The Florida Industry has been dubbed, not so fondly, "Big Sugar" in the state and is comprised of the United States Sugar Corporation, Florida Crystals Corporation (owned by the Fanjul brothers' Fanjul Corporation), both of which are integrated producers, and the Sugar Cane Growers Cooperative of Florida. The industry is in Palm Beach, Hendry and Glades County. Three quarters of its production comes from Palm Beach County south and east of Lake Okeechobee. There are four mills and two refineries in the area to process the raw sugar cane and sugar. (Baucum and Rice, 2009).

Even though the industry has always been a very high cost and uncompetitive producer relative to those in other countries, it has been very effective in lobbying the U.S. Government for the protective trade policies it needed to thrive. The protection started in the 1920s and 1930s, but took a quantum leap after the Cuban Embargo, which eliminated Cuba's sugar quota in 1961, shutting the United States' largest supplier out of our market and freeing the domestic industry from competition. (Caraway, 2003).

A sharp jump in Florida sugar cane production occurred in 1961 and 1962 as Florida producers moved to fill the gap created by the 3.1-million-ton reduction in Cuban supply resulting from the abolition of its quota (Chart 55). Florida production continued to expand through 2000, followed by a setback due to increased Mexican supply, which was eventually resolved by an agreement with Mexico to limit exports and maintain minimum export prices. This enabled production to recover. The value of sugar production exhibited a similar pattern allowing for the different time horizon of the charts and adjusting for the different scale (Chart 56).

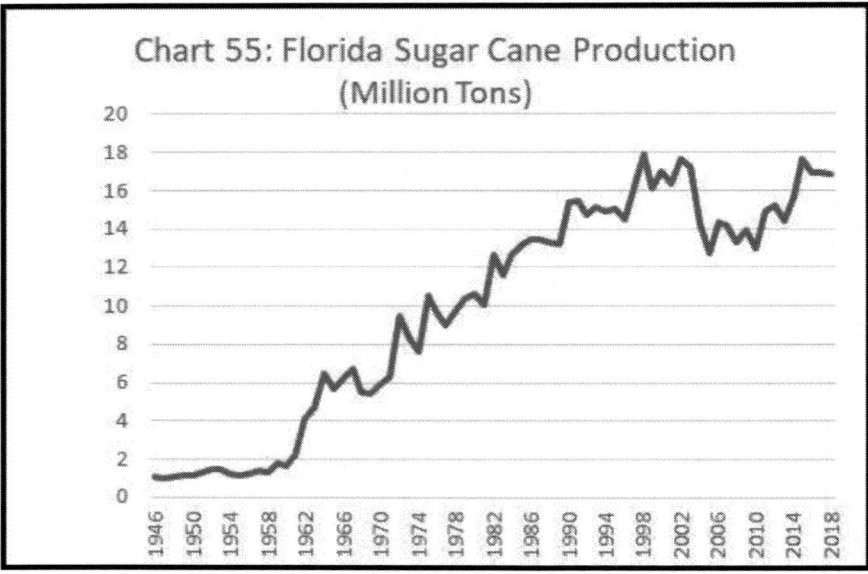

Chart 55: Florida Sugar Cane Production (Million Tons)

Source: U.S. Department of Agriculture, 2018.

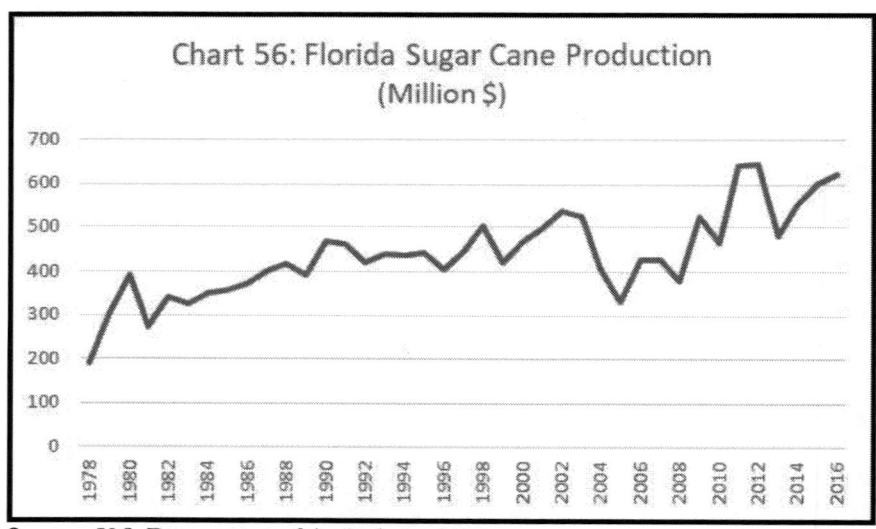

Chart 56: Florida Sugar Cane Production (Million $)

Source: U.S. Department of Agriculture, 2018.

The U.S. Sugar Program under the 2014 Farm Bill supports domestic sugar production by providing implicit subsidies for the industry. It works by setting a loan rate of 18.75 cents per pound for raw sugar which allows processors to take out non-recourse loans on their raw sugar inventories. It also establishes sugar tariff quotas. These work by setting quotas consistent with the loan rate on which low tariffs of 0.625 cents per pound are charged. Imports in excess of the quotas are charged a prohibitively high rate of 15.36 cents per pound or 82 per cent, which discourages imports in excess of the quota and supports the raw sugar price at the loan rate. (U.S. Department of Agriculture, Sugar Policy, 2018). A similar scheme also exists for beet sugar, but that's not what the Florida industry produces.

The Heritage Foundation estimated that the U.S. price of raw sugar was 6 cents a pound higher than the world price in Fiscal Year 2013 due to the Sugar Program and that, as a result, U.S. consumers pay $1.4 billion more per year for sugar (Riley, 2014). Since the Florida industry accounts for around 24 per cent of U.S. production, its share of this additional revenue could be estimated at $336 million. From the point of view of the United States, this is a loss for American consumers. But from a narrower Florida point of view, it's a gift to the state's producers. (There is also a deadweight loss to American consumers that is larger the more elastic the demand for sugar, but that is more complicated than we need to go into here.)

US Sugar Mill in Clewiston.

Fishing

Fishing is still an important economic activity in Florida. The commercial fishing industry continues to harvest finfish and shellfish at commercially viable levels, provided, of course, that the red tide abates and does not permanently damage the fishery (a topic covered in Chapter 26).

Total landings revenue increased gradually over the 2006 to 2015 period to $241 million (Chart 57). The revenue was divided with 63 per cent coming from shellfish and 37 per cent from finfish. The seafood caught by the commercial fishers in the state is very important to the tourism industry as it adds to the state's appeal as a destination. One of the many reasons that tourists come to Florida is to enjoy fresh seafood like shrimp, stone crabs, spiny lobsters, grouper and snapper. If the seafood is served in a seaside restaurant that looks like a Chickee Hut designed by Jimmy Buffet, all the better. The seafood caught also generates income for those who process, transport and distribute it that must be taken into consideration in any calculation of its contribution to the Florida economy.

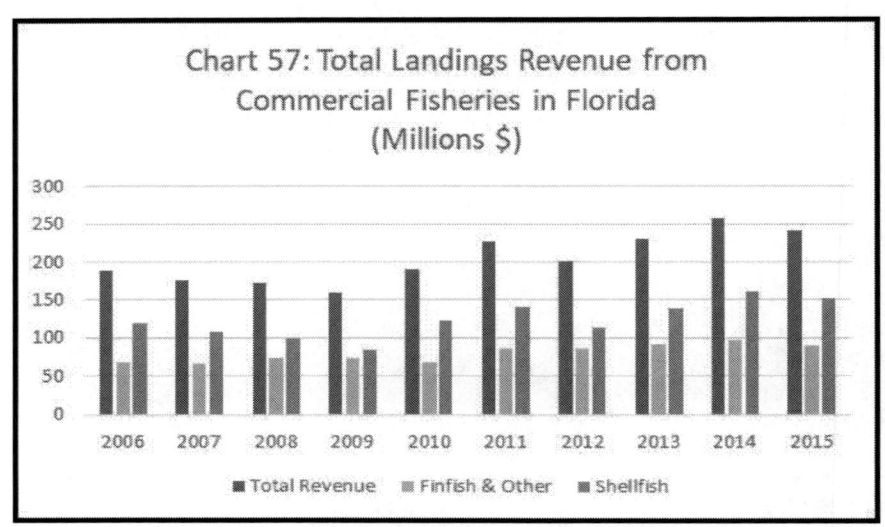

Chart 57: Total Landings Revenue from Commercial Fisheries in Florida (Millions $)

Source: U.S. Department of Commerce, National Marine Fisheries Service, 2017, p.142&174.

Fish are not only for eating, but also for the pure fun of catching. This satisfies something primitive, buried deep in our ancestral hunter-gatherer DNA. The recreational fishing industry in Florida is a big draw bringing millions into the state to spend their money, just simply fishing. In 2015, there were 5.6 million anglers, who took 22 million fishing trips, providing $4.1 billion in income for the captains and crews taking them out, and creating 97,000 jobs. In many areas of Florida, like Charlotte Harbor, fishing boat captains, who serve as guides for tourists and others, can earn a reasonable income. However, the livelihood of captains and fishing guides is threatened by the red tide that has been wreaking havoc up and down the coasts, causing massive fish kills, and raising health concerns about consuming the fish caught (Carloni, 2018). Some local captains in the Punta Gorda area are already seeking alternative employment.

And just in case you were wondering, the business of selling live alligators or alligator products by Florida aquaculturalists earned $8 million gross in 2012 (Fl DofA, 2017, p.16). In addition, there is some extra money made by hunters, or those who remove nuisance gators from ponds or swimming pools. By the way, contrary to what many tourists tell their children, alligators hanging around residential areas are not relocated, except to the Great Swamp in the sky. Granted the alligator business does not raise much money, but it does help keep the alligators under control. Incidentally alligators have made quite a comeback in Florida in recent years and now number 1.25 million.

Exaggerated Claims About the Importance of Agriculture for Florida

Efforts have been made to portray agriculture as much larger and more important for the Florida economy than it actually is (Hodges, Rahmani and Stevens, 2015). Vastly exaggerated claims, counter to the facts set out in this chapter, have been made by the Florida Chamber of Commerce to the effect that "14 per cent of Florida jobs are connected to the agricultural industry" and that "15.4 per cent of our gross state product [is] tied to the industry" (Roberts, 2016). Nonsense! These claims are based on an overly expansive definition of the industry that includes food industries and other natural resource industries, which really aren't agriculture at all in most people's eyes. While it would be a reasonable extension to include the processing of agricultural commodities like oranges and sugar, which is included in the manufacturing sector, it is a bridge too far to include all food-related industries like food service establishments (restaurants and bars), food stores, and food distribution. Another problem is that the estimates put forward incorporate multipliers from a regional economic modelling system, which is a methodology that has been subject to criticism for inflating impacts (Grady and Muller, 1988). Similarly, the job estimates advanced are based on an overly wide definition of employment that incorporates full-time, part-time, and seasonal positions, and not more narrowly just on full-time equivalents.

The employment prospects in agriculture may be even grimmer than its declining production suggests. There has been an increasing trend in the industry to mechanize by utilizing mechanical harvesters produced by companies like Oxbo. In the orange industry, for example, while less than 10 per cent of the crop is mechanically harvested at present, studies have concluded that mechanical harvesters can harvest sweet oranges more cheaply and with no long term damage to the trees (Moseley, House and Roka, 2012). How they work is amazing and worth checking out on the web. This technology has wider applicability to the whole labor-intensive agricultural sector, and casts a giant cloud over the long-run prospect for employment in agriculture.

It's necessary to highlight the overdrawn nature of the employment and output estimates for the agricultural sector that have been promoted by the Florida Chamber of Commerce because their purposes are primarily political, not analytical or informational. A realistic appreciation of the true relative importance of agriculture to the Florida economy is necessary for economic and environmental policy makers in Florida. They may be called on to make some hard decisions involving trade-offs between sectors, particularly if agriculture is adversely affecting the environment. Agriculture should not be regarded as a sacred cow, but as an economic sector, like all the others, based on its present contribution to our economic welfare, and not on its past glories.

25
HOW MANY PEOPLE CAN SHARE IN THE FLORIDA DREAM?

Florida has been growing exponentially now for more than a hundred years. It went from less than a million in 1920 to about 5 million in 1960, almost 10 million in 1980, approximately 16 million in 2000, and is now in the vicinity of 21 million, with growth still chugging along at a good clip. Over the scant course of a century, Florida has gone from being one of the least densely populated states to the 8th densest with 391 people per square mile inhabiting its low-lying terrain in 2017 (Chart 58). This was more than four times the U.S. average of 92 people per square mile. It was way higher than the 108 people per square mile in Texas and much greater than the 254 people per square mile in California. And it was almost as high as the 421 people per square mile in New York, but not so elevated as in the Megalopolis that stretches from Boston to Washington, D.C., including Rhode Island, which had a population density of 1,225 people per square mile. The nation's capital, if it had been included in the Chart, would have distorted the scale as it had 11,337 people per square miles. Large population densities like this may be okay in small urban areas, but as they spread over large states and multistate areas, they raise serious ecological and congestion issues. Hence, the probably unanswerable question posed in this chapter's title about how many people can share in the Florida Dream.

The data on the density of Florida's population per square mile may even be understated. There were an estimated 11.4 million acres of wetlands in Florida in 1996 occupying 29 percent of the land area of the state. This is a larger share than in any of the other lower 48 states. Wetlands are fragile and cannot be developed as easily as other land areas, and, if they are, there can be serious environmental consequences for water flows and wildlife. Wetlands have important roles in storing water, alleviating flooding, protecting shorelines, replenishing the aquifer, cleansing water, and providing a habitat for many plants and animals species like alligators and wading birds (Haag and Lee, 2016).

FLORIDA DREAMS

Chart 58: People Per Square Mile, 2017

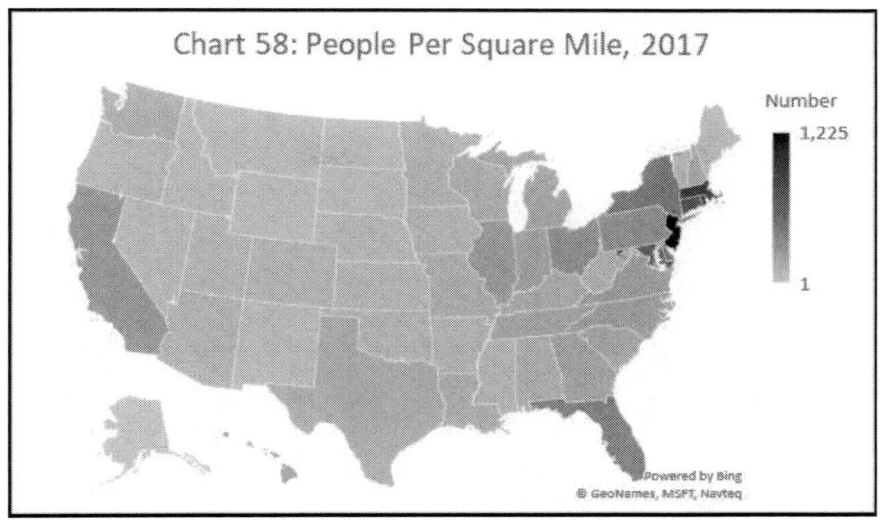

Number: 1 to 1,225

Source: U.S. Census Bureau, 2018.

The Florida Chamber Foundation suggests in its report, *Florida 2030*, that Florida will be home to 26 million by 2030, the end of its planning horizon. This is not a pipe dream, but a realistic projection based on a continuation of the existing trend. Is that too many people? And even if it is, there is little that can be done about it. Barring an environmental catastrophe, people will continue to follow their dreams to Florida from other states and throughout the world, especially from Latin America. The Sunshine State will continue its phenomenal rise in population at least for the foreseeable future. It's like a steamroller. There's no stopping it. All you can do is get out of the way.

Where are all these people coming to Florida going to live? In the state's largest cities and suburbs, which will continue to grow, spreading over larger and larger rural areas, is where they'll make their homes. The city likely to experience the greatest growth is Orlando. Walt Disney wasn't just whistling Dixie when he consecrated it the capital of his Florida Empire. He recognized its central position astride the state's main thoroughfares and away from the hurricane-exposed coasts. He saw that Orlando is different. Unlike Miami, it's not hemmed in on one side by the Atlantic Ocean and on the other by the Everglades. Nor, as we now know, is it exposed to sunny day tidal flooding. Tampa-St. Petersburg and Jacksonville are also limited by their coastlines. While the miles of orange groves surrounding Orlando have already been replaced by suburbs, the city still has plenty of room to grow. The rapidly-growing Villages has almost become a suburb of Orlando.

While Miami ranked 1st in congestion in Florida (and 12th nationally), according to the Texas Transportation Institute's Urban Mobility Scorecard, Orlando was 2nd in Florida and 27th in the country. This ranking is based on three mobility measures: yearly delay per auto commuter; travel time index; and excess fuel per auto commuter. Tampa-St. Petersburg and Jacksonville ranked right behind Orlando. (Texas Transportation Institute, 2015, p.2).

Road Construction to Counter Congestion in Orlando.

A large and rapidly growing population also puts demands on the water resources provided by the Florida Aquifer and poses problems in disposing of solid and liquid wastes. If these problems are not dealt with adequately and expeditiously, they can threaten the sustainability of Florida's rise, and thwart Florida Dreams.

The only thing you can do to reduce congestion is to build more and better transportation infrastructure. The same applies to solid and liquid waste treatment facilities. Congestion and pollution, if allowed to worsen, can kill the tourism goose that lays the golden egg, as well as lower the quality of life of all Floridians.

26
DREAMS THREATENED BY ENVIRONMENTAL CHALLENGES

The environmental hazards threatening Florida Dreams are not the alligators in Florida swamps and lakes, or the sharks cruising off Florida's lovely sand beaches, or even the ferocious seasonal lightning storms. Between 2000 and 2016 only seven people a year were bitten by gators, so one is unlikely to get you unless you are stupid enough to go wading in a murky pond at night or try to rescue your little doggy from a hungry gator's jaws (Nala Rogers, 2018). Even though Florida may be billed as the shark attack capital of the world with 31 recorded incidents in 2017, representing 35 per cent of the world-wide total, tourists still swarm to the beach without a worry in their heads (Florida Museum, 2018). And, while Florida is the state with the highest lightening fatalities averaging 5 a year in the 10-year period ending in 2006, it's not enough to keep anybody off the golf course (Sosnowski, 2018). Florida's environmental challenges are on a much bigger scale than these small individual risks.

Over the years, Florida has sought to protect the environment by pursuing one of the most ambitious programs of land acquisition for conservation and recreation in the country. Almost 10 million acres of conservation land are now under government management, with 2.5 million acres added under the Florida Forever Program, launched in July 2001, and its predecessor, Preservation 2000. This has done much to preserve Florida's natural beauty for future generations and to protect habitats for the state's distinct flora and fauna. However, the environmental challenges Florida now faces are even greater and will require a much more active and creative approach.

Red Tide

The greatest threat currently facing Florida, in the short- to medium term, is the red tide. It has the potential to severely damage the tourism industry, which is the engine of the Florida economy. While dead fish can be cleaned up, not very many tourists are going to come down to Florida beaches if the fresh sea air is replaced by aerosolized toxins that burn their lungs.

Red tide is caused by a toxic dinoflagellate called Karenia brevis, which permanently and naturally resides in the waters as much as 120 miles off the coast. It is especially prevalent on the inner West Florida Shelf from Tampa to Naples but can also occur off the Panhandle and the east coast. Periodically, for reasons not fully understood, it approaches the shore where it feeds on the nutrients brought down the coastal rivers such as the Caloosahatchee, the Peace, and the Manatee. The more nutrients it gets the greater its biomass becomes. Large increases, called blooms, sporadically occur usually starting 10 to 40 miles off shore. They emit brevetoxins, which are a type of neurotoxin that can kill vertebrates like fish, turtles and even manatees and porpoises. The toxins can also become airborne as the microorganisms are broken up by wave action causing respiratory problems for people and marine animals.

Professor Larry Brand is a respected marine biologist at the University of Miami, who has studied the phenomena of red tide most closely. He and his laboratory assistant Angela Compton found that K. brevis was 20 times more abundant 3 miles off the coast than 12 to 18 miles off and that it was 13 to 18 times as profuse in the most recent period studied (1994-2002)-than in an earlier period (1954-63). They attribute these findings to increased run-offs of fertilizers and other nutrient-rich pollutants closer to the shore, as the population of Southwest Florida has increased. (Brand and Compton, 2007). This is consistent with an earlier study by Stanford University researchers, which, using satellite imagery, found a link between dumps of irrigation water, laden with fertilizers, and red tide blooms in the Gulf of California (Ahrens et al, 2008). In a more recent paper, Maze, Olascoaga and Brand (2015) note that "Many aspects relating to such blooms remain poorly known, including environmental conditions during their occurrence." However, they also find that large blooms "occur only when the Loop Current [which is the current in the Gulf that comes up between the Yucatan and Cuba and loops clockwise before exiting the Florida Straits] is in its northern position, due to the enhanced retention on the [Florida] shelf."

The recent bout of red tide has persisted since October 2017. This is unusually long as blooms mostly occur in the summer and fall and are broken up by northerly winds in the winter (Brand, Campbell, Bresnan, 2012; Reuters, 2018). It's only now in December 2018 that it seems to be fading, but it could come back at any time, especially next spring when the Gulf warms up again, or even earlier (Reilly, 2018).

The red tide bloom has caused enormous kills of fish that have littered primarily Southwest Florida beaches with piles of rotting stinking dead fish of all varieties, including enormous goliath groupers and a 26-foot whale shark. The decaying carcasses of manatees, dolphins and turtles have also washed up on the beaches. This disgusting spectacle has been duly reported in lurid detail by the national media for those who weren't able to see it with their own eyes and smell it with their nose. If this wasn't enough to discourage tourism, those who did make it to the beach were greeted by not-so-fresh sea air loaded with toxins that burned the throat and lungs and induced fits of coughing or even worse for those with chronic lung diseases like asthma and emphysema. Substantial damages from the red tide have already been incurred and documented (Walton, 2018).

FLORIDA DREAMS

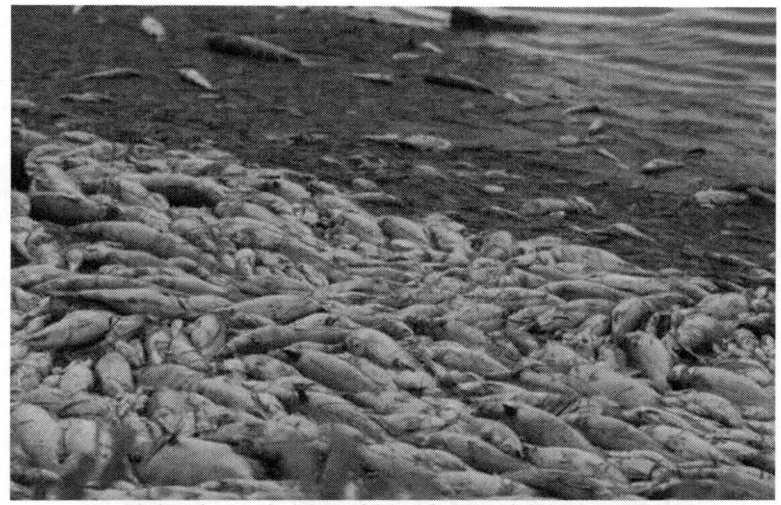

Red Tide Sanibel Island Florida. Dead fish along the shell covered beaches in Southwest Florida. Photo Taken August 5, 2018. ID 123090508
© Melanie Kowasic | Dreamstime.com

    The situation was considered sufficiently grave that Governor Rick Scott issued Executive Order 18-221 on August 13, 2018 declaring a state of emergency in Pinellas, Hillsborough, Manatee, Sarasota, Charlotte, Lee, and Collier Counties on the Gulf Coast. As such a declaration can only apply for a 60-day period, he issued Executive Order 18-275 on October 4 prolonging the emergency for another 60 days and extending it to St. Lucie, Martin, Palm Beach, Broward, and Miami-Dade Counties on the east coast. The Executive Orders names the Director of the Division of Emergency Management as the State Coordinating Officer and the Department of Environmental Protection as the lead agency in managing the crisis and requires state government departments to cut through the red tape to take any needed action. The Governor also announced a series of budgetary measures and other initiatives to deal with the crisis on September 19th. None of the steps taken so far, while useful, will make the red tide go away. But it could, of course, go away on its own, as it seems to be doing, or perhaps not. Nobody knows for sure. Ay, there's the rub, to steal the bard's words.

    Since much is at stake and important economic sectors like tourism and agriculture have conflicting interests, the issue has become highly politicized with much finger pointing all around. Adding to the confusion is that even the scientists are not all in full agreement on the causes and cures of the red tide. However, since I'm an economist, not a scientist, I'm not constrained by the lack of consensus from offering my observations.

    Okeechobee means "plenty big water" in Seminole. That's what it used be. Now a more accurate name would be "plenty dirty water." Lake Okeechobee has become the recipient of all the water coming down the Kissimmee River from near Orlando.

This water contains all the run-off from the cattle and citrus industry along its shores. Around 800 thousand head of cattle defecate in the water daily, if not directly then indirectly after a rain. Much of the orange industry, which has been struggling with greening and other diseases through increased use of fertilizers and pesticides, is drained by the river as are other agricultural producers. Many of the homes along the way are on septic tanks, so human waste can be added to the toxic brew. Golf courses contribute their share of pollutants. Some phosphate mines also add to the problems on the Kissimmee basin and in other coastal rivers. All the waste water, rich in phosphates and nitrogen, collects in Lake Okeechobee, where it stews. That is until the Army Corp of Engineers decides that there is, or is likely to be, too much water in the lake for the poor old Herbert Hoover Dike to hold. Not wanting to let the dike be breached and flood the agricultural area south of the lake, the Corp flushes the water out, usually 70 per cent down the Caloosahatchee to the Gulf, and 30 per cent down the St. Lucie to Stuart and the Atlantic Ocean.

Lake Okeechobee from the Herbert Hoover Dike in Clewiston.
If you look hard, you can see it in the distance past the
marshy island or islandy marsh.

Sometimes, like in 2018 for instance, the nutrients spawn a fresh water blue-green algae (cyanobacteria) bloom in the two rivers draining Lake Okeechobee. The blue-green algal blooms contain the toxin microcystin that is harmful to humans. The blooms also cut off sunlight in the water and lower oxygen, killing plants and fish. When the blue-green algae reach salty water, they die and break down into nutrients that can feed the red tide if the K. brevis happen to be around. Blue-green algae are found in many waterways in Florida like the Indian River Lagoon and not just the Caloosahatchee and the St. Lucie. (Wright, 2018; Schneider,2018).

The sugar industry is often blamed as the main culprit for the red tide. But this is a stretch since most of the industry is located south and downstream from Lake Okeechobee. Their effluent can end up in Lake Okeechobee primarily if it is pumped back up into the lake. The industry's claim is that such back-pumping only contributes 1 per cent of the flow out of Lake Okeechobee and 99 per cent of the water in the lake comes down the Kissimmee. But its claim that its hands are clean is disputed. While less water is being back pumped than there used to be, there are still "legacy" nutrients in the lake from past back-pumping that can be released by the wind, resuspending sediment containing sugar cane nutrients, so they can flow down the two rivers feeding coastal algal blooms.

Scientists at the Mote Marine Research Laboratory have been working on a cure for red tide. They have succeeded in purifying large 25,000-gallon tanks of infected water using ozone and have been trying other naturally occurring substances. However, the remedies that they have been researching are still experimental and would have to be applicable on the mega-scale required to combat red tide on 150 miles of coastline. (Reuters, 2018).

There are practical steps that need to be taken to clean up Lake Okeechobee, and to prevent the spread of blue-green algae and the feeding of the red tide. Some are already underway. Others are well known but have been delayed. They include: repairing the Herbert Hoover Dike so that there's no danger of a breach, and releases can be better controlled; pursuing the planned 35-year, $10.5 billion Comprehensive Everglades Restoration Program (CERP) more aggressively to restore the flow of clean water through the Everglades (Chart 59); and reducing the flow of agricultural, mining and residential pollution in the rivers and streams flowing into Lake Okeechobee.

Restoring the water flow through the Everglades is more than just a project to protect plants and wildlife, as important as that may be. It is also essential to increase the water flow in the Biscayne Aquifer to mitigate the intrusion of salt water in the aquifer, which according to a recent study is progressing (Prinos et al, 2014). This is critical as the Biscayne Aquifer is the source of Miami's water supply.

The Federal budget proposed for 2019 includes $169 million for Herbert Hoover Dike repairs and the state government has chipped in another $50 million. The Army Corps of Engineers plans to have the work completed by 2025, but the state government has been pushing for 2022. (Treadway, 2018). The earlier the work can be completed, the better. Seepage is an ongoing threat to an earthwork dam like the Herbert Hoover Dike and a breach could be disastrous.

The Water Resources Development Act, which was pushed through both Houses of Congress by Congressman Brian Mast, and Senators Marco Rubio and Bill Nelson, was signed into law by President Trump on October 23, 2018. It authorizes a storage reservoir in the Everglades Agricultural Area South of Lake Okeechobee and contains other provisions to reduce the discharge of pollutants from Okeechobee and to help restore more water flow through the Everglades. While it will still be necessary to secure the required funding in the budget for the Federal Governments $800 million share of the $1.6 billion project, the Florida government has already budgeted its share of the cost in the spring of 2017 (Treadway and Schmitz, 2018).

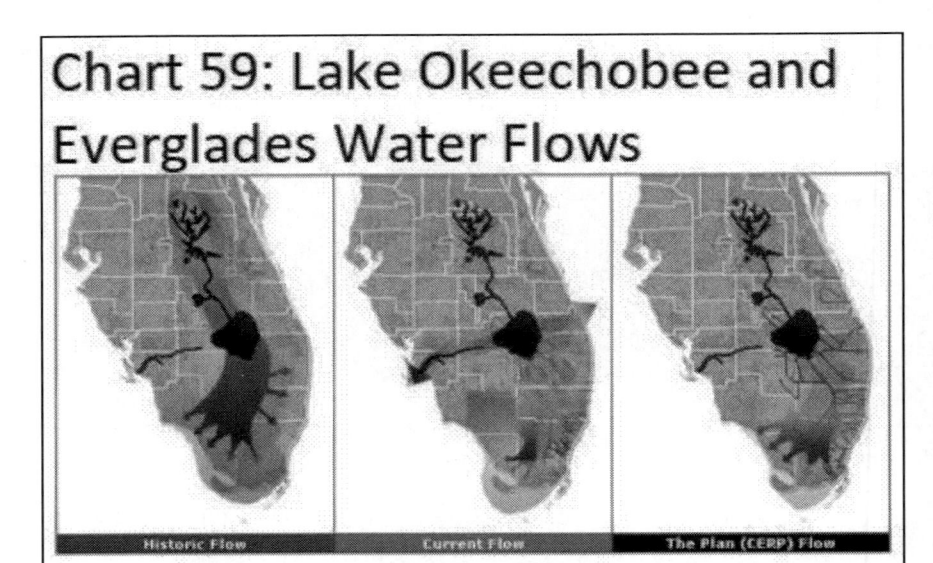

Chart 59: Lake Okeechobee and Everglades Water Flows

[Historic Flow | Current Flow | The Plan (CERP) Flow]

Source: Courtesy of EvergladesPlan.org, which is now EvergladesRestoration.gov. Chart was produced by the Army Corps of Engineers.

The next step in the CERP was to acquire land south of Lake Okeechobee to use as a reservoir for treating the water before releasing it south through the Everglades. The state government is going to have to take a very hard line on this as it has already lost some of the available land. The South Florida Water Management District (SFWMD) just extended expiring leases on some state owned land in the area until 2027 to Florida Crystals for the growing of sugar cane. This extension totally ignored the direct request for delay made by Governor-elect Ron DeSantis whose environmental plan calls for putting a greater priority on restoring the water flow from Okeechobee through the Everglades into Florida Bay.

It's not the first time the SFWMD put obstacles in the way of the planned reservoir. In 2015, by letting an option on the land expire, the district scuttled a deal to buy 46,800 acres of land in the Everglades Agricultural Area from U.S. Sugar. This followed its earlier failure to exercise the initial option, to acquire the land at $7,400 per acre, which had expired in 2013. Not exercising the earlier option at that time had raised the cost of the land under option from $346 million to an estimated $500 to $700 million at fair market value. This amount, which the SFWMD claimed was too much, was used as a justification for its 2015 decision to take a pass on the option, even though the money for the land purchase had already been set aside in the Land Acquisition Trust Fund from 33 per cent of the net revenues from the excise tax on documents for just such a purpose by the Florida Water and Land Conservation Amendment in 2012. By not acting on the options, the district was left with only the 26,800 acres it originally acquired in 2010 for $194 million. (Staletovich, 2018).

The existing state-owned land south of the lake is not large enough to accommodate a reservoir of the required size to treat the planned flow according to the Everglades Coalition of 62 environmental groups (Treadway, 2018). BullSugar.org estimates that an additional 6,500 acres would be necessary to treat the targeted amount of water to the specified standards (BullSugar.org, 2018).

The new governor's task has been made more difficult by the SFWMD. If he is going to be able to make progress with his environmental plan, which includes continuing to raise the Tamiami Trail as well as a reservoir south of Okeechobee and Everglades restoration, he needs to replace the existing Governing Board members with people who are more committed to expeditiously implementing the CERP and who won't sabotage his program before he even gets out of the gate. (Update: Since publication of the Kindle of this book on January 1, 2019, Governor DeSantis got off to a good start by calling for the resignation of all the SFWMD Board members. As of January 17, 2019, two have resigned leaving six more to go [Schmitz, 2019].)

The third step is to cut down the flow of pollutants coming into Lake Okeechobee, which is mainly from the Kissimmee drainage basin. The primary focus should be on curtailing the phosphates and nitrogen that feed the growth of blue-green algae and the red tide. It would require, at a minimum, tightening controls on agricultural and residential emissions. If that doesn't work, more extreme measures will have to be considered. At stake is the health of residents living all along the Southwest Gulf and Atlantic Coasts, and the livelihood of those who depend on the coastal tourism industry.

Global Warming and Rising Sea Levels

Long before Al Gore discovered *An Inconvenient Truth*, the Intergovernmental Panel on Climate Change (IPCC) was established by the United Nations to bring together scientists from around the globe to provide the world with scientific advice on climate change and its economic and political implications. Its main finding was that the continuing increase in greenhouse gasses (mostly carbon dioxide, but also methane, nitrous oxide, fluorinated gases, and even water vapor) is contributing to global warming. They do this by absorbing and emitting radiation within the thermal infrared range that laypeople call heat. To put it more simply, it is like the earth is enclosed in a giant greenhouse that gets increasingly warmer the more of these gasses the atmosphere contains. The corollary to this finding of the IPCC is that greenhouse gasses must be reduced to halt global warming. The IPCC's past and ongoing research form the scientific basis on which the Kyoto Protocol and the subsequent Paris Agreement to reduce greenhouse gas emissions is based.

In its report, the IPCC (2018) estimates that an increase of 1°C in global temperatures has already occurred and that the increase is likely to reach 1.5°C (2.7°F) by 2030 to 2052 and to keep increasing thereafter unless net greenhouse gas emissions are heroically cut 45 per cent from 2010 levels by 2030 and further reduced to a net zero by 2050 (IPCC, 2018). Anthropogenic global warming is estimated to be proceeding at 0.2°C per decade (between 0.1°C and 0.3°C). A 0.5°C increase is estimated to be associated with a 0.1-meter (4 inch) rise in sea levels. These estimates of warming and sea level rises may be low because they assume that countries participating in the Paris Agreement successfully follow through on their commitments to reduce greenhouse gases. The required cuts are so large that it's hard to see how they can be made without unprecedented international cooperation to implement drastic action to get off fossil fuels.

The U.S. Government's *Fourth National Climate Assessment* estimates that "global sea level is very likely to rise by 0.3–0.6 feet by 2030, 0.5–1.2 feet by 2050, and 1.0–4.3 feet by 2100 (U.S. Global Change Research Program, 2018). It also specifically warns, in its chapter dealing with the Southeast region, about the risks to Florida of coastal flooding, compromises to drinking and waste water treatment, increases in vector-borne diseases spread by mosquitos, increasing severity of hurricanes, and coral reef mortality (USGCRP, 2018).

The Florida Chamber Foundation provided a slightly more optimistic estimate in its report, *Florida 2030*, that "sea levels in Southeast Florida are projected to rise from 2018 levels by a median amount of 2.5 inches by 2030 and 10.5 inches by 2060" and noted that "nearly 80 per cent of Florida's population lives in coastal areas (Florida Chamber Foundation, 2018, p.13).

Putting aside the need to reach net zero anthropogenic carbon emissions globally to stabilize global temperatures, even a rise in temperatures of 0.5 °C over the next 10 to 20 years, which appears to be already in the cards, would have significant implications for a low lying, semitropical state like Florida, particularly in a place like Miami that already has localized flooding during heavy rains and unusually high tides, the so-called sunny day flooding. (IPCC, 2018). The Global Change Research Group noted that, in 2015, Miami had an all-time record of 15 occurrences of flooding (USGCRP, 2018). Maybe, it's because of their regular exposure to water-filled streets that Miamians not only believe in climate change, but also think that it will harm them personally (Elfrink, 2017). (If you live on the coast and want more information on how you could be affected by sea level rises, check out the National Oceanographic and Atmospheric Administration's sea level rise viewer on its website. It will show you the impact of various scenarios for sea level rise on your own locality.)

Unfortunately, like King Canute, there is little that the Florida state government can do to halt rises in the sea level. But it can implement climate change adaptations to alleviate the effects of temperature increases and sea level rises, which will, of course, cost lots of money (Lausche, 2009). At the same time, it would be irresponsible not to participate in broader national and international efforts to reduce greenhouse gasses like the Paris Agreement. This is something we should urge our political representatives to do. Anthropogenic climate change is a reality we can't afford to ignore.

Hurricanes

Hurricanes are seared into the consciousness of Floridians. Years afterwards, when memories of the torrential wind and rain should have faded, people still talk about past hurricanes as if they happened yesterday. My town of Punta Gorda was hit by Hurricane Charley at 4:29 pm on August 13, 2004. The town was devastated. An empty space still stands in the center of town that used to be a shopping center anchored by a Publix, all of which was flattened as if hit by a bomb. Rebuilding of the rest of the town took several years. A touching memorial comprised of a bent, but intact, palm tree and sundial marking the fateful hour was erected in our Laishley Park to the Spirit of Punta Gorda in surviving the hurricane and its aftermath. Fourteen years later the disastrous event is still remembered by the local affiliate of NBC News (NBC, 2018).

Marion Avenue in Punta Gorda the morning after Hurricane Charley.

People from all over the country associate Florida with hurricanes. Maybe that's because, other than during elections, it's when Florida gets the most attention from the national media. Or perhaps, it's because some of Florida's best novels are about hurricanes. Zora Neale Hurston's *Their Eyes Are Watching God* climaxes in the 1928 Hurricane, the one that burst the dike on Lake Okeechobee, killing 2,500 people. Carl Hiassen's *Stormy Weather* fictionalizes Hurricane Andrew's buzz saw path through South Florida and its tragicomic aftermath for a bunch of colorful misfits.

Many will be surprised to hear that hurricanes are not an annual occurrence for most Floridians. So far in the 21st Century, hurricanes have only made landfall in Florida 9 times (Chart 60; Table 12). Large areas of Florida have not been directly hit by a hurricane in this century. Hurricanes are also not, like the red tide, a direct threat to the tourism industry because the hurricane season is usually from June to November with a peak in August and September (6 of the 9 were in those months), which is when most prospective tourists misguidedly shun Florida anyway, as hell on earth. Hurricanes can be very costly, particularly in terms of property damage. Hurricane Irma is reported to have caused estimated insured losses in Florida of $10.5 billion as of August 24, 2018 (not including flood damage and uninsured losses) and the costs are still rising (Brink, 2018). The tourism industry in the Keys was especially impacted by Irma, both in terms of the property damage incurred and the lost business (Tourism Economics, 2018).

Since Hurricane Irma was a monster storm that ripped right up the state, it also forced the largest evacuation in Florida history with around 7 million leaving, a couple of millions of whom, me included, were under mandatory evacuation orders (Kimberly Miller, 2018). Hurricane Irma also directly took 11 lives, most of which were in Florida and in total caused 123 fatalities indirectly as well as directly (Issa et al, 2018).

Chart 60: Florida Hurricanes, 2000-2017

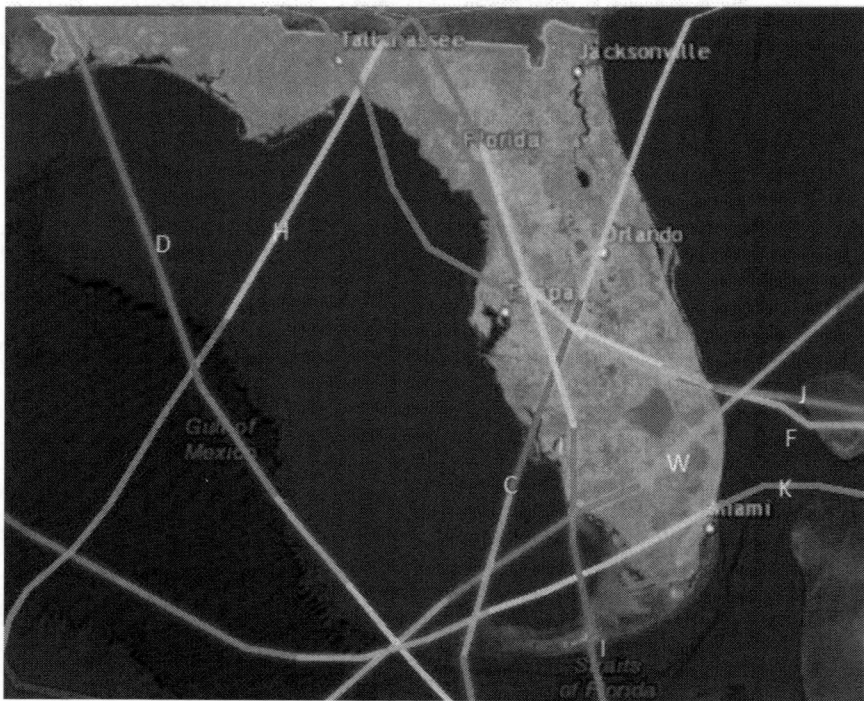

Notes: Map codes are given on Table 12. The letters next to the paths are the first letters of the hurricane's names shown in Table 12. Hurricanes weaken in category after landfall the longer they are over land, as they draw their energy from the water's heat.
Source: National Oceanographic and Atmospheric Administration, 2018.

Floridians are used to coping with hurricanes. We consider them to be an unavoidable cost of living in a semitropical paradise. If the hurricanes continue as in the past, we will be able to survive and prosper. Building codes are tighter and construction is more hurricane proof than ever. Emergency procedures are in place to ensure everybody stays safe and to assist those in need. These procedures have been tested and worked well. However, complaisance is the enemy of safety. There is a risk that many will not observe mandatory evacuation orders in the future. On the other hand, problems are also created if people evacuate who don't need to go and who can safely shelter in place. Much unnecessary congestion is created on the evacuation routes and fuel shortages and long lines at service stations can occur. This poses an impediment for those who really need to get out.

There is also a risk that global warming will contribute to larger and more frequent hurricanes. That ratchets the challenges posed by hurricanes up an order of magnitude.

Table 12: Florida Hurricanes, 2000-2017

Name	Map Code	Dates	Category at Florida Landfall
Charley	C	August 9-15, 2004	4
Frances	F	Aug. 25 to Sept. 10, 2004	2
Jeanne	J	September 13-29, 2004	3
Dennis	D	July 4-18, 2005	3
Katrina	K	August 23-31, 2005	1
Wilma	W	October 15-26, 2005	3
Hermine	H	Aug. 28 to Sept. 8, 2016	2
Irma	I	Aug. 30 to Sep. 13, 2017	4
Michael		October 7-16, 2018	4

Note: Michael is not on Chart 60 but it made landfall in Mexico Beach in the Panhandle as a category 4.

Source: National Oceanographic and Atmospheric Administration, 2018.

Managing the Environmental Challenges

The environmental problems that threaten the Florida Dream should be manageable if growth does not continue as strongly as in the past, raising population past the absorptive capacity of the state. Given that the baby boomers are the biggest group of retirees, the smaller groups coming up behind them should be able to take their place without adding excessively to the population. On the other hand, immigration cannot continue forever without putting unsustainable pressure on resources, particularly in Southeast Florida, which is squeezed between the Atlantic Ocean and the Everglades.

Floridians voted overwhelmingly in the November 2018 election in favor of Amendment 9 that embeds the state's ban on offshore oil and gas drilling as an amendment to the state constitution (which, anomalously and questionably from a constitutional point of view, also added vaping to the prohibition on indoor smoking). This constitutionally enshrined ban puts in place an additional political hurdle to any efforts to authorize off-shore drilling, which may be made by the Federal Government as part of the Trump Administration's proposed five-year offshore drilling plan. As an economy based on tourism, Florida cannot afford the risk of a Deepwater Horizon disaster off our shores.

The Everglades is a national treasure that must be preserved for future generations. The bordering coastal mangrove forests and the interior strands of sawgrass, making up the Seminole's Pa-hay-okee or Marjorie Stoneman Douglas's

"River of Grass," are precious. Together they comprise a wild and savagely beautiful, eco-system where alligators bask, ospreys soar, and wading birds feed in the shallow water.

Development has restricted the Everglade's natural water flow, gradually almost strangling it. The CERP promises to restore a larger flow, hopefully before it is too late, and to produce needed freshwater resources for Southeast Florida. It's costly and will take a long time, but it can work if we seriously and expeditiously pursue it as we must.

The "River of Grass" near the Shark Valley Observation Tower.

27
RED OR BLUE DREAMS?

Political junkies who've gotten this far will be pleased to see that I've not forgotten the Sunshine State's sphinxlike politics. Whether Florida will end up in the red column or the blue is the question that preoccupies, indeed obsesses, the American media every two years. Since 1964, Florida has voted for the winning side in every presidential election but one (1992 when Florida voters went for the posthumously canonized George H. W. Bush against Bill Clinton). The 2000 electoral battle between George W. Bush and Al Gore came down to a legal catfight before the Florida Supreme Court, which was settled amidst heated arguments about hanging-chads, with an unbelievably scant margin of only 537 votes out of a total of almost 6 million. Equally significant was the victory of Donald J. Trump in 2016 which pushed him over the top, transforming Mar-a-Lago in Palm Beach into the Florida White House, thrusting Florida ever more prominently into the national political spotlight.

The political weight of Florida in the Congress and Electoral College has been growing with every census, unlike the other increasingly blue mega-states of California and New York. California hasn't gotten any more electoral votes since 2003 and New York hasn't picked up any since Harry Truman. Only the red mega-state of Texas, which is growing fast, largely because of Mexican and Central American immigration, is also racking up more electoral votes.

There are offsetting factors at work here that make predicting future outcomes a mug's game. The support of the Republican Party has been waning in the Cuban community as the old anti-Castro hard-liners pass on and the younger community comes to reflect more traditional Hispanic and youth voting preferences for Democrats. In addition, there is the ever-growing Hispanic Ola from Latin America, including Mexico and our own territory, Puerto Rico, that is also swelling the ranks of the Democrats. African-Americans will continue to vote solidly Democrat. On the other hand, the wave of retirees moving into Florida are disproportionately Republican. And white voters, particularly in rural areas, are increasingly voting as a block as they do in many of the other Southern States and as is traditionally done by other ethnic groups.

As Fox commentator Chris Stirewalt so colorfully put it, "Florida is the biggest alligator in the swing state swamp." The 2018 mid-term election bore this out with a vengeance. Republicans kept possession of the Governor's mansion with Ron DeSantis's narrow victory over Andrew Gillum, and Rick Scott, the outgoing two-term Republican Governor, beat Bill Nelson, the incumbent three-term Senator, by an even narrower margin. However, all was not red in Florida. A Democrat Nicole "Nikki" Fried, was elected to statewide office as the Commissioner of Agriculture and Consumer Affairs. The Democrats also garnered a few seats in the U.S. House of Representative and in the Florida State House and Senate elections. But the state government does still remain firmly in Republican hands.

A Geographic Breakdown of Florida Voting Patterns by Party

A good indicator of the current party line breakdown of the vote in Florida for a year, in which there are no Presidents like Trump or Obama heading up the ticket, is provided by the 2018 Senate race between Republican Governor Rick Scott and Democratic Senator Bill Nelson. It took two weeks after the polls closed finally to declare Rick Scott the winner. The election was hard fought and very close, right down till the last vote was recounted in a mandatory hand recount under the not-so-watchful eye of Broward County Supervisor of Elections, Brenda Snipe. This contest is profiled here as a good indicator of the voting preferences of Floridians because it is the one that elicited the greatest number of votes, more than even those cast in the gubernatorial race.

The total number of votes for U.S. Senator in Florida was 8,190,005. The votes broke 4,099,505 or 50.1 per cent for Rick Scott (R) and 4,089,472 or 49.9 per cent for Bill Nelson (D), with a few hundred votes going to five write-in candidates. This gave Republican Scott a margin of victory of only 10,033 votes.

The Democratic strength in the Senatorial contest was concentrated in: Southeast Florida in Miami-Dade and Broward Counties; in Orange County and the surrounding counties of Osceola and Seminole in Central Florida around Orlando; in Alachua County in the north central part of the state where Gainesville, the home of the University of Florida Gators, is located; and in Leon County the site of our capital Tallahassee; and in neighboring Gadsden County (Chart 61). The Democrats also had more votes in Hillsborough and Pinellas counties on the Gulf Coast where the Tampa-St. Petersburg metropolitan area is found, and managed to squeak by in the Northeast in Duval County, whose county seat is Jacksonville.

The Republican support was everywhere else in smaller cities, towns and suburbs, and especially in rural areas. In many of the rural counties, the Republican margin of victory was over 50 per cent, reaching a high of 75 per cent in Holmes County. The highest margin the Democrats had was 38 per cent in Broward County, the domain of the controversial and now nationally famous Supervisor of Elections, Brenda Snipes.

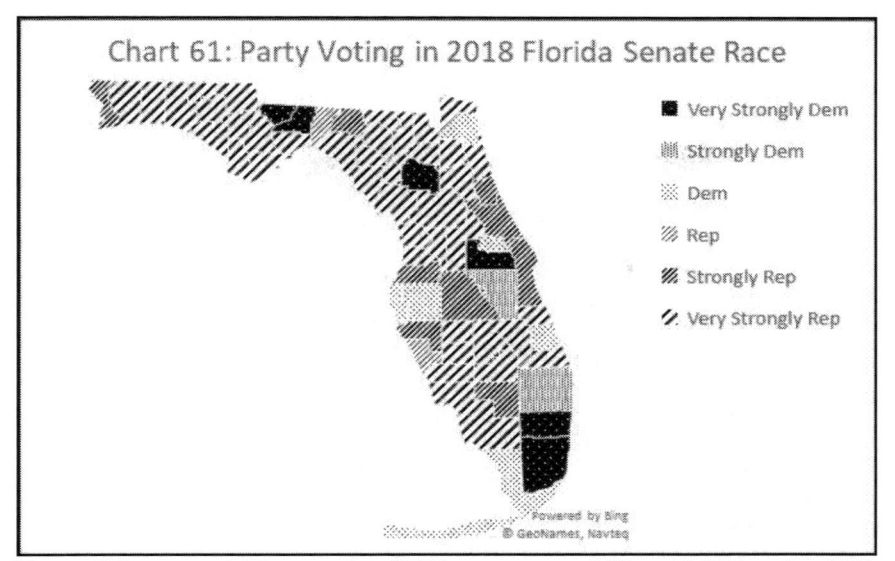

Chart 61: Party Voting in 2018 Florida Senate Race

Legend:
- Very Strongly Dem
- Strongly Dem
- Dem
- Rep
- Strongly Rep
- Very Strongly Rep

Notes: "Very strongly" is a margin of 20% or greater, and "Strongly" is less than 20%, but 10% or more. For less than 10% the winning party is shown as "Dem" or "Rep."
Source: Florida Department of State, Division of Elections, 2018.

Republicans Win State-Wide Races Except for One

Florida has a political system under its 1968 Constitution whereby the Governor and other members of the Florida Cabinet are elected by statewide voting. The Lieutenant Governor runs with the Governor as a ticket. But the Attorney General, the Chief Financial Officer, and Commissioner of Agriculture and Consumer Relations are all on the ballot separately. This unique Cabinet System of Government was first implemented under the 1885 State Constitution, which was enacted following the end of Reconstruction after the Civil War. Under it, there were six separately elected members: the Secretary of State; the Attorney General; the Comptroller; the Treasurer; the Superintendent of Public Instruction; and the Commissioner of Agriculture. An independently elected Cabinet was established to counter the centralization of power in the Governor's Office during Reconstruction by putting governmental power in the hands of six other elected officers not beholden to the Governor for their jobs. (Benton, 2008, pp.196-97). The number of statewide officers was reduced in the 1968 Constitution, and a series of activist governors, particularly Jeb Bush, who took office in 1999, succeeded in making the Governor's Office a much more powerful and dominant force in the machinery of state government (Corrigan, 2018).

The Gubernatorial race was the most important state-wide political race. It pitted Ron DeSantis, a lawyer, war-veteran, and three -term Freedom Caucus Congressman from Palm Coast, against Andrew Gillum, the young charismatic African-American mayor of Tallahassee. Ideologically, the two were poles apart with DeSantis a conservative and Tea Partyer and Gillum a champion of the progressive wing of the Democratic Party. DeSantis got lots of support from President Trump who came to Florida to rally the base for both him and Rick Scott, twice in the last week of the election (Mahoney, 2018). Gillum also brought in his big gun, President Obama, to rev up his supporters for the final push. All around, it was a high-profile campaign. A criminal investigation of municipal corruption in Tallahassee looked like it might damage Gillum's campaign, but never did much harm (Mower and Smiley, 2018). DeSantis chose Jeanette Nuñez, a Cuban-American Florida House member as his running mate. Gillum picked Chris King, an Orlando businessman and self-described "Christian progressive" to round out his ticket and to appeal to more conservative elements in his party.

The election was close, but DeSantis/Nuñez managed to squeeze out a victory with a narrow margin of 32,463 votes after a machine recount. This was just large enough not to require a hand recount under Florida election law. DeSantis/Nuñez received 4,076,186 votes or 49.6 per cent of the total; Gillum/King got 4,043,723 or 49.2 per cent.

Republican Ashley Moody, a respected former Florida Circuit Judge, beat Democrat attorney Sean Shaw by a larger margin of 52.1 per cent to 46.1 to become Florida's new Attorney General, replacing outgoing term-limited Attorney General, Pam Bondi.

Republican incumbent Jimmy Patronis retained his position as Chief Financial Officer over Democratic challenger Jeremy Ring by a margin of 51.7 per cent to 48.3 per cent.

The only statewide office won by the Democrats was the Commissioner of Agriculture and Consumer Affairs, which was taken by Nicole "Nikki" Fried, by a razor thin margin of 6,753 votes. Not an overwhelming victory for the Democrats, but a victory, nevertheless.

In the 2018 mid-term elections, the Republicans, thus, won all the state-wide offices except for the Commissioner of Agriculture and Consumer Affairs, preserving their dominance, if not total control, of the administrative side of the state government of Florida. This contrasts sharply with the outcome in two of the other mega-states. While Florida is a little purple, California is pure blue with no Republican statewide office holders, and Texas is solid red with no Democrats.

The Democrats Pick Up Seats in the Congress and State Legislature

The attrition of Republican seats in the U.S. House of Representatives, the State House and the State Senate persisted in the 2018 mid-term election. The Democrats gained 2 seats in the House of Representatives and the Republicans lost 2, which was broadly in line with the national trend that saw control of the House of Representatives pass to the Democrats. The Republicans lost 5 seats in the State House, and 2 in the State Senate, with the Democrats picking up the loss, but still the Republicans managed to retain control of both Houses of the State Legislature.

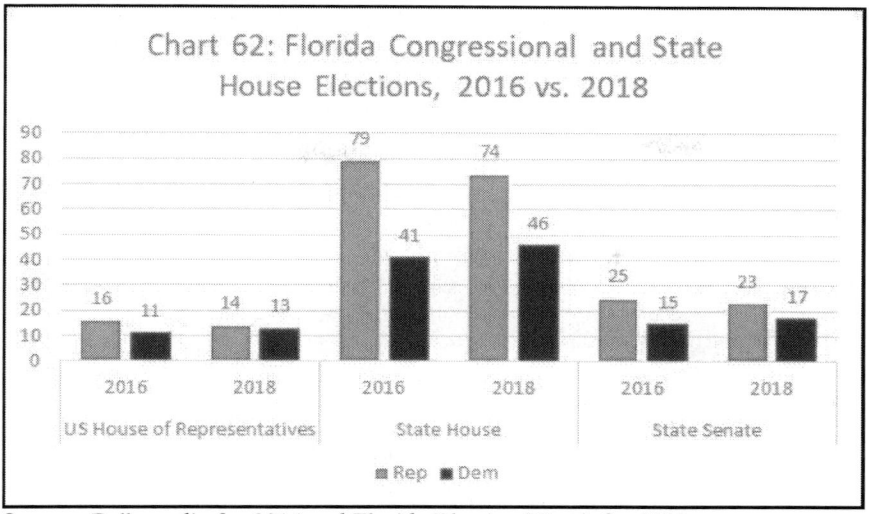

Chart 62: Florida Congressional and State House Elections, 2016 vs. 2018

Office	2016 Rep	2016 Dem	2018 Rep	2018 Dem
US House of Representatives	16	11	14	13
State House	79	41	74	46
State Senate	25	15	23	17

Source: Ballotpedia for 2016 and Florida Election Watch for 2018.

Wither Goeth Florida?

This is the $64,000 question for media pundits. While the Republicans clearly came out on top in the 2018 mid-term elections, winning the Governorship, the U.S. Senate seat, all but one statewide office, and retaining control of the state legislature, their margins were slim for statewide offices and they dropped seats in the U.S. House, and in both houses of the state legislature.

Exit polls of the gubernatorial race in Florida show that Republicans did less well among women, younger people (under 44 years old), minorities, and upper income (above $100,000) (CNN, 2018). On the other hand, they did better with whites, married people, evangelicals, and gun owners. While Democrats had a 54/46 margin among Hispanics in Florida, this was much less favorable than their national margin of 69/29 from the same survey for the U.S. House (CNN, 2018; Tyson, 2018). This reflects the unique make-up of Florida's Hispanic population where many Cuban-Americans, particularly older ones, have a long tradition of voting Republican. While the African-American vote went overwhelmingly Democratic, as always, a surprising result of the exit poll is that Andrew Gillum, the African-American candidate for Governor, who polled an 86/14 margin among African-Americans, polled behind the 90/9 national average margin for Democratic House of Representative candidates and behind the 90/10 advantage that Democratic Senator Nelson received in the losing race for his own Florida U.S. Senate seat. Ironically, Gillum's less impressive showing among African-Americans, particularly women, may have made the difference between victory and defeat (Parker, 2018).

Given the party preferences revealed by the exit poll, and the likely continuing rise of younger Hispanic voters, the attrition of Republican officeholders is likely to grind on. But the continuation of this trend is not certain. Republicans still have an opportunity to deliver the good government they have promised and stave off the Democrats for a while longer. Success at the national level is obviously important, as

President Trump played a big role in pushing the Republicans over the top in the state's Gubernatorial and Senatorial contests. But success at the state level in delivering the economic and environmental policies necessary to keep the state's economy on track may be more critical given that the state often marches to its own drummer.

Another factor that people don't consider is the extent to which retirees push Florida in a more conservative direction than their numbers suggest. According the Department of Elder Affairs, there were 4,163,882 elderly (age 60 and above) registered voters in Florida representing 34.4 per cent of all voters. Not only that, elderly voters, with more time on their hands, and perhaps an old-fashioned sense of civic responsibility, are more likely to turn out than younger, particularly minority voters.

A red herring that has been thrown into the mix is the passage in the 2018 election of Amendment No. 4, which restores voting rights to 1.5 million convicted felons. This sounds like a lot of additional votes that could swing elections one way or the other. However, two political scientists, one a professor at the University of Pennsylvania, and the other a graduate student at Yale and Harvard, carried out an interesting analysis based on a previous similar episode in 2007 when then-Governor Charlie Christ restored voting rights to 150,000 ex-felons. They found some important facts about the voting behavior of this group that they used to estimate the impact of Amendment No. 4. First, contrary to the heartfelt belief of many Republicans, ex-felons do not all vote Democratic, but instead have differing political party preferences just like everyone else. While 87 per cent of the blacks registered as Democrats, they account for only a quarter of the ex-felons likely to benefit from Amendment No. 4. In contrast, 40 per cent of non-blacks, who account for the remaining three-quarters of ex-felons, registered as Republican, and only 34 per cent as Democrat. Second, the ex-felons in the previous group whose voting rights were restored had extremely low participation rates. Only 16 per cent of black ex-felons and 12 percent of non-blacks voted. (Is it so surprising that the civic virtue of political participation is weaker among ex-felons?) Applying all these ratios to the 1.5 million convicted felons who would have their voting rights restored under the Amendment, the estimate was that it could generate another 48,000 net votes for the Democrats, a significant, but not overwhelming, increase (Meredith and Morse, 2018). On the other hand, this would have been enough to tip the big races for Senator and Governor that went Republican (Lopez, 2018), and likewise for all the other statewide races with narrow Republican margins. However, the key factor in the analysis is the voter participation rate. For example, if the participation rate of white ex-felons turned out to be higher than black, the results would be quite different given that they tend to vote Republican.

For the present, though, Florida is a red state trending blue. Whether or not this will continue depends very much on unpredictable future developments. And even if it does go blue, it will be more of a purply shade of blue given the preferences of Floridians, even Democrats, for more limited government than in states like California and New York, and given the constitutional restrictions on taxation, including the prohibition of an income and estate tax.

28
THE FLORIDA DREAM LIVES ON

Florida Dreams will continue to inspire Americans from other states and immigrants from abroad to come to Florida in droves seeking a new and better life for themselves in America's only subtropical haven. They will come, rich and poor, and will live in condos, apartments, mobile homes, and houses, ranging from modest to luxurious, in cities, small towns, out in the country, with plenty of palm trees, and maybe even near the beach or next to swamps filled with alligators. And other Americans and people from all over the world will come to visit and to share their enjoyment of Florida's climate and many amazing attractions, not the least of which is our diverse and friendly population. This should keep our most important industry, tourism, going full tilt.

The Sunshine Mega-State has the people, the warm sunshine, the economic climate, the social capital, the infrastructure, the resources, and the ideas necessary to continue to grow and prosper.

Florida will keep on attracting people from other states for as long as its taxes remain low (no income and estate taxes) and it has good jobs to offer those wanting them. A business-friendly economic climate is key. And a right-to-work law, enshrined in the state constitution, will ensure the labor market remains flexible and open to new job seekers. If Florida wants to remain a rising mega-state, it will have to avoid the policies that drive people out of the state like those being pursued in California and New York.

The challenge will be to accommodate all the people whose dream is to share in the richness that is Florida, while at the same time preserving our fragile environment and not destroying the thing that makes Florida such a Promised Land. The most immediate and acute problem that needs to be addressed is the red tide, which has its origins in Lake Okeechobee and spills out on both coasts poisoning our waters, killing our fish and marine life, and polluting our air and water.

There is agreement among Florida scientists that the natural flow of water out of Okeechobee into the Everglades and down into Florida Bay must be restored. This is the best way to cleanse the water of the pollutants that feed the red tide and to stem the salinization of the water supply required by the fast-growing Miami metropolitan region. It will require that some of the land now being used to cultivate sugar cane for U.S. Sugar, and Florida Crystals be utilized to facilitate the flow of water and reinvigorate the River of Grass.

Global warming is a more long-term threat. There's very little a state, even a mega-state like Florida, can do by itself to stem the trend, which is, of course, not to say that Florida and Floridians should not participate in national or global schemes that offer a reasonable hope of countering climate change. However, we have limited resources and should concentrate them on what Florida can do on its own to best deal with the looming problem. This would include taking the required steps to harden our infrastructure and housing and protect our population from more severe tropical storms and hurricanes. The difference in the emergency response and results in Florida and Puerto Rico when faced with recent hurricanes highlights the importance of preparedness and capabilities in dealing with natural disasters. Hurricane Irma did serious damage in Florida, but there was little loss of life and damage to property was manageable. Hurricane Marie, on the other hand, devastated Puerto Rico and a full recovery will be many years, if ever, and will be heavily dependent on external assistance.

A rise in the sea level is a likely consequence of global warming. This would be particularly problematic for Florida, which is the flattest state in the union and has so much low-lying coastal lands. Large cities like Miami, Tampa-St. Petersburg, and Jacksonville have large population concentrations and extremely valuable land, situated only a tad above sea level. There are already problems of flooding in heavy rains and unusually high tides. Cost-benefit analysis argues in favor of allocating substantial funding to infrastructure designed to mitigate the effects of rising sea levels. If places like New Orleans and Holland didn't build dikes and sea gates to keep out the water, they would be under water. And many coastal cities in Florida may have to do the same. Miami is already starting to raise its sea walls and to install an elaborate pumping system.

Another big challenge facing Florida is accommodating its newcomers. The two main groups that require the greatest accommodation are retirees and immigrants. Each is different and will have different problems.

Retirees will be aging. Many will be dependent on Social Security for a large share of their income. The nation will have to put Social Security on a solvent footing and make sure that the money keeps flowing. Most retirees will be dependent on Medicare to pay for their health care. Steps will have to be taken to control soaring healthcare costs and to ensure that the elderly retain the needed access. Both Social Security and Medicare will require nation-wide solutions, which are well beyond the scope of the state government. The elderly will also require many additional services like assisted living and long-term care as they become unable to care for themselves. With the largest elderly population in the country, Florida will have to pioneer new approaches.

Immigrants, largely from Latin America and the Caribbean, will have to be integrated into the Florida economy. They bring the Spanish language with them. It is a global language spoken by over 500 million people throughout Latin American and Europe. Unlike the tongues of earlier generations of immigrants, it will not disappear in a generation or two. The critical mass of Spanish speakers will transform Florida into a bilingual state where people can dream in two languages and will create closer economic and social ties with Latin America. It will also give rise to social tensions in

Florida, but people should be able to work out their differences. Many immigrants will begin their work lives in Florida in low-skilled jobs, but they will be able to move on up to higher-paid jobs as they gain experience and acquire more education, following the example of Cuban-Americans who have been so successful. Poor English language skills will be less of a barrier to economic success as Spanish becomes more widespread.

While Florida builds on its status as a retirement Mecca, it cannot afford to ignore the young who still represent the state's future. Even though the Florida educational system is already pretty good, we will still have to strive to remedy its deficiencies and to provide the best education in the world to our students, so they are prepared to compete in the global information economy.

Will the Florida Dreams be red or blue? Obviously, some will be one, some the other, and some neither or indifferent. The retirees, being elderly, will lean towards the red and the Hispanic immigrants to the blue. Cuban-Americans who were red are becoming bluer. African Americans will remain very blue. Identity politics may intensify block voting. All of this means that, at least through the next few electoral cycles, Florida should keep pundits up guessing on election nights.

If Floridians can dream, they can also rely on their imagination and creativity to overcome the bumps and even blockages on the road to the future. Florida Dreams are made up of a mix of Old and New Florida. The biggest challenge of all will be to preserve what is best of Old Florida, while building a New Florida, that is dynamic, modern and prosperous – the number one Mega-State, not necessarily in size, but for the quality of its life and its innovativeness.

Long live the Florida Dream!
© Joeybear | Dreamstime.com

Postscript
"DREAMS" AS A MOTIVATING FORCE IN ECONOMICS

"Dreams" is not a technical term commonly used by economists. So, in the interest of protecting my professional reputation, a word or two of explanation might be prudent. Neoclassical static microeconomics was built on an elaborate theoretical framework that required economic agents to make economic choices based on mathematical optimization. Individuals were assumed to have consistent preferences and maximize their utility given their resource constraints and prices, and entrepreneurs were assumed to maximize profits given their production functions and the prices they face in product and resource markets. Perfect competition was also assumed, which means that there were large numbers of independent economic actors and that no one of them was large enough to influence prices.

While the static neoclassical model has not yet been overturned in academia, it has been challenged on several fronts. Theories of imperfect and monopolistic competition were developed and awkwardly and incompletely incorporated in microeconomic decision-making (Chamberlin, 1933; Robinson, 1933). During the Great Depression, John Maynard Keynes emphasized "animal spirits" as the driving factor behind business investment (Keynes, 1936). More recently, psychologists like Amos Tversky and Daniel Kahneman have applied a cognitive approach to economic decision-making under risk and uncertainty that spawned a new field of economics called behavioral economics, which offers a more realistic view of economic decision-making than the classical rational model by allowing for psychological, social, cultural and emotional factors (Kahneman, 2011). A subfield of behavioral economics is behavioral finance, which was developed by Richard Thaler and Robert Shiller. It applies the same insights to financial markets (Thaler, 2015; Shiller, 2015).

Dreams are psychological and emotional phenomena like others studied by behavioral economists. As applied here, they refer to deeply and emotionally held aspirations for the future, not necessarily those that only occur during our sleep, which we often can't remember anyway, and which we'll leave to psychoanalysts, who have fallen into disfavor in recent years, maybe because of their dogged attachment to interpreting nighttime dreams. No one can deny that dreams defined in the broader sense used here have an important role to play in our lives and often provide the overriding visions that shape our economic decisions even if they've never been systematically studied by social scientists.

The economic decisions that can be covered by the dream paradigm are not the little ones like buying one or two cups of coffee or even choosing between Starbucks and Dunkin' Donut, but the big important ones like those make-or-break life decisions of marriage, family, location and migration, education and career choice, and the establishment and expansion of firms. Entrepreneurs like Henry Flagler, Henry Plant, Barron Collier, Carl Fisher, Walt Disney, Harold Schwartz, Ted Arison and Chief Jim Billies were all following their dreams as they developed modern-day Florida. If they had only made cold, hard-headed rational decisions, they'd have accomplished much less, and I probably wouldn't be writing about them now. The same could be said for the many migrants and immigrants, snowbirds and tourists, who came to Florida and who made their contributions on a smaller, but still important scale.

In this work, "dreams" is not used as a scientific economic term. Rather, for the present, let's just say it's a metaphor for the deep-seated desires and ambitions that drive us all to do great things for mankind, our country, our state, our towns, our families, and even ourselves. But who knows? Someday "dreams" could even become a subject for study in behavioral economics. If it does, remember you heard it here first.

BIBLIOGRAPHY

Note: The websites referenced were all accessed in the first week of December 2018. If any of the hyperlinks to the references in the text get broken, you can usually find the reference by Googling it without the "url". This will show the new correct "url" unless the material has been taken down, and not just moved. The easiest way to follow the "urls" in this book is to use the Kindle version where they are all "hot."

Ahrens, D., J. M. Beman, J. A. Harrison, P. K. Jewett and P. A. Matson. "A synthesis of nitrogen transformations and transfers from land to the sea in the Yaqui Valley agricultural region of northwest Mexico." *Water Resources Journal.* Vol. 44. 2008.
<https://agupubs.onlinelibrary.wiley.com/doi/full/10.1029/2007WR006661>

Airbnb. "The U.S. Midwest, Ryokans and Brazilian Beaches: Airbnb's 2018 Travel Trends." December 17, 2017. <https://press.airbnb.com/the-u-s-midwest-ryokans-and-brazilian-beaches-airbnbs-2018-travel-trends/>

Aisch, Gregor, Robert Gebeloff and Kevin Quealy. "Where We Came From and Where We Went, State by State." *New York Times.* UPDATED August 19, 2014.
<https://www.nytimes.com/interactive/2014/08/13/upshot/where-people-in-each-state-were-born.html>

Alvarado, Francisco. "1981: Miami's Deadliest Summer." *Miami New Times.* August 10, 2011. <https://www.miaminewtimes.com/news/1981-miamis-deadliest-summer-6565290>

Baker Tilley. "Dual state residency can result in dual taxation." April 28, 2011.
<https://www.bakertilly.com/insights/dual-state-residency-can-result-in-dual-taxation/>

Ballotpedia. "State Credit Ratings." 2018.
<https://ballotpedia.org/State_credit_ratings>

Baucum, L. E. and R. W. Rice. "An Overview of Florida Sugarcane." University of Florida IFAS Extension. Revised August 2009.
<http://ufdc.ufl.edu/IR00003414/00001>

Beckett, Samantha. "Florida Seminole Casinos Generating Massive Revenues for Tribe." August 9, 2017. <https://www.casino.org/news/florida-seminole-casinos-generating-massive-revenues-for-tribe>

Becnel, Thomas. "Top 10 reasons you should salute Freedom Swim across Peace River." *Herald-Tribune.* July 3, 2013.
<http://ticket.heraldtribune.com/2013/07/03/here-are-the-top-10-reasons-to-salute-annual-freedom-swim-across-peace-river/>

Benton, J. Edwin (ed.). *Government and Politics in Florida,* 3rd Edition. Gainesville. 2008. <https://www.amazon.com/Government-Politics-Florida-Edwin-Benton/dp/0813031702/ref=sr_1_1?s=books&ie=UTF8&qid=1544791974&sr=1-1&keywords=j+edwin+benton>

Blechman, Andrew. *Leisureville: Adventures in America's Retirement Utopias.* New York: Atlantic Monthly Press. 2008. <https://www.amazon.com/Leisureville-Adventures-World-Without-Children/dp/0802144187/ref=sr_1_1?s=books&ie=UTF8&qid=1544792036&sr=1-1&keywords=andrew+blechman>

Bloom, Jane. "Did you get the Safe Sex memo?" VillagesNews.com. June 4, 2014.
<https://www.villages-news.com/get-safe-sex-memo/>

Bodenner, Chris. "The Science Behind Florida's Sinkhole Epidemic Reports of these ground-chasms have been swelling in the past few years. Geology helps explain why." Smithsonian.com. May 2018.
<https://www.smithsonianmag.com/science-nature/science-behind-floridas-sinkhole-epidemic-180969158/>

Bonogofsky, Alexis. "'This State Is on the Front Lines': Floridians Mobilize Against Sabal Trail Natural Gas Pipeline." Truthout. June 8, 2017.
<https://truthout.org/articles/water-protectors-rise-up-to-stop-florida-s-sabal-trail-pipeline/>

Borjas, George J. "The Wage Impact of the Marielitos: a Reappraisal." *Industrial and Labor Relations Review.* Vol. 70, No. 5. October 2017.
<https://sites.hks.harvard.edu/fs/gborjas/publications/journal/ILRR2017.pdf>

Brand, Larry E. and Angela Compton. "Long-term increase in Karenia brevis abundance along the Southwest Florida Coast." *Harmful Algae.* 6(2). 2007.

<https://www.ncbi.nlm.nih.gov/pmc/articles/PMC2330169/>

Brand, Larry E, Lisa Campbell and Eileen Bresnan. "Karenia: The biology and ecology of a toxic genus." *Harmful Algae*. Vol. 14. February 2012. <https://www.sciencedirect.com/science/article/pii/S156898831100148X?via%3Dihub>

BREA Business Research & Economic Advisors. "The Contribution of the International Cruise Industry to the U.S Economy in 2016." Prepared for Cruise Lines International Association. August 2017. <https://cruising.org/news-and-research/research/2018/december/the-global-economic-contribution-of-cruise-tourism-2017>

Breakstone, Noah. "As economy expands, housing market struggles to recover." *Miami Herald*. September 14, 2018. <https://www.miamiherald.com/latest-news/article218774970.html>

Brink, Graham. "Hurricane Irma's price tag in Florida passes $10 billion." *Tampa Bay Times*. August 24, 2018. <https://www.tampabay.com/news/business/Hurricane-Irma-s-price-tag-in-Florida-passes-10-billion_171176633>

Brown, Chris. "Russian space program in 'crisis' as David Saint-Jacques set to blast off." CBC News. November 28, 2018. <https://www.cbc.ca/news/world/russian-space-program-in-crisis-as-david-saint-jacques-set-to-blast-off-1.4922114>

Brown, Helen. "The Palm Beach Season." The Helen Brown Group. December 17, 2017. <https://www.helenbrowngroup.com/the-palm-beach-season/>

Browning, Lynnley and Gillian Tan. "Fund Managers Are Ditching Wall Street for Florida." Bloomberg. June 4, 2018. <https://www.bloomberg.com/news/articles/2018-06-04/florida-nabs-money-managers-as-property-tax-cap-boosts-its-pitch>

BullSugar.org. "Scientists Grade the Everglades Reservoir Plan: F" 2018. <https://www.bullsugar.org/eaa_reservoir_plan_fails_evaluation>

Bunch, T. Jared. "The Heart Health Benefits of Going South for the Winter." Everyday Health. Accessed November 5, 2018. <https://www.everydayhealth.com/columns/jared-bunch-rhythm-of-life/the-heart-health-benefits-of-going-south-for-the-winter/>

Burns, Robert. "Trump space force - a real need but hazy planning." *Miami Herald*. October 22, 2018. <https://www.miamiherald.com/news/business/article220426125.html>

Burnson, Patrick. "Top 30 U.S. Ports 2017: Preparing for the uncertain." *Logistics*

Management. May 7, 2017.
<https://www.logisticsmgmt.com/article/top_30_u.s._ports_2017_preparing_for_the_uncertain>

Business Development Board (BDB) of Palm Beach County. "Financial Services and Hedge Funds." 2018. <https://www.bdb.org/targeted-industries/financial-services-and-hedge-funds/>

Buss, Dale. "Best And Worst States For Business In 2018." *Chief Executive.* May 3, 2018. <https://chiefexecutive.net/best-worst-states-business-2018/>

Buss, Dale. "Five States To Watch: Texas, Florida, Indiana, Colorado And Alabama." *Chief Executive.* May 2, 2018. <https://chiefexecutive.net/5-states-to-watch-texas-florida-indiana-colorado-and-alabama/>

Campbell, Elizabeth. "Jacksonville education poll: Teachers should be paid more: Most residents say education 2nd most important issue, after crime." News4Jax. January 19, 2018. <https://www.news4jax.com/education/jacksonville-education-poll-teachers-should-be-paid-more>

Cannon, Jeff. "The Florida Tuberculosis Sanatorium: Located in the northeastern community of Trilby, the Florida Tuberculosis Sanatorium is believed to be the first TB sanatorium in Florida." *New Port Richey Patch.* April 21, 2012. <https://patch.com/florida/newportrichey/the-florida-tuberculosis-sanatorium>

Card, David. "The Impact of the Mariel Boatlift on the Miami Labor Market." *Industrial and Labor Relations Review.* Vol. 43, No. 2. January 1990. <http://davidcard.berkeley.edu/papers/mariel-impact.pdf>

Caraway, Rose. "Post-embargo Cuba: Economic Implications and the Future of Socialism." The University of Texas at Austin, Teresa Lozano Long Institute of Latin American Studies. December 2003.
<http://lanic.utexas.edu/project/etext/llilas/ilassa/2004/caraway.pdf>

Carloni, Brittany. "As red tide lingers in the Gulf, Southwest Florida fishing captains try to save their livelihoods." *Naples Daily News.* August 1, 2018. <https://www.naplesnews.com/story/news/local/communities/the-banner/2018/08/01/red-tide-hurting-fishing-tour-companies-swfl-captains-say/873463002/>

Carroll, Paul. Big Blues: *The Unmaking of IBM.* Three Rivers Press: 1994. <https://www.amazon.com/Big-Blues-Unmaking-Paul-Carroll/dp/0517882213>

Carruth, Erika. "Top Florida Residential Builders – December 2017." HBWeekly. January 12, 2018. <http://blog.hbweekly.com/top-florida-residential-builders-december-2017/>

Carter, Phillip M. "This is why Spanish won't sideline English in the U.S. — not even in Miami." Market Watch. January 28, 2018. <https://www.marketwatch.com/story/this-is-why-spanish-wont-sideline-english-in-the-us-2018-01-25>

Castaldo, Joe. "Intrigue at Sloan's Curve: A dispute between a Toronto businessman and a comic-book mogul escalated into allegations of hate mail, extortion and DNA theft. And it all started with tennis courts." *Maclean's*. August 28, 2017. <https://www.macleans.ca/intrigue-at-sloans-curve/>

Chamberlin, Edward. *The Theory of Monopolistic Competition*. Cambridge: Harvard University Press. 1933. <https://www.amazon.com/Theory-Monopolistic-Competition-Re-orientation-Eighth/dp/B0007H0A38/ref=sr_1_1?s=books&ie=UTF8&qid=1544792223&sr=1-1&keywords=edward+chamberlin+monopolistic+competition>

Chenevert, Rebecca, Alfred Gottschalck, Mark Klee, and Xingyou Zhang. "Where the Wealth Is: The Geographic Distribution of Wealth in the United States." Social, Economic and Housing Statistics Division, U.S. Census Bureau. 2017. < https://www.census.gov/content/dam/Census/library/working-papers/2017/demo/FY2016-129.pdf>

Chevreau, Jonathan. " Snowbird? Learn the 'substantial presence' test: Learn the tax pitfalls of retiring to the sun in the U.S." *MoneySense*. Jun 30, 2017. < https://www.moneysense.ca/spend/real-estate/tax-pitfalls-canadian-snowbirds-to-the-u-s-need-to-know/>

Cision PR Newswire. "The 55 Best 55+ Communities in America for 2015." January 20, 2015. <https://www.prnewswire.com/news-releases/the-55-best-55-communities-in-america-for-2015-300022954.html>

Clark, James C. *A Concise History of Florida*. Charleston, SC: The History Press, 2014. <https://www.amazon.com/Concise-History-Florida-Brief-ebook/dp/B00XRUEH7M/ref=sr_1_5?s=books&ie=UTF8&qid=1544792286&sr=1-5&keywords=james+clark+florida>

Clemens, Michael. "What the Mariel Boatlift of Cuban Refugees Can Teach Us about the Economics of Immigration: An Explainer and a Revelation." Center for Global Development. May 22, 2017. <https://www.cgdev.org/blog/what-mariel-boatlift-cuban-refugees-can-teach-us-about-economics-immigration>

Clough, Alexandra. "Crocker Partners pays $170 million for former IBM campus in Boca Raton." *The Palm Beach Post*. April 10, 2018. <https://www.palmbeachpost.com/business/crocker-partners-pays-170-million-for-former-ibm-campus-boca-raton/EWx4oSnnrz68i7LopGhuUO/>

Clough, Alexandra. "Former IBM campus in Boca: Once tech hub, now set for housing?" *The Palm Beach Post.* November 10, 2017. <https://www.palmbeachpost.com/business/former-ibm-campus-boca-once-tech-hub-now-set-for-housing/B8jbqXcBBVqx8DHG4kkyUO/>

CNN. "Exit Polls." 2018. <https://www.cnn.com/election/2018/exit-polls/florida/governor>

Cohen, Alina. "Art Basel Miami Beach 2017: The Good, the Bad and the Biggest Sales." *Observer.* December 11, 2017. <https://observer.com/2017/12/art-basel-miami-beach-2017-review-best-worst-and-what-sold/>

Cohen, Howard. "Florida ranks No. 1 in higher education, survey says. But K-12 still lags." *Miami Herald.* March 07, 2018. <https://www.miamiherald.com/news/local/education/article204004094.html>

Cohen, Joshua. "Texas Judge Deals Obamacare A Major Blow." *Forbes.* December 13, 2018. <https://www.forbes.com/sites/joshuacohen/2018/12/16/texas-judge-deals-obamacare-a-major-blow/#5f93bd6d23e0>

Cohen, Stefanie. "Romance and STD's: Inside Florida's wild retirees getaway." *New York Post.* January 25, 2009. <https://nypost.com/2009/01/25/retire-to-the-bedroom/>

Colburn, David R and Lance Dehaven-Smith. *Government in the Sunshine State: Florida Since Statehood.* Gainesville: University Press of Florida. 1998. <https://www.amazon.com/Government-Sunshine-State-Florida-Statehood/dp/0813016525/ref=sr_1_5?s=books&ie=UTF8&qid=1544792410&sr=1-5&keywords=david+r.+colburn>

Colburn, David R. *From yellow dog Democrats to red state Republicans: Florida and its politics since 1940.* Gainesville: University Pres of Florida s. 2007. <https://www.amazon.com/Yellow-Dog-Democrats-State-Republicans-ebook/dp/B00FDX5658/ref=sr_1_1?s=books&ie=UTF8&qid=1544792370&sr=1-1&keywords=david+r.+colburn>

Colburn, David R. *Florida's Megatrends: Critical Issues in Florida.* Gainesville: University Press of Florida. 2011.<https://www.amazon.com/Floridas-Megatrends-Critical-Issues-Florida/dp/0813035198/ref=sr_1_3?s=books&ie=UTF8&qid=1544792410&sr=1-3&keywords=david+r.+colburn>

CollegeBoard. "AP Program Participation and Performance Data 2018." 2018. <https://research.collegeboard.org/programs/ap/data/participation/ap-2018>

CollegeBoard. "The College and Career Readiness Benchmarks for the SAT Suite of Assessments." 2016. <https://collegereadiness.collegeboard.org/pdf/educator-benchmark-brief.pdf>

Comarow, Avery. "The Best Hospitals 2018-19 Honor Roll: These 20 hospitals outperformed all others in U.S. News' Best Hospitals rankings." U.S. News and World Report. August 14, 2018. <https://health.usnews.com/health-care/best-hospitals/slideshows/the-honor-roll-of-best-hospitals?onepage>

Copage, Eric V. "C. D. Atkins, 86, Inventor of Orange Juice Process." *New York Times*. June 8, 2000. <https://www.nytimes.com/2000/06/08/business/c-d-atkins-86-inventor-of-orange-juice-process.html>

Cordeiro, Monivette. "Brightline changes name to Virgin Trains USA in new partnership with billionaire Richard Branson." *Orlando Weekly*. November 16, 2018. <https://www.orlandoweekly.com/Blogs/archives/2018/11/16/brightline-changes-name-to-virgin-trains-usa-in-new-partnership-with-billionaire-richard-branson>

Corrigan, Matthew T. *Conservative Hurricane: How Jeb Bush Remade Florida*. Gainesville: University Press of Florida, 2018. <https://www.amazon.com/Conservative-Hurricane-Florida-Government-Politics-ebook/dp/B00PKGLFD0/ref=sr_1_1?s=books&ie=UTF8&qid=1544792531&sr=1-1&keywords=matthew+t+corrigan>

Dahlberg, Nancy. "California hedge fund Universa moving its base to Miami." *Miami Herald*. February 19, 2014. <https://www.miamiherald.com/news/article1960533.html>

Dahlberg, Nancy. "Miami to Orlando in 26 minutes is one step closer to hyperloop reality." *Miami Herald*. September 17, 2017. <https://www.miamiherald.com/news/business/article173847151.html>

Danielson, Richard. "Brightline's combination of rail and development in Miami makes believers of Tampa leaders." *Tampa Bay Times*. August 24, 2018. <https://www.tampabay.com/news/transportation/masstransit/Brightline-s-combination-of-rail-and-development-in-Miami-makes-believers-of-Tampa-leaders_171132359>

Danielson, Richard. "Water Street Tampa plans downtown's first new office towers in decades." *Tampa Bay Times*. September 6, 2018. <https://www.tampabay.com/news/business/realestate/Water-Street-Tampa-plans-downtown-s-first-new-office-towers-in-decades_171514928>

Dargan, Michele. "Five years after Madoff: 'We've shed the tears'." *Palm Beach Daily News*. October 20, 2015. <https://www.palmbeachdailynews.com/news/local/five-years-after-madoff-shed-the-tears/aZqDMD8Sb4cdrEz03Lc3oO/>

Darrah, Nicole. "More than 450 people in Florida ordered to give up guns under new law, report says." Fox News. July 30, 2018.

<https://www.foxnews.com/us/more-than-450-people-in-florida-ordered-to-give-up-guns-under-new-law-report-says>

Das, Avik and Shilpa Phadnis. "Indian-American couple make $2 billion from sale of firm." *The Times of India.* July 24, 2018.<https://timesofindia.indiatimes.com/nri/us-canada-news/indian-american-couple-make-2-billion-from-sale-of-firm/articleshow/65110957.cms>

Daszkowski, Don. "The Biography of Red Lobster Founder Bill Darden." The Balance Small Business. May 11, 2018. <https://www.thebalancesmb.com/bill-darden-biography-1350946>

Deloitte. "US Gift and Estate Tax Rules for Resident and Non-Resident Aliens." 2016. <https://www2.deloitte.com/content/dam/Deloitte/us/Documents/Tax/us-tax-us-estate-and-gift-tax-rules-for-resident-and-nonresident-aliens.pdf>

Denslow, David and Ray Schaub. "The Net Impact of Retirees on Florida's State And Local Budgets." Bureau of Economic and Business Research, University of Florida. September 18, 2013. <https://www.bebr.ufl.edu/sites/default/files/Research%20Reports/retiree_net_impact_on_floridas_budgets_final_7-8-13.pdf>

Dewey, James and David Denlow. *Tougher Choices: Shaping Florida's Future.* Bureau of Economics and Business Research, University of Florida and Leroy Collins Institute. February 14, 2014.<http://collinsinstitute.fsu.edu/sites/default/files/Tougher%20Choices%20FINAL%202-20-14.pdf>

Doty, Rich and Suzanne Roulston-Doty. "The Aging of Florida." Bureau of Economic and Business Research, University of Florida. August 6, 2015. <https://www.bebr.ufl.edu/population/website-article/aging-florida>

Dyckman, Martin A. *Floridian of His Century: The Courage of Governor LeRoy Collins.* Gainesville: University Press of Florida. 2006. <https://www.amazon.com/Floridian-His-Century-Courage-Governor/dp/0813029694/ref=sr_1_5?s=books&ie=UTF8&qid=1544792598&sr=1-5&keywords=Martin+A+Dyckman>

Dyckman, Martin A. *Reubin O'D. Askew and the Golden Age of Florida Politics.* Gainesville: University Press of Florida. 2011. <https://www.amazon.com/Reubin-Golden-Florida-Politics-Government-ebook/dp/B00LMJCVIC/ref=sr_1_3?s=books&ie=UTF8&qid=1544792598&sr=1-3&keywords=Martin+A+Dyckman>

Economist. "Florida's snowbirds: A chilly welcome." March 8, 2014. <https://www.economist.com/united-states/2014/03/08/a-chilly-welcome>

Echeniique, Martin and Luis Melgar. "Mapping Puerto Rico's Hurricane Migration with Mobile Phone Data." CityLab.com. May 11, 2018.
<https://www.citylab.com/environment/2018/05/watch-puerto-ricos-hurricane-migration-via-mobile-phone-data/559889/>

Elfrink, Tim. "Florida Believes in Global Warming, but Only Miami Thinks It Will Be Harmful." *Miami New Times*. March 22, 2017.
<https://www.miaminewtimes.com/news/south-florida-wells-fargos-keep-getting-sued-for-racism-10917703>

Enterprise Florida. "Florida Merchandise Trade: 2017 Summary Tables." 2018.
<https://www.enterpriseflorida.com/wp-content/uploads/top-fl-trade-ranking-tables.pdf>

Erisman, Ryan. *Inside the Bubble: The Unauthorized Guide to Florida's Most Popular Community*. 2018. <https://www.insidethebubble.co/82-cool-facts-the-villages/>

Federal Reserve Board. "Structure Data for the U.S. Offices of Foreign Banking Organizations." March 31, 2018.
<https://www.federalreserve.gov/releases/iba/201709/bycntry.htm>

Florida Chamber Foundation. "A Strategic Look at Florida's Medical Tourism Opportunities." <http://www.flchamber.com/wp-content/uploads/2016/06/Research_A-Strategic-Look-at-Floridas-Medical-Tourism-Opportunities.pdf>

Florida Chamber Foundation. *Florida 2030: The Blueprint to Secure Florida's Future*. 2018. <https://www.flchamber.com/wp-content/uploads/2018/09/ES_FLChamber2030_TargetsandStrategies_Sep12.pdf>
<http://www.flchamber.com/wp-content/uploads/2018/06/ES_FLChamber2030_Mar18_9x12_reduced.pdf>

Florida Department of Agriculture and Consumer Services. "2016 Florida Agriculture by the Numbers." 2017.
<https://www.nass.usda.gov/Statistics_by_State/Florida/Publications/Annual_Statistical_Bulletin/FL_Agriculture_Book/2016/Florida_Agriculture_by_the_Numbers_Brochure_2016.pdf>

Florida Department of Education. "Student Achievement in Florida's Charter Schools: A Comparison of the Performance of Charter School Students with Traditional Public School Students." March 2017.
<http://www.fldoe.org/core/fileparse.php/7778/urlt/Charter_Student_Achievement_Report_1516.pdf>

Florida Department of Elder Affairs. "2016 Profile of Older Floridians." 2016.
<http://elderaffairs.state.fl.us/doea/pubs/stats/County_2016_projections/Counti

es/Florida.pdf>

Florida Legislative Office of Economics and Demographic Research "Florida: Long-Range Financial Outlook as Adjusted by Hurricane Irma." Updated October 12, 2017. <http://edr.state.fl.us/Content/presentations/long-range-financial-outlook/3YearPlan2017FallUpdate_Hurricane%20Irma.pdf>

Florida Museum. "Yearly Worldwide Shark Attack Summary." 2018. <https://www.floridamuseum.ufl.edu/shark-attacks/yearly-worldwide-summary/>

Florida Power & Light. "Ten Year Power Plant Site Plan 2018-2027." Submitted to Florida Public Service Commission. April 2018. <https://www.fpl.com/company/pdf/10-year-site-plan.pdf>

Florida Revenue Estimating Conference. *Florida Tax Handbook*. Tallahassee, FL. <http://edr.state.fl.us/content/revenues/reports/tax-handbook/>

Florida Tax Watch. "Buying In – An Analysis of International Homebuyers in Florida." June 2014. <https://www.floridatrend.com/public/userfiles/news/pdfs/InternationalHomes FINAL.pdf

Florida Tax Watch. "2018 How Florida Compares Taxes: State and Local Tax Rankings for Florida and the Nation." June 19, 2018. <https://floridataxwatch.org/Research/Full-Library/ArtMID/34407/ArticleID/15609/2018-How-Florida-Compares-Taxes>
Florida Trend. "Florida's 125 Biggest Public Companies Ranked by Revenue." June 28, 2017. <https://www.floridatrend.com/article/22390/floridas-125-biggest-public-companies>

Forbes, Alexander. "What Sold at Art Basel in Miami Beach." *Artsy*. December 9, 2017. <https://www.artsy.net/article/artsy-editorial-sold-art-basel-miami-beach>

Forgione, Mary. "World's busiest cruise ports are in Florida." *Los Angeles Times*. July 25, 2017. <http://www.latimes.com/travel/cruises/la-tr-cruises-worlds-busiest-cruise-ports-20170721-story.html>

Fortado, Lindsay. "Greenwich: the rich town on the frontline of US hedge fund fight." *Financial Times*. April 24, 2018. <https://www.ft.com/content/3bffaf1c-3e35-11e8-b9f9-de94fa33a81e>

Fortune. "The Fortune 500 Issue: Ranking America's Biggest Companies." June 1, 2018. <http://fortune.com/fortune500/list/>
Fox News. "Florida Mayor's Bilingual Push Hits Brick Wall." February 15, 2013. <http://www.foxnews.com/politics/2013/02/15/florida-mayor-bilingual-push-hits-brick-wall.html>

Frank, Robert. "Mar-a-Lago membership fee doubles to $200,000." CNN Inside Wealth. January 25, 2017. <https://www.cnbc.com/2017/01/25/mar-a-lago-membership-fee-doubles-to-200000.html>.

Friedlander, Joshua P. and Matthew Bass. "RIAA Mid-Year 2018: Latin Music Report." 2018. <https://www.riaa.com/wp-content/uploads/2018/10/RIAA_LatinMidYear_100918a.pdf>

Fry, Erika and Matt Heimer. "Change the World." *Fortune*. September 2018. p.67. <http://fortune.com/2018/08/20/small-companies-change-the-world/>

Gale, Kevin. "1986 Flashback: The birth of Office Depot in Lauderdale Lakes Mall." *Sun-Sentinel*. February 15, 2015. <https://www.sun-sentinel.com/sfl-1986-flashback-the-birth-of-office-depot-in-lauderdale-lakes-mall-20150205-story.html>

Garcia, Gustovo. "Why Miami is Latin America's Center of Interconnection: How American and Caribbean businesses get connected to the world." Interconnections – The Equinix Blog. May 1, 2018. <https://blog.equinix.com/blog/2018/05/01/why-miami-is-latin-americas-center-of-interconnection/>

Gardner, Eriq. "Marvel's Ike Perlmutter Sued for Allegedly Sending Court Filing to Hollywood Reporter." *Hollywood Reporter*. July 3, 2018. <https://www.hollywoodreporter.com/thr-esq/marvels-ike-perlmutter-sued-allegedly-sending-court-filing-hollywood-reporter-1124851>

Garfield, Leanna. "The largest mall in the US is coming to Miami, and it will have a massive indoor water park and ice rink." *Business Insider*. May 25, 2018. <https://www.businessinsider.com/largest-mall-us-american-dream-miami-2018-5>

Gensler, Lauren. "An Alligator Wrestler, A Casino Boss and a $12 Billion Tribe." *Forbes*. October 19, 2016. <https://www.forbes.com/sites/laurengensler/2016/10/19/seminole-tribe-florida-hard-rock-cafe/#692a58505bbc>

Gilbertson, Dawn. "Allegiant's $420M bet: Airline building its own $200-a-night hotel to upsell flyers." *USA Today*. September 25, 2018. <https://www.usatoday.com/story/travel/flights/2018/09/25/sunseeker-resort-allegiant-air-building-new-high-end-florida-property/1301222002/>

Gollom, Mark. "The trouble with Harry: Canadian businessman Harold Peerenboom is no stranger to feuds, but his latest clash is straight out of a comic book." Canadian Broadcasting Corporation. November 24, 2017. <https://www.cbc.ca/news2/interactives/sh/og1dB3kAlj/harold-peerenboom-perlmutter-marvel-florida-feud/>

Governing the States and Localities. "Military Active-Duty Personnel, Civilians by

State." 2018. < http://www.governing.com/gov-data/public-workforce-salaries/military-civilian-active-duty-employee-workforce-numbers-by-state.html>

Grady, Patrick and Andrew Muller. "On the Use and Misuse of Input-Output Based Impact Analysis in Evaluation." *Canadian Journal of Program Evaluation.* Vol. 3, No.2. October/November 1988. <http://www.global-economics.ca/input.output.multipliers.pdf>

Gray, Tom and Robert Scardamalia. "The Great California Exodus: A Closer Look." Manhattan Insitute. Civic Report Number 71. September 20, 2012. <https://www.manhattan-institute.org/pdf/cr_71.pdf>

Griffen, Justine. "Water Street Tampa unveils video showing downtown's transformation." *Tampa Bay Times.* August 23, 2017. <http://www.tampabay.com/news/business/water-street-tampa-unveils-illustrations-showing-downtowns-transformation/2334688>

Greenspan, Donna M. "Florida's Official English Amendment." *Nova Law Review.* Volume 18, Issue 2, Article 7. 1994. <https://nsuworks.nova.edu/cgi/viewcontent.cgi?referer=https://www.google.com/&httpsredir=1&article=1563&context=nlr>

Grunwald, Michael. *The Swamp: The Everglades, Florida, and the Politics of Paradise.* New York: Simon and Schuster. 2006. <https://www.amazon.com/Swamp-Everglades-Florida-Politics-Paradise-ebook/dp/B000MGATWQ/ref=sr_1_1?s=digital-text&ie=UTF8&qid=1547637577&sr=1-1&keywords=the+swamp>

Guttman, Amy. "Why Bill Gates and Jeff Vinik Are Investing Billions To Build An Ecosystem In Tampa." *Forbes.* November 8, 2016. <https://www.forbes.com/sites/amyguttman/2016/11/08/why-bill-gates-and-jeff-vinik-are-investing-billions-to-build-an-ecosystem-in-tampa/#416f52784d6d>

Haag, K.H., and Lee, T.M. "Hydrology and ecology of freshwater wetlands in central Florida—A primer." U.S. Geological Survey Circular 1342. 2010. <https://pubs.usgs.gov/circ/1342/>

Hemlock, Doreen and Kerry Close. "Brazil's Embraer flying high in the United States." *Sun Sentinel.* August 14, 2014. < http://www.sun-sentinel.com/fl-embraer-florida-profile-20140815-story.html>

Herrera, Chabeli. "How the Seminole Tribe came to rock the Hard Rock empire." *Miami Herald.* May 22, 2016. <https://www.miamiherald.com/news/business/biz-monday/article79172817.html>

Herrera, Chabeli. "With last beam in place, Hollywood Hard Rock's guitar-shaped hotel is almost finished." *Miami Herald.* July 9, 2018. <https://www.miamiherald.com/news/business/tourism-

cruises/article214567760.html>

Hobbs, Wayne. "Free Wasps to Control Citrus Greening Offered." IFAS Extension, University of Florida. August 14, 2017.
<http://blogs.ifas.ufl.edu/clayco/2017/08/14/wasps-help-greening/>

Hodges Alan W., Mohammad Rahmani, and Thomas J. Stevens. "Economic Contributions of Agriculture, Natural Resources, and Food Industries in Florida in 2013." IFAS Extension, University of Florida. FE969. August 23, 2015.
<https://fred.ifas.ufl.edu/pdf/FE969-FullReport.pdf>
Hoffower, Hillary. "Florida is one of the best places to retire in America — here's exactly how much it costs for a dream retirement in the Sunshine State." *Business Insider*. Jul. 21, 2018. <https://www.businessinsider.com/can-i-afford-retirement-in-florida-budget-breakdown-2018-7>

Hofheinz, Darrell. "Renovations at Paul Tudor Jones' estate may total $6.4 million." *Palm Beach Daily News*. May 19, 2017.
<https://www.palmbeachdailynews.com/business/real-estate/report-renovations-paul-tudor-jones-estate-may-total-million/akCB5HaiKZFdrL8AS7GpeL/>

Hollis, Tim. *Selling the Sunshine State: A Celebration of Florida Tourism Advertising*. Gainesville: University of Florida Press, 2008. <https://www.amazon.com/Selling-Sunshine-State-Celebration-Advertising/dp/0813032660/ref=sr_1_1?s=books&ie=UTF8&qid=1544792715&sr=1-1&keywords=tim+hollis+sunshine+state>

IBM. "The birth of the IBM PC." <https://www-03.ibm.com/ibm/history/exhibits/pc25/pc25_birth.html>

Insinna, Valerie. "How much will the Space Force cost, and what's it going to look like?" August 9, 2018. <https://www.defensenews.com/space/2018/08/09/no-answers-yet-on-cost-structure-of-space-force/>

Intergovernmental Panel on Climate Change (IPCC). *Global Warming of 1.5 °C*. United Nations. October 2018. <http://www.ipcc.ch/report/sr15/>

Issa A, K Ramadugu, P Mulay, et al. "Deaths Related to Hurricane Irma — Florida, Georgia, and North Carolina, September 4–October 10, 2017." Morbidity and Mortality Weekly Report. 2018.
<https://www.cdc.gov/mmwr/volumes/67/wr/mm6730a5.htm#suggestedcitation>
Kahneman, Daniel. *Thinking Fast and Slow*. New York: Farrar, Straus and Giroux. 2011. <https://www.amazon.com/Thinking-Fast-Slow-Daniel-Kahneman/dp/0374533555/ref=sr_1_1?s=books&ie=UTF8&qid=1544826846&sr=1-1&keywords=Kahneman%2C+Daniel%2C+Thinking+Fast+and+Slow>.

Kaye, Ken. "Will All Aboard transform Florida as others rails have?" *Sun Sentinel*.

April 10, 2015. <http://www.sun-sentinel.com/local/broward/fl-florida-railroad-history-20150410-story.html>

Kalesan, Bindu, Marcos D Villarreal, Katherine M Keyes, and Sandro Galea. "Gun ownership and social gun culture" *Injury Prevention*. doi:10.1136. 2015. <https://injuryprevention.bmj.com/content/injuryprev/early/2015/06/09/injuryprev-2015-041586.full.pdf?keytype=ref&ijkey=doj6vx0laFZMsQ2>

Kaufman, Michelle. "Is Miami such a bad place to live? It's 'the worst,' this study says." *Miami Herald*. June 28, 2016. <https://www.miamiherald.com/news/local/community/miami-dade/article86476492.html>

Kennedy Space Center Visitor Complex. "History of Kennedy Space Center Visitor Complex." July 31, 2017. <https://www.kennedyspacecenter.com/blog/31/history-of-kennedy-space-center-visitor-complex>

Keynes, John Maynard. *The General Theory of Employment, Interest, and Money*. London: Macmillan. 1936. <https://www.amazon.com/General-Theory-Employment-Interest-Money/dp/0156347113/ref=sr_1_3?s=books&ie=UTF8&qid=1544792766&sr=1-3&keywords=john+maynard+keynes>

Kimel, Earle. "Allegiant Air Sunseeker Resort on track in Charlotte County." *Herald-Tribune*. April 6, 2018. <http://www.heraldtribune.com/news/20180406/allegiant-air-sunseeker-resort-on-track-in-charlotte-county>

Kisa, Zahid, Melissa Dyehouse, Toby Park, Brian Andrews-Larson and Carolyn Herrington. "Evaluation of the Florida Tax Credit Scholarship Program: Participation, Compliance and Test Scores in 2016-17." Learning Systems Institute, Florida State University. July 2018. <http://www.fldoe.org/core/fileparse.php/5606/urlt/FTC-Report1617.pdf>

Kingsley, G. Thomas, Robin Smith, and David Price. "The Impact of Foreclosures on Families and Communities." The Urban Institute. May 2009. <https://www.urban.org/sites/default/files/publication/30426/411909-The-Impacts-of-Foreclosures-on-Families-and-Communities.PDF>

Kizito, Owusu. "Understanding the Negative Effects of Home Foreclosures On Mental And Physical Health." The ExecRanks. November 15, 2015. <https://www.execrank.com/board-of-directors-articles/understanding-the-negative-effects-of-home-foreclosures-on-mental-and-physical-health>

Knight-Ridder/Tribune. "3 Cubans Windsurf to Freedom." *Chicago Tribune*. May 1, 1994. <https://www.chicagotribune.com/news/ct-xpm-1994-05-01-9405010193-

story.html>

Kotkin, Joel and Wendell Cox. "Where Talent Wants to Live." *Chief Executive*. May 2, 2018. <https://chiefexecutive.net/where-talent-wants-to-live/>

Krogstad, Jens Manuel. "Rise in English proficiency among U.S. Hispanics is driven by the young." Pew Research Institute. April 20, 2016.
<http://www.pewresearch.org/fact-tank/2016/04/20/rise-in-english-proficiency-among-u-s-hispanics-is-driven-by-the-young/>
Langone, Alix. "Walt Disney World Agrees to Raise Its Minimum Wage to $15 By 2021." *Money*. August 26, 2018. <http://time.com/money/5378529/walt-disney-world-minimum-wage-contract/>

Lausche, Barbara J. "Synopsis of an Assessment: Policy Tools for Local Adaptation to Sea Level Rise." Technical Report No. 1419. Mote Marine Laboratory. October 2009. <https://mote.org/media/uploads/files/Synopsis-Policy_Tools_for_Local_Adaptation_to_Sea_Level_Rise(fin).pdf>

Layden, Laura. "6 Southwest Florida residents among world's billionaires." *Naples Daily News*. March 21, 2017a.
https://www.naplesnews.com/story/news/local/2017/03/21/southwest-florida-residents-among-worlds-billionaires/99442022/

Layden, Laura. "Naples family might sell 70 'amazing and unique' acres that include beach." Naples Daily News. March 3, 2017b.
<https://www.naplesnews.com/story/money/real-estate/2017/03/03/70-acres-beachfront-property-keewaydin-island-gordon-pointe-could-up-sale/98686366/>

Layden, Laura. "SWFL move was part of bumpy road for Hertz; new CEO maps turnaround." *Naples Daily News*. August 5, 2017c.
<https://www.naplesnews.com/story/money/business/2017/08/05/hertz-has-tough-road-ahead/475080001/>

Leary, Alex. "Still booming with retirees, The Villages gives Trump, GOP edge in Florida: Remarkable growth fuels a demographic trend in the GOP's favor." *Tampa Bay Times*. October 5, 2017. <https://www.tampabay.com/florida-politics/2017/10/05/still-booming-with-retirees-the-villages-gives-trump-gop-edge-in-florida/>

LeMieux, George S. and Laura E. Mize. *Florida Made: The 25 Most Important Figures Who Shaped the State*. Charleston, SC: The History Press. 2018.
<https://www.amazon.com/Florida-Made-Important-Figures-Shaped-ebook/dp/B07DXBJZS5/ref=tmm_kin_swatch_0?_encoding=UTF8&qid=1544791878&sr=1-1>

Lincoln Journal Star. "The 30 cities with the highest murder rates in the US." March 6, 2018. <https://journalstar.com/news/local/911/the-cities-with-the-highest-

murder-rates-in-the-us/collection_153b5890-f3bb-5b58-93cc-dfbda5aa1d8d.html#1>

Lopez, German. "Florida's Bill Nelson would have likely beat Rick Scott if ex-felons had been able to vote." *Vox*. November 19, 2018. <https://www.vox.com/policy-and-politics/2018/11/19/18102579/florida-senate-midterm-election-results-felons-nelson-scott>

Luhby, Tami. "Hispanics are climbing the social mobility ladder faster than blacks." CNN. June 22, 2018. <https://www.msn.com/en-us/money/markets/hispanics-are-climbing-the-social-mobility-ladder-faster-than-blacks/ar-AAz1GBq?li=BBnbfcN>

Lunhow, David. "Latin America Is the Murder Capital of the World." *Wall Street Journal*. September 20, 2018. <https://www.wsj.com/articles/400-murders-a-day-the-crisis-of-latin-america-1537455390>

Maher, Jimmy. "Starting MS-DOS — The complete history of the IBM PC, part one: The deal of the century: Bill Gates, mysterious deaths, and the business machine that sparked a home revolution." *ArsTechnica*. June 30, 2017. <https://arstechnica.com/gadgets/2017/06/ibm-pc-history-part-1/>

Mahoney, Emily L. "Trump makes closing argument for Ron DeSantis, Rick Scott in Pensacola rally." *Tampa Bay Tribune*. November 3, 2018. <https://www.tampabay.com/florida-politics/buzz/2018/11/03/trump-makes-closing-argument-for-ron-desantis-rick-scott-in-pensacola-rally/>

Man, Anthony. "With population growth, Haitian community in South Florida sees more political clout." *Sun Sentinel*. June 2, 2017. <http://www.sun-sentinel.com/news/politics/fl-reg-florida-haitian-political-clout-20170601-story.html>

Marquis, Christopher. "Jorge Mas Canosa dead at 58." *Miami Herald*. November 24, 1997. <https://www.miamiherald.com/article213289789.html>

Marshall, Barbara. "Adios, snowbirds: Glad Palm Beach County's tourist season is over?" *Palm Beach Post*. April 18, 2017. <https://www.palmbeachpost.com/lifestyles/adios-snowbirds-glad-palm-beach-county-tourist-season-over/j1U0Rqq0sCYbZmZuGGotKL/>

Maze, G., M. J. Olascoaga and L.E. Brand. "Historical analysis of environmental conditions during Florida Red Tide. *Harmful Algae*. No. 50. 2015. <https://doi.org/10.1016/j.hal.2015.10.003>

McKnight, Robert. "The impact of the Mariel Boatlift still resonates in Florida after 38 years." *Miami Herald*. April 18, 2018. <https://www.miamiherald.com/opinion/op-ed/article209282994.html>

Meredith, Marc and Michael Morse. "Why letting ex-felons vote probably won't swing Florida." *Vox.* November 2, 2018. <https://www.vox.com/the-big-idea/2018/11/2/18049510/felon-voting-rights-amendment-4-florida>

Miller, Carlos. "The Miami River Cops Case The most corrupt case in the history of the Miami Police Department." *Miami Beach 411.* May 20, 2009. <http://www.miamibeach411.com/news/miami-river-cops>

Miller, Kimberly. "Irma forced mass evacuations; officials urge staying home next time." *Palm Beach Post.* April 4, 2018. <https://www.palmbeachpost.com/weather/hurricanes/irma-forced-mass-evacuations-officials-urge-staying-home-next-time/KippDb0Dnw3reWRT0oH3rM/>

Miller, Michael J. "The Rise of DOS: How Microsoft Got the IBM PC OS Contract." *PC Magazine.* August 10, 2011. <https://forwardthinking.pcmag.com/software/286148-the-rise-of-dos-how-microsoft-got-the-ibm-pc-os-contract>

Millsap, Adam. "Florida's Population Is Booming--But Should We Worry About Income Growth?" *Forbes.* Jun 6, 2018. <https://www.forbes.com/sites/adammillsap/2018/06/06/floridas-population-is-booming-but-should-we-worry-about-income-growth/#bac7b7f134db>

Modys, JoNell. "Celebrities Find Their Own Paradise in Naples & Marco Island." ParadiseCoast.com. 2018. <https://www.paradisecoast.com/article/celebrities-find-their-own-paradise-naples-marco-island>

Moore, Thomas Gale. "Life, Death, and Climate." Hoover Institution, Stanford University. 1998. <https://web.stanford.edu/~moore/HealthBenefitsofWarmer.html>

Moreno, Carolina. "Miami Is Where Most Latin Americans Would Like to Live, Survey Says." *Huffington Post.* August 27, 2013. <https://www.huffingtonpost.com/2013/08/27/miami-latin-americans_n_3825447.html>

Mormino, Gary. "Roadsides and Broadsides: A History of Florida Tourism," *FEH Florida Forum.* Vol. 10, No. 3. 1987. <https://digital.usfsp.edu/cgi/viewcontent.cgi?article=1001&context=forum_magazine>

Moseley Katrina R., Lisa A. House, and Fritz Roka. "Adoption of Mechanical Harvesting for Sweet Orange Trees in Florida: Addressing Grower Concerns on Long-Term Impacts." *International Food and Agribusiness Management Review.* Volume 15, Issue 2. 2012. <http://ageconsearch.umn.edu/record/127108/files/20110048_Formatted.pdf>

Mower, Lawrence and David Smiley. "New Andrew Gillum documents show FBI agent might have paid for fundraiser dinner." *Tampa Bay Times*. October 26, 2018. <https://www.tampabay.com/florida-politics/buzz/2018/10/26/new-andrew-gillum-documents-show-fbi-agent-might-have-paid-for-fundraiser-dinner/>

Mower, Lawrence, Caitlin Johnston and Steve Contorno. "Rick Scott announces potential high-speed rail linking Tampa and Orlando." *Tampa Bay Times*. June 2, 2018. <http://www.tampabay.com/florida-politics/buzz/2018/06/22/rick-scott-announces-potential-high-speed-rail-linking-tampa-and-orlando/>

Munzenrieder, Kyle. "Art Basel Miami Beach 2018: All the Gossip You May Have Missed." *W Magazine*. December 9, 2018. <https://www.wmagazine.com/story/art-basel-miami-beach-2018-celebrities-parties-gossip-recap>

Munzenrieder, Kyle. "Florida Has the Second Fewest Native Residents of Any State." *Miami New Times*. August 18, 2014. <https://www.miaminewtimes.com/news/florida-has-the-second-fewest-native-residents-of-any-state-6548292>

NASA. Fiscal Year 2019 Budget Estimates. 2018. <https://www.nasa.gov/sites/default/files/atoms/files/fy2019_presidents_budget_nasa.pdf>

National Association of Realtors "2017 Profile of International Residential Real Estate Activity in Florida." Conducted for Florida Realtors. October 2017. <https://www.floridarealtors.org/ResearchAndStatistics/Other-Research-Reports/upload/Florida2017_FinalReport.pdf>

National Education Association. "Estimates of School Statistics 2018." April 2018. <http://www.nea.org/assets/docs/180413-Rankings_And_Estimates_Report_2018.pdf>

Nehamas, Nicholas. "21 Miami-Dade, Broward banks win highest ratings." *Miami Herald*. September 25, 2015. <https://www.miamiherald.com/news/business/banking/article36545811.html>

NBC2. "Hurricane Charley hit Punta Gorda 14 years ago today." August 13, 2018. <http://www.nbc-2.com/story/38874836/hurricane-charley-hit-punta-gorda-14-years-ago-today>

NBC. "In Miami, Spanish Becoming Primary Language: 55.8 Per Cent Speak Spanish; Some English Speakers Feel Marginalized." NBCNews.com. May 29, 2008. <http://www.nbcnews.com/id/24871558/ns/us_news-life/t/miami-spanish-becoming-primary-language/#.W7ihN2hKhPa>

Nikolewski, Rob. "Regulators vote to shut down Diablo Canyon, California's last nuclear power plant." *Los Angeles Times*. January 11, 2018. <https://www.latimes.com/business/la-fi-diablo-canyon-nuclear-20180111-story.html>

Norcross, Eileen and Olivia Gonzalez. "Ranking the States by Fiscal Condition, 2017 Edition. State and Local Policy Research Paper/Study. Mercatus Center, George Mason University. July 11, 2017. <https://www.mercatus.org/system/files/norcross-fiscalrankings-2017-mercatus-v1.pdf>

O'Donnell, Christopher. "High-speed rail firm scouting land for station and development around proposed Rays ballpark site." *Tampa Bay Times*. August 4, 2018. <https://www.tampabay.com/news/transportation/masstransit/High-speed-rail-firm-scouting-land-for-station-and-development-around-proposed-Rays-ballpark-site_170561134>

Office Depot. "Office Depot Announces Termination of Merger Agreement with Staples." May 26, 2016. <http://investor.officedepot.com/phoenix.zhtml?c=94746&p=irol-newsArticle&ID=2168737>

Ousley, Edie. "Florida's Economy Hits New $1 Trillion GDP Milestone." Florida Chamber of Commerce. July 13, 2018. <https://www.flchamber.com/breaking-floridas-economy-hits-new-1-trillion-gdp-milestone/>

Oxford Economics. "The Economic Impact of Out-of-State Visitors in Florida: 2016 Calendar Year Analysis." Study Prepared for VisitFlorida. January 2018. <https://www.visitflorida.org/media/30679/florida-visitor-economic-impact-study.pdf>

Parker, Star. "A Lesson in Racial Politics from Florida." The Daily Signal. November 22, 2018. <https://www.dailysignal.com/2018/11/22/a-lesson-in-racial-politics-from-florida/>

Passell, Peter. "I.B.M. and the Limits of a Consent Decree." *New York Times*. June 9, 1994. <https://www.nytimes.com/1994/06/09/business/ibm-and-the-limits-of-a-consent-decree.html>

Patterson, Gordon. *The Mosquito Wars: A History of Mosquito Control in Florida*. Florida History and Culture Series, Gainesville, FL: University of Florida Press, 2004. <https://www.amazon.com/Mosquito-Wars-History-Control-Florida/dp/0813027209/ref=sr_1_1?s=books&ie=UTF8&qid=1544792839&sr=1-1&keywords=gordon+patterson+mosquito+wars>

Peters, Sarah. "Here's what's happening with Palm Beach Gardens' biggest new development." *The Palm Beach Post*. August 23, 2018. <https://www.palmbeachpost.com/news/local/here-what-happening-with-palm-

beach-gardens-biggest-new-development/dCF8tkRqGi5WHUoCnrzBSM/>

Pew Charitable Trust. "Rainy Day Funds and State Credit Ratings: How well-designed policies and timely use can protect against downgrades." May 2017. <https://www.pewtrusts.org/~/media/assets/2017/05/statesfiscalhealth_creditratingsreport.pdf>

Price, Wayne T. "Embraer to assemble two new classes of business jets in Melbourne," *Florida Today*. October 14, 2018.<https://www.floridatoday.com/story/news/2018/10/14/embraer-assemble-two-new-classes-business-jets-melbourne/1613743002/>

Prinos, Scott T., Michael A. Wacker, Kevin J. Cunningham, and David V. Fitterman. "Origins and Delineation of Saltwater Intrusion in the Biscayne Aquifer and Changes in the Distribution of Saltwater in Miami-Dade County, Florida." U.S. Department of the Interior, U.S. Geological Survey, Scientific Investigations Report 2014–5025. Prepared in cooperation with Miami-Dade County. 2014. <https://www.nrc.gov/docs/ML1621/ML16216A235.pdf>

Radcliff, Darby. "Top 10 Unique Cruise Ship Attractions: From go-carts to skydiving, your days spent at sea will be anything but boring." *Islands*. June 20, 2017. <https://www.islands.com/top-10-unique-cruise-ship-attractions/>

Radley, David C., Douglas McCarthy, and Susan L. Hayes. "2018 Scorecard on State Health System Performance." The Commonwealth Fund. May 2018. <https://interactives.commonwealthfund.org/2018/state-scorecard/files/Radley_State_Scorecard_2018.pdf>

Rayer, Stefan. "Natural Decrease." Bureau of Economic and Business Research, University of Florida. January 22, 2016. <https://www.bebr.ufl.edu/population/website-article/natural-decrease-florida>

Rayer, Stefan and Ying Wang. "Projections of Florida Population by County, 2020–2045, with Estimates for 2017." Bureau of Economic and Business Research, University of Florida. Florida Population Studies. Volume 51, Bulletin 180. January 2018. <https://www.bebr.ufl.edu/population/population-data/projections-florida-population-county-2020%E2%80%932045-estimates-2017>

Reilly, Steve. "Red tide may be fading away." *Englewood Sun*. December 13, 2018. <https://www.yoursun.com/englewood/news/red-tide-may-be-fading-away/article_b6394552-ff0c-11e8-a268-fb680973f0ac.html>

Realtytrac. "Florida Real Estate Trends & Market Info." 2018. < https://www.realtytrac.com/statsandtrends/foreclosuretrends/fl/>

Reuters. "Scientists seek new ways to combat Florida's 'red tide'." August 20, 2018. <https://www.theweathernetwork.com/us/news/articles/florida-red-tide-new-

science-solution-gulf-algae-bloom-karenia-brevis-dead-marine-creatures/109696>

Riley, Bryan. "U.S. Trade Policy Gouges American Sugar Consumers." The Heritage Foundation. June 5, 2014. <https://www.heritage.org/trade/report/us-trade-policy-gouges-american-sugar-consumers>

Roberts, Melissa. "14 Percent of Florida Jobs Are Connected to the Agriculture Industry." Florida Chamber of Commerce. 2016. <https://www.flchamber.com/dyk-14-percent-florida-jobs-connected-agriculture-industry/>

Roberts, Melissa. "The Statewide Impact of Florida's Military Economy is More Than $70 Billion." Florida Chamber of Commerce. 2014. <https://www.flchamber.com/know-statewide-impact-floridas-military-economy-70-billion/>

Robinson, Joan. *The Economics of Imperfect Competition*. New York: Macmillan. 1933. <https://www.amazon.com/Economics-Imperfect-Competition-2nd/dp/0333102894/ref=sr_1_1?s=books&ie=UTF8&qid=1544792894&sr=1-1&keywords=joan+robinson>

Rodriquez, Rene. "The Miami sound is gone. But the beat goes on. Here is what replaced it." *Miami Herald*. June 26, 2016. <https://www.miamiherald.com/entertainment/music-news-reviews/article85906062.html>

Rogers, Katie. "Trump Orders Establishment of Space Force as Sixth Military Branch." *New York Times*. June 18, 2018. <https://www.nytimes.com/2018/06/18/us/politics/trump-space-force-sixth-military-branch.html>

Rogers, Nala. "Why Are Alligator Bites on the Rise in Florida?" *Inside Science*. August 20, 2018. <https://www.insidescience.org/news/why-are-alligator-bites-rise-florida>

Rohternov, Larry. "Jorge Mas Canosa, 58, Dies; Exile Who Led Movement Against Castro." *New York Times*. November 24, 1997. <https://www.nytimes.com/1997/11/24/us/jorge-mas-canosa-58-dies-exile-who-led-movement-against-castro.html>

Romo, Vanessa and Lucian Kim. "Soyuz Rocket Launches, Docks Successfully To Relief Of NASA, Russia Space Agency." National Public Radio. December 3, 2018. <https://www.npr.org/2018/12/03/672838733/soyuz-rocket-launches-successfully-to-relief-of-nasa-russia-space-agency>

Rosica, Jim. "Deal 'em: Rick Scott, Seminole Tribe agree on gambling money." *Florida Politics*. April 18, 2018. <http://floridapolitics.com/archives/261678-rick-scott-seminole-gambling>

Saunders, Jim. "The fight over Miami Beach's minimum wage law continues before Florida Supreme Court." *Miami Herald.* October 30, 2018. <https://www.miamiherald.com/news/local/community/miami-dade/miami-beach/article220863435.html>

Scarboro, Morgan. "State Corporate Income Tax Rates and Brackets for 2017." Tax Foundation. February 27, 2017. <https://taxfoundation.org/state-corporate-income-tax-rates-brackets-2017/>

Scarboro, Morgan. "State Individual Income Tax Rates and Brackets for 2018." Tax Foundation. March 5, 2018. <https://taxfoundation.org/state-individual-income-tax-rates-brackets-2018/>

Schlink, Bruce. *Americans Held Hostage by the Environmentalist Movement.* Pittsburg: Rose Dog Books. 2012.
https://books.google.com/books?id=7mkXBaIFpuAC&pg=PA261&lpg=PA261&dq=environmentalists+oppose+expansion+of+electrical+generating+plants+in+california&source=bl&ots=XaSA7PgvEo&sig=KWoBUvmdfkN02ijZQKJQ4PbqSk0&hl=en&sa=X&ved=2ahUKEwiV6YmvppXfAhXNuFkKHe4PAo44FBDoATAFegQIABAB#v=onepage&q=environmentalists%20oppose%20expansion%20of%20electrical%20generating%20plants%20in%20california&f=false>

Schmitz, Ali. "Two SFWMD board members resign at Gov. Ron DeSantis' request; leaving six holdouts." *TCPalm.* January 14, 2019.
<https://www.tcpalm.com/story/news/local/indian-river-lagoon/politics/2019/01/14/sfwmd-two-board-members-resign-after-gov-ron-desantis-call/2569492002/>

Schneider, Karl. "Florida algae crisis: What's the difference between red tide and blue-green algae?" *News Press.* August 3, 2018. <https://www.news-press.com/story/tech/science/environment/2018/08/03/red-tide-blue-green-algae-whats-difference/901808002/>

Schulz, Max. "California's Potemkin Environmentalism: A celebrated green economy produces pollution elsewhere, ongoing power shortages, and business-crippling costs." *City Journal.* Spring 2008. <https://www.city-journal.org/html/california%E2%80%99s-potemkin-environmentalism-13079.html>

Schumpeter, Joseph A. *Capitalism, Socialism and Democracy.* New York: Harper. 1942.

Seemuth, Mike. "The 25 wealthiest South Floridians." *Miami Herald.* October 11, 2014. <https://www.miamiherald.com/news/business/biz-monday/article2673915.html>

Shammas, Brittany. "Miami Is Only U.S. City Where Most Language Learners Are

Studying English." *Miami New Times.* October 13, 2017.
<https://www.miaminewtimes.com/news/miami-is-only-us-city-where-most-studied-language-is-english-9743341 >

Shenot, Christine. "Founder of Red Lobster, William B. Darden, Dies." *Orlando Sentinel.* March 30, 1994. <http://articles.orlandosentinel.com/1994-03-30/business/9403300598_1_red-lobster-darden-seafood-restaurant>

Shiller, Robert. *Irrational Exuberance.* Princeton: Princeton University Press. Third Edition. 2015. <https://www.amazon.com/Irrational-Exuberance-Revised-Expanded-Third/dp/0691173125/ref=sr_1_1?s=books&ie=UTF8&qid=1544792952&sr=1-1&keywords=robert+shiller>

Sitler, Nevin D. "Selling St. Petersburg: John Lodwick and the Promotion of a Florida Paradise." An MA thesis submitted to the University of South Florida. 2006.
<https://www.stpete.org/historic_preservation/docs/Selling_St_Petersburg.pdf>
Smith, Stanley K. "Florida Population Growth: Past, Present and Future." Bureau of Economic and Business Research, University of Florida. June 2005.
<https://www.bebr.ufl.edu/sites/default/files/Research%20Reports/FloridaPop2005_0.pdf>

Smith, Stanley K. and Mark House. "Snowbirds, Sunbirds, and Stayers: Seasonal Migration of Elderly Adults in Florida." *The Journals of Gerontology*: Series B. Volume 61, Issue 5. September 1, 2006.
<https://academic.oup.com/psychsocgerontology/article/61/5/S232/604064>

Sommeiller, Estelle and Mark Price. "The new gilded age Income inequality in the U.S. by state, metropolitan area, and county." Economic Policy Institute. July 19, 2018. <https://www.epi.org/publication/the-new-gilded-age-income-inequality-in-the-u-s-by-state-metropolitan-area-and-county/>

Sortal, Nick. "Seminoles vote to oust Billie as chairman." *Miami Herald.* September 28, 2016. <https://www.miamiherald.com/news/local/community/miami-dade/article104710976.html>

Sosnowsky, Alex. "Why Florida ranks highest for lightning fatalities in the US." AccuWeather. 2018. <https://www.accuweather.com/en/weather-news/why-florida-ranks-highest-for-lightning-fatalities-in-the-us/70004543>

Soule, Alexander. "Connecticut financiers latching onto tax workaround." *Greenwich Time.* September 21, 2018.
<https://www.greenwichtime.com/business/article/Report-Connecticut-financiers-latching-onto-tax-13248277.php>

Staletovich, Jenny. "Big sugar land buy for Everglades restoration hits road block."

Miami Herald. April 20, 2018.
<https://www.miamiherald.com/news/local/environment/article17992718.html>

Statistica. "Domestic market share of leading U.S. airlines from October 2017 to September 2018." 2018. < https://www.statista.com/statistics/250577/domestic-market-share-of-leading-us-airlines/>

Stebbins, Samuel and Evan Comen. "50 Worst Cities to Live In" 24/7 Wall Street. June 10, 2018. <https://247wallst.com/special-report/2018/06/10/50-worst-cities-to-live-in-3/3/>

Stebbins, Samuel and Thomas C. Frohlich. "Geographic disparity: States with the best (and worst) schools." *USA Today*, 24/7 Wall Street. February 12, 2018. <https://www.usatoday.com/story/money/economy/2018/02/08/geographic-disparity-states-best-and-worst-schools/1079181001/>

Stronge, William B. *The Sunshine Economy: An Economic History of Florida Since the Civil War.* Gainesville: University Press of Florida. 2011.
<https://www.amazon.com/Sunshine-Economy-Economic-History-Florida/dp/0813032016/ref=sr_1_1?s=books&ie=UTF8&qid=1544793019&sr=1-1&keywords=william+b.+stronge>

Storey, Ken. "Site ranks Latitude Margaritaville over The Villages as Florida's best retirement community." *Orlando Weekly.* Posted Jun 11, 2018.
<https://www.orlandoweekly.com/Blogs/archives/2018/06/11/site-ranks-latitude-margaritaville-over-the-villages-as-floridas-best-retirement-community>

Tan, Gillian "I Squared Raises $7 Billion for Infrastructure Investments." Bloomberg. September 4, 2018.
<https://www.bloomberg.com/news/articles/2018-09-04/i-squared-capital-raises-7-billion-for-infrastructure-deals>

Taylor-Martin, Susan. "One of Florida's 'most exclusive' collection of properties hits the market." March 3, 2017. <https://www.tbo.com/news/one-of-floridas-most-exclusive-collection-of-properties-hits-the-market-20170303/>
Texas Transportation Institute. "Congestion in Florida: Findings from the 2015 Urban Mobility Scorecard." September 2015.
<http://www.fdot.gov/planning/trends/special/flcongestion.pdf>

Thaler Richard H. *Misbehaving: The Making of Behavioral Economics.* New York: Norton. 2015. <https://www.amazon.com/Misbehaving-Behavioral-Economics-Richard-Thaler/dp/039335279X/ref=sr_1_1?s=books&ie=UTF8&qid=1544793063&sr=1-1&keywords=richard+h.+Thaler>

Themed Entertainment Association. TEA/AECOM. "2017 Theme Index and Museum Index: The Global Attractions Attendance Report." 2018.

<http://www.teaconnect.org/images/files/TEA_268_653730_180517.pdf>

Thompson, Buster. "Nuke plant reaches milestone: Final fuel assembly removed from CR3." *Citrus County Chronicle*. January 29, 2018.
<https://www.chronicleonline.com/news/local/nuke-plant-reaches-milestone/article_831b4354-0562-11e8-be13-8f0cb5697c03.html>

Tierney, Mike. "Amid Rising Discord Over Indian Images, F.S.U. Has Harmony." *New York Times*. October 23, 2013.
<https://www.nytimes.com/2013/10/24/sports/ncaafootball/amid-rising-discord-over-indian-images-florida-state-has-harmony.html>

Toadvine, Mel and Kevin Shea. "Obama will tour Lehigh Acres Tuesday: Nobody from Lehigh expected to be on Obama tour of community." LehighAcresCitizen.com. February 7, 2009.
<http://www.lehighacrescitizen.com/page/content.detail/id/500226/Obama-will-tour-Lehigh-Acres-Tuesday.html>

Tourism Economics. "The Impact of Hurricane Irma on the Florida Tourism Economy." January 2018. <https://www.visitflorida.org/media/46680/fl-hurricane-impacts.pdf>

Touropia. "10 Largest Malls in the World." Updated on October 24, 2017.
<https://www.touropia.com/largest-malls-in-the-world/>

Touropia. "25 Top Tourist Attractions in the USA." Updated January 26, 2018.
<https://www.touropia.com/tourist-attractions-in-the-usa/>

Treadway, Tyler. "Herbert Hoover Dike: Florida gives Army Corps $50 million for Lake Okeechobee repairs." *TCPalm*. April 19, 2018.
<https://www.tcpalm.com/story/news/local/indian-river-lagoon/health/2018/04/19/herbert-hoover-dike-florida-gives-army-corps-50-million-lake-okeechobee-repairs/531590002/>

Treadway, Tyler. "Lake Okeechobee reservoir could be completed in 7-9 years, SFWMD chief Ernie Marks says." *TCPalm*. January 17, 2018.
<https://www.tcpalm.com/story/news/local/indian-river-lagoon/health/2018/01/17/lake-okeechobee-reservoir-could-completed-7-9-years-sfwmd-chief-ernie-marks-says/1039527001/>

Treadway, Tyler and Ali Schmitz. "President Trump signs law authorizing reservoir to cut Lake Okeechobee discharges." *TCPalm*. October 23, 2018.
<https://www.tcpalm.com/story/news/local/indian-river-lagoon/health/2018/10/23/president-trump-scheduled-sign-wrda-law-reservoir-cutting-lake-okeechobee-discharges/1598546002/>

Tribou, Richard. "NASA's manned missions slate now has Boeing Starliner ahead

of SpaceX Dragon." *Orlando Sentinel.* January 11, 2018.
<https://www.orlandosentinel.com/business/space/go-for-launch/os-manned-missions-spacex-boeing-starliner-20180111-story.html>

Trigaux, Robert. "New study ranks Raymond James among top ten firms for financial adviser misconduct." *Tampa Bay Times.* March 3, 2016.
<https://www.tampabay.com/news/business/banking/new-study-ranks-raymond-james-among-top-ten-firms-for-financial-adviser/2267704>

Tsai, Alexander C. and James Coyne. "Home Foreclosure, Health, and Mental Health: A Systematic Review of Individual, Aggregate, and Contextual Associations." *PLoS One.* v.10(4). 2015.
<https://www.ncbi.nlm.nih.gov/pmc/articles/PMC4388711/>

Tyson, Alec. "The 2018 midterm vote: Divisions by race, gender, education." Pew Research Center. November 8, 2018. <http://www.pewresearch.org/fact-tank/2018/11/08/the-2018-midterm-vote-divisions-by-race-gender-education/>

U.S. Census Bureau. "2020 Census Residence Criteria and Residence Situations." 2018a. <https://www.census.gov/programs-surveys/decennial-census/2020-census/about/residence-rule.html>

U.S. Census Bureau. How the Census Bureau Measures Poverty. 2018b.
<https://www.census.gov/topics/income-poverty/poverty/guidance/poverty-measures.html>

U.S. Census Bureau. Income and Poverty in the United States: 2017. September 12, 2018. <https://www.census.gov/library/publications/2018/demo/p60-263.html>
U.S. Census Bureau. "The Nation's Older Population Is Still Growing, Census Bureau Reports." Release Number CB17-100. June 22, 2017.
<https://www.census.gov/newsroom/press-releases/2017/cb17-100.html>

U.S. Conference of Mayors. *Report on Hunger and Homelessness.* December 2016.
<https://endhomelessness.atavist.com/mayorsreport2016>

U.S. Department of Agriculture. "2017-18 Citrus Summary." August 28, 2018.
<https://www.nass.usda.gov/Statistics_by_State/Florida/Publications/Citrus/Citrus_Summary/Citrus_Summary_Prelim/cit82818.pdf>

U.S. Department of Agriculture. "Florida County Estimates 2017-18." May 2018.<https://www.nass.usda.gov/Statistics_by_State/Florida/Publications/County_Estimates/2018/FLCattle2018.pdf>

U.S. Department of Agriculture. Economic Research Service. "Policy." May 2018.
<https://www.ers.usda.gov/topics/crops/sugar-sweeteners/policy.aspx#sugar>

U.S. Department of Commerce. "Fisheries Economics of the United States 2015."

National Marine Fisheries Service. NOAA Technical Memorandum NMFS-F/SPO-170. May 2017.
<https://www.st.nmfs.noaa.gov/Assets/economics/publications/FEUS/FEUS-2015/Report-Chapters/FEUS%202015%20All%20Chapters_Final4_508.pdf>

U.S. Department of Housing and Urban Development. *The 2017 Annual Homeless Assessment Report (AHAR) to Congress: Part 1: Point-in-Time Estimates of Homelessness.* Office of Community Planning and Development. December 2017.
<https://www.hudexchange.info/resources/documents/2017-AHAR-Part-1.pdf>

U.S. Department of Transportation. Office of Aviation Analysis. "U.S. International Air Passenger and Freight Statistics." December 2017.
<https://www.statista.com/statistics/250577/domestic-market-share-of-leading-us-airlines/>

U.S. Global Change Research Program. Fourth National Climate Assessment: Volume II Impacts, Risks, and Adaptation in the United States. 2018.
<https://nca2018.globalchange.gov/>

U.S. News and World Report. "Best Hospitals in Florida."2018a.
<https://health.usnews.com/best-hospitals/area/fl>

U.S. News and World Report. "Health Care Rankings: Measuring how well states are meeting citizens' health care needs." 2018b.
<https://www.usnews.com/news/best-states/rankings/health-care>

U.S. News and World Report. "Higher Education Rankings: Measuring which states are the most educated." 2018c.<https://www.usnews.com/news/best-states/rankings/education/higher-education>

USA Today. "The 20 most visited theme parks in North America." Updated December 14, 2016.
<https://www.usatoday.com/story/travel/experience/america/2016/06/14/20-most-visited-theme-parks-north-america-2015/85839968/>

United Healthcare. "America's Health Rankings."2018.
<https://www.americashealthrankings.org/>

Van Velzer, Ryan. "Cocaine comes roaring back to South Florida — and then some." *Sun Sentinel.* May 26, 2017. <http://www.sun-sentinel.com/news/florida/fl-reg-cocaine-surge-fueling-overdoses-20170523-story.html>

Vartabedian, Ralph. "Cost for California bullet train system rises to $77.3 billion." *Los Angeles Times.* March 9, 2018. <http://www.latimes.com/local/california/la-me-bullet-train-cost-increase-20180309-story.html>

Vaughan, Jessica. "Immigration Multipliers Trends in Chain Migration" Center for

Immigration Studies. November 2017. <https://cis.org/sites/default/files/2017-09/vaughan-chain-migration_1.pdf>

Veiga, Christina. "The uncertain future of español in Miami-Dade classrooms." *Miami Herald*. May 25, 2015.
<https://www.miamiherald.com/news/local/education/article22190205.html>

Walton, Chelle Koster. "In the Wake of the Red Tide." Florida Weekly. November 21, 2018. <https://fortmyers.floridaweekly.com/articles/in-the-wake-of-red-tide/>

Walton, Justin. "Florida's Economy: The 6 Industries Driving GDP Growth." Investopedia. January 13, 2016.
<https://www.investopedia.com/articles/investing/011316/floridas-economy-6-industries-driving-gdp-growth.asp#ixzz5FydsekBZ>

Walczak, Jared and Scott Drenkard. "State and Local Sales Tax Rates, Midyear 2018." Tax Foundation. July 16, 2018. <https://taxfoundation.org/state-local-sales-tax-rates-midyear-2018/>

Wenner, Kurt. "2018 How Florida Compares: Taxes: State and Local Tax Rankings for Florida and the Nation." Florida Tax Watch. June 2018.
<http://www.floridataxwatch.org/portals/3/pdfs/2018_HFCTaxes_FINAL_web.pdf>

White, Randy Wayne. "Red Tide, Take Warning: Perhaps the disaster that struck Florida's southwest coast this summer will cause residents to rethink the way they live." *New York Times*. September 29, 2018.
<https://www.nytimes.com/2018/09/29/opinion/sunday/red-tide-florida-tourism.html>

Wilde, Claire. "Cruise Industry Heroes: Ted Arison." February 10, 2016.
<https://www.cruise1st.co.uk/blog/cruise-lines/carnival-cruises/cruise-industry-heroes-ted-arison/>

Williams, Roger. "Green is the New Orange." Charlotte County Florida Weekly. August 23-29, 2018. <https://charlottecounty.floridaweekly.com/articles/green-is-floridas-new-orange/>

Wurth, Julie. "Report: Public schools pay presidents a pretty penny." *News Gazette*. July 18, 2018. <http://www.news-gazette.com/news/local/2018-07-16/report-public-schools-pay-presidents-pretty-penny.html>

Wohl. Jessica. "Dick Portillo reflects on sale of eponymous restaurant chain." *Chicago Tribune*. May 22, 2015. <http://www.chicagotribune.com/business/ct-dick-portillo-0524-biz-20150522-story.html>

World Nuclear News. "Regulator approves license for new Florida units." April 6,

2018. <http://www.world-nuclear-news.org/NN-Regulator-approves-licences-for-new-Florida-units-0604184.html>

Zhao, Helen. "AutoNation and Waste Management founder H. Wayne Huizenga dies at age 80." CNBC. March 23, 2018.
<https://www.cnbc.com/2018/03/23/autonation-and-waste-management-founder-h-wayne-huizenga-dies-age-80.html>

Zimmerman, Bill. "Florida's GDP hits $1 trillion mark: As a country, it'd rank 17th in world." *Orlando Sentinel.* July 13, 2018.
<http://www.orlandosentinel.com/business/consumer/os-bz-florida-gdp-1-trillion-20180713-story.html>